# Mission Mathematics II

## Grades 9–12

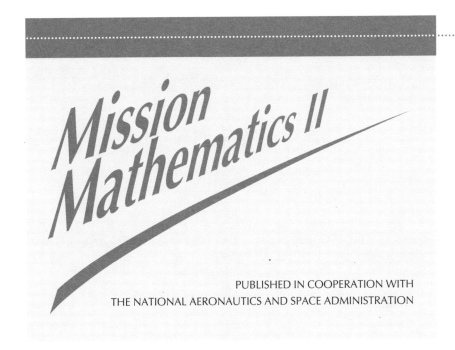

PUBLISHED IN COOPERATION WITH
THE NATIONAL AERONAUTICS AND SPACE ADMINISTRATION

**Edited by**

Peggy A. House
Roger P. Day

**Contributors**

Mary Jo Aiken
Margaret Butler
Alice Foster
Adele Hanson
Richard A. Hanson
Minot H. Parker

**Project Director**

Michael C. Hynes

NATIONAL COUNCIL OF
**NCTM** | TEACHERS OF MATHEMATICS

Library of Congress Cataloging-in-Publication Data

Mission mathematics II. Grades 9–12 / edited by Peggy A. House and
Roger P. Day.
    p. cm.
  Includes bibliographical references.
  ISBN 0-87353-573-1
1. Mathematics—Study and teaching (Secondary) I. House, Peggy A.
II. Day, Roger P.
  QA11.2.M582 2004
  510'.71'2—dc22
                   2004024794

Cover photograph © ESO, European Southern Observatory/Y. Nazé, G. Rauw, J. Manfroid, J. Vreux, and Y. Chu. All rights reserved. Used with permission. Nebulas Surrounding Wolf-Rayet Binary BAT99-49.

Text photographs, unless otherwise credited, are courtesy of NASA.

The National Council of Teachers of Mathematics is a public voice of mathematics education, providing vision, leadership, and professional development to support teachers in ensuring mathematics learning of the highest quality for all students.

The publications of the National Council of Teachers of Mathematics present a variety of viewpoints. The views expressed or implied in this publication, unless otherwise noted, should not be interpreted as official positions of the Council.

# Dedication

*Mission Mathematics II is dedicated to the memory of Pamela Louise Mountjoy. Her passion for NASA, mathematics, and teaching served as the inspiration for Mission Mathematics II and has promoted the expectation that this series will make a valuable contribution to the lives of the students and teachers in our great nation.*

# Contents

## *Unit 5: Communicating through Space* ........155

# Foreword

MISSION MATHEMATICS: Linking Aerospace and the NCTM Standards is a collaborative project of the National Aeronautics and Space Administration (NASA) and the National Council of Teachers of Mathematics (NCTM). The vision of Frank Owens, director of educational programs for NASA, and James Gates, executive director of NCTM at the time of the conception of this project, inspired this unprecedented effort to link the science of aeronautics to the standards NCTM has developed for all aspects of mathematics education.

The books of the *Mission Mathematics* series have been well received by teachers each year since their initial publication. However, both NCTM and NASA have experienced exciting changes, and the time for updating the series has arrived. The revision of *Mission Mathematics* has focused on aligning the activities with NCTM's *Principles and Standards for School Mathematics* (2000). To accomplish this alignment, two separate books for elementary school teachers are being published—one for prekindergarten–grade 2 and the other for grades 3–5. In addition, the series now includes a new book for middle school teachers. The activities in the current grades 9–12 volume have been modified and updated to reflect advancements in aerodynamics and space exploration.

The original project director, Michael C. Hynes, and the contributors to the first edition, Mary Jo Aiken, Margaret Butler, Alice Foster, Adele Hanson, Richard A. Hanson, and Minot H. Parker, gave many, many hours to this project. The editors are grateful for their hard work, creative ideas, enthusiasm, and support throughout the project.

A special note of thanks is extended to Harry Tunis and the production and editorial staff of NCTM and posthumously to Pamela Mountjoy of NASA. Each provided the support, guidance, and expertise that have made the project enjoyable from the first day.

*Peggy A. House and Roger P. Day, Editors*

# Preface

IN ITS 2003 strategic plan, NASA (http://www.nasa.gov/pdf/1968main_strategi.pdf) described its mission as follows:

> To understand and protect our home planet,
> To explore the universe and search for life,
> To inspire the next generation of explorers
> ... as only NASA can.

Since its creation in 1958, NASA has been built on vision: the vision to land humans on the Moon and return them safely to Earth, the vision to explore distant planets, the vision to peer deeply into the depths of space and witness the birth of stars, the vision to construct a space station in orbit, the vision to create futures as yet unimagined. Forty-six years later, NASA's vision for space exploration continues, a vision of "charting a bold new course into the cosmos, a journey that will take humans back to the Moon, and eventually to Mars and beyond" (http://www.nasa.gov/externalflash/Vision/index.html).

NCTM, too, is an organization with a vision: a vision of a dynamic mathematics curriculum that promotes deep understanding of important mathematics and its uses; a vision of dynamic, stimulating teaching and learning in environments that actively engage, challenge, and motivate students; a vision of ongoing assessment that is integral to, and aligned with, instruction; a vision of mathematical power and success for every child. NCTM, like NASA, strives to inspire the next generation of mathematicians and intelligent consumers and explorers of mathematics.

The visions of NASA and NCTM are compatible and complementary. From the context of aerospace arises important mathematics that can give students a glimpse into contemporary applications that are engaging and challenging, that permeate all aspects of modern life, and that invite students to become personally involved in open-ended investigations. These contemporary applications of mathematics, and the technology that makes them accessible to secondary school students, portray mathematics as dynamic and very much alive and well in the modern world. The mathematics of aerospace significantly furthers the goals expressed in NCTM's vision for mathematics education. At the same time, the attainment of NCTM's vision of mathematical power for every student will be essential if NASA is to find the next generation of mathematical thinkers needed to realize its ever-evolving vision of new futures.

Neither the vision of NASA nor the vision of NCTM would be achievable were it not for the dedicated and creative individuals who compose the two organizations. During the development of the original Mission Mathematics series, as well as during the preparation of this revised second edition, the senior authors of the Mission Mathematics books visited several NASA Space Centers and met with many NASA staff members engaged in all aspects of the aerospace enterprise. From the beginning, two characteristics of these people made a deep impression: their genuine enthusiasm for the work they were doing, and their realization of the importance of each individual's work and its contribution to the total NASA mission.

Returning to the Kennedy Space Center visitor complex immediately after viewing a spectacular night launch of the Space Shuttle, we were struck by the sign already in place at the entrance to the grounds. It hailed the successful launch completed less than an hour earlier, bade the astronauts God speed, and then proclaimed gratitude and recognition for the contributions of the countless thousands of Earthbound NASA personnel who had made the mission possible. We need to clearly communicate this powerful message to students, for when young people think about the space program and their possible interest in it, the majority naturally think about becoming an astronaut. This response is not unlike the dream of every high school player who has ever dribbled a basketball down the court to someday star in the NBA. Students have a level of understanding of what astronauts do; unfortunately, they lack insight into the vast array of important activities performed by the legion of professionals without whom there could be no astronauts. Thus, *Mission Mathematics: Grades 9–12* was developed in the hope that it will introduce students to some of the exciting and significant ways in which mathematics might continue to engage them in whatever career paths they may ultimately choose.

The selection of topics for inclusion in *Mission Mathematics: Grades 9–12* was guided by the following goals:

✦ To present significant mathematics at a level attainable by high school students

✦ To engage students in reasoning and problem solving

✦ To lay a conceptual foundation for understanding mathematical ideas

✦ To show contemporary applications of mathematics in an important context and using contemporary methodologies

✦ To motivate and inspire

*Mission Mathematics: Grades 9–12* strives to elucidate further the NCTM vision for meaningful mathematics, but individual teachers in their individual classrooms must make that vision come alive for students. Teachers do so when they convey the consistent message that no matter what students want to do in life, mathematics will help them achieve it. The authors hope that the materials in this volume will help teachers launch their students to a new level of mathematical awareness and interest.

In the predawn hours of February 11, 1997, as the first edition of Mission Mathematics was being readied for press, we again stood on the grounds of the Kennedy Space Center and watched the Space Shuttle Discovery light up the night sky as mission STS-82 lifted off Launch

Pad 39A en route to its rendezvous with the Hubble Space Telescope. During the next ten days, astronauts made repairs and installed new technologies that significantly improved Hubble's ability to expand our vision of the universe. On board Discovery with the astronauts was the mission patch illustrated on the covers of the Mission Mathematics books, a fitting tribute to the partnership between NASA and NCTM that made the series possible. It served as a timely lift-off for the Mission Mathematics project and a reminder that our mission as mathematics teachers is to introduce students to the vastness and wonder of the universe of mathematics.

In the years following the launch of the first edition of Mission Mathematics, both NASA and NCTM have further clarified and focused their visions, adapting to new knowledge, new technologies, new needs, and new dreams. NASA continues to move forward "into the cosmos, … back to the Moon,… to Mars and beyond" (http://www.nasa.gov/ externalflash/Vision/index.html). Educational programs have always been an essential component of every major NASA activity; now NASA has elevated education to the status of an Education Enterprise, comparable with the Life on Earth, Humans in Space, and Exploring the Universe enterprises that frame NASA's activities. Meanwhile, NCTM has continued to evolve its vision and goals in the form of *Principles and Standards for School Mathematics* (NCTM 2000). Mission Mathematics, too, has been updated to keep pace with the evolution of both NASA's and NCTM's visions.

Now, as before, the mission is in the hands of the teachers who accept the challenge to introduce their students to the vastness and wonder of the universe of mathematics. We wish both teachers and students an exciting and productive journey of knowledge and discovery.

# Scaling Up

## Scaling the Heights

At night, when we gaze at the sky and marvel at the beauty of the twinkling stars, we often contemplate the vastness of the universe, yet truly conceptualizing the immensity of space is difficult. From an intellectual perspective, we can talk about the length of time required for light to travel to Earth from distant stars. We have learned in school that light travels at a speed of nearly 300,000 kilometers per second; in a year, light travels $9.86 \times 10^9$ kilometers. Light emanating from a star that is ten light-years from Earth began its journey ten years before we see it. Another way to think about this distance is to consider that we are seeing the star where it was ten years ago. These intellectual musings make sense but may still not yield an intuitive notion of the vastness of space.

People today are not the first to try to comprehend distances in the universe. Our natural human need to understand the world around us has prompted others throughout history to search for answers to questions about the size of our universe. More than two thousand years ago, scientists in ancient Greece were using the known mathematics of the day to estimate the distance to the Moon and the Sun. As new mathematics was invented, our ability to measure those distances improved, but not until the seventeenth century did Cassini make the first reasonably accurate calculation of the distance from Earth to the Sun. Using more refined mathematics and improved technology, humans have continued to measure the distances between celestial bodies. As the age of space exploration began, distances in the universe became the province of all kinds of people, not just scientists. Daily newspapers printed reports of manned and unmanned space ventures, comic books carried fictitious stories about interstellar travel, and schoolbooks began to include more data about the universe.

Today, satellite launches and Space Shuttle missions seem rather ordinary and routine. We are aware that men and women are living in orbit high above Earth. We see pictures of Earth taken by astronauts on the Space Shuttle and International Space Station from more than a hundred miles in space. Although such photographs make our planet seem small, if Earth were an orange, the astronauts would be no farther from the edible part of the orange than the outer edge of the skin. Again, these notions are difficult to grasp because of the vastness of space and the sizes of planets and stars.

In grades 9–12 all students should ... develop a deeper understanding of very large and very small numbers and of various representations of them....

*(NCTM 2000, p. 290)*

These activities presume the use of spreadsheet software because a spreadsheet is a natural tool to use in performing the required calculations; however, the activities can also be done using a calculator. Because doing the calculations with a calculator is tedious, you may want to have different groups of students complete different parts of the charts and pool their results.

Information about planetary sizes and distances is readily available from numerous publications and Internet sites. You may wish to use this investigation as an opportunity for student inquiry by assigning students to research the data themselves instead of giving them the tables.

High school students should become increasingly facile in dealing with very large and very small numbers as part of their deepening understanding of number. Such numbers occur frequently in the sciences....

*(NCTM 2000, p. 291)*

NASA reports to us about the travels of unmanned space vehicles, such as *Pioneer 10, Voyager 1,* and *Voyager 2*. These spacecraft have traveled for years to reach a distance of more than 5 billion miles from Earth and are continuing on journeys that may last well into the current millennium. With these unmanned spacecraft, humankind is searching for the boundary of the solar system, the heliopause. This edge of the solar system may be 9 to 11 trillion miles from Earth. As spacecraft make their way through the solar system, scientists are learning a great deal about the planets from data sent back to NASA laboratories.

Given humankind's continuing fascination with the mysteries of space, all people should gain insight into the size and nature of the solar system. We must begin to scale up our understanding of sizes and distances in the context of space.

Mars view

# Modeling the Solar System

ooking out into the vastness of space, we cannot help but marvel at the enormous sizes and distances of bodies in our universe. Both students and teachers may have difficulty comprehending just how large and how far away the objects are in our solar system and beyond, but an understanding of such magnitudes is important for other activities in *Mission Mathematics: Grades 9–12*. Thus, we begin with this unit on scaling as a way to help put measurements in perspective.

All the investigations in this unit and others throughout the book are directed toward students. Tips for teachers and other useful information appear in the margins, and solutions and additional notes for teachers are found at the end of each unit.

Opportunities to use and understand measurement arise naturally during high school in other areas of mathematics, in science, and in technical education. Measuring the number of revolutions per minute of an engine, vast distances in astronomy, or microscopic molecular distances extends students' facility with derived measures and indirect measurement.

*(NCTM 2000, p. 321)*

Mars view

## Distribution of Matter in the Solar System

| | |
|---|---|
| Sun | 99.85% |
| Planets | 0.135% |
| Comets | 0.01% |
| Satellites | 0.00005% |
| Minor planets | 0.0000002% |
| Meteoroids | 0.0000001% |
| Interplanetary medium | 0.0000001% |

## Investigation 1—Scaling Planetary Sizes

The solar system—our Sun, its nine planets, their moons, and other orbiting bodies—can be described only in measurements of millions, or even hundreds of millions, of miles or kilometers. With numbers of that magnitude, comprehending the enormous sizes of objects in the universe and the vast distances between them is difficult. We can gain a better sense of size and distance, however, by scaling down these objects to more familiar measurements and evaluating the relative proportions of our models. Such scaling is not difficult with the aid of spreadsheet software or the table functions of a calculator.

The table below shows information about the equatorial diameters of the Sun, the planets, and our moon. Note that because a planet rotates on its axis, it is not perfectly spherical. Instead, the planet is an oblate spheroid, bulging slightly at its equator and somewhat flattened at the poles. For example, Earth's equatorial diameter is given as 12,756 kilometers (7,909 miles), whereas its polar diameter is 12,714 kilometers (7,883 miles). Because the difference is so small compared with the size of Earth, however, we are justified in treating

*The Solar System: Sizes*

| Body | Equatorial Diameter (Kilometers) | Equatorial Diameter (Miles) | Diameter Compared with Earth's | Solar System Diameters Scaled to ... |
|---|---|---|---|---|
| Mercury | 4,880 | | | |
| Venus | 12,100 | | | |
| Earth | 12,756 | | 1 | |
| Mars | 6,794 | | | |
| Jupiter | 143,200 | | | |
| Saturn | 120,536 | | | |
| Uranus | 51,800 | | | |
| Neptune | 49,528 | | | |
| Pluto | 2,330 | | | |
| Moon | 3,476 | | | |
| Sun | 1,392,000 | | | |

the planet as a sphere. In fact, in most computations involving the size of Earth in this unit, these measurements will be rounded even further.

Create a spreadsheet and copy the information from the table into it, then complete the next two columns of the table as follows:

1.  Use the spreadsheet to calculate the diameters of the planets, Sun, and moon in miles. Remember that 1 mile equals 1.61 kilometers and that 1 kilometer equals 0.62 mile.

2.  Calculate the ratio of the diameters of the other bodies compared with Earth's diameter. How many Plutos are needed to line up across the diameter of Earth? Of Saturn? How many Earths are needed to line up across the diameter of Jupiter? Of the Sun?

## Investigation 2—The Exploration Begins

Suppose that you want to make a model of our solar system in which Earth is represented by a basketball and the Sun, moon, and other planets are all proportional. Create a column on your spreadsheet or calculator table titled "Solar System Diameters Scaled to 'Earth = Basketball.'" The diameter of a basketball is 24 centimeters. After you determine the diameters of the other bodies, find objects that you could use to represent each, and add their names to your table.

1.  Think of all of the spheres you have ever seen. If the smallest sphere represents the smallest planet, what spheres could you find to represent the other planets? Would the Sun fit into your classroom?

2.  Add several columns to your table similar to the "Solar System Diameters Scaled to …" column, and change the scale each time. For example, you might decide that the basketball should serve as a model for the Sun, or you might represent one of the planets with a marble. Remember, you are trying to show the relative sizes of the bodies in the solar system. Try to locate a set of physical objects that you can bring into the classroom to illustrate one of your models.

3.  On a large local or state map, find the two landmarks or cities that are the farthest apart. Use the distance between those places to represent the diameter of Jupiter, then scale the other planets, the moon, and the Sun to that distance. Name the landmarks or cities at the endpoints of each diameter. For example, in the state of Wisconsin, the diameter of Jupiter would be represented by the distance from Kenosha to Superior, and the diameter of Earth would be represented by the distance from Kenosha to Milwaukee.

If Earth is represented by a basketball, Jupiter will be nearly 270 centimeters in diameter and the Sun, more than 26 meters. If the basketball represents the Sun, however, Earth shrinks to less than $1/4$ centimeter. Using a spreadsheet allows students to ask "What if …?" easily and to try a number of comparisons such as these.

In a subsequent unit in *Mission Mathematics,* the properties of elliptical orbits and the concept of eccentricity are discussed in more detail, and methods of modeling elliptical orbits are explored. In this unit, the exploration is simplified by assuming that the planetary orbits are circular. Why is that assumption reasonable?

## Investigation 3—Scaling Planetary Distances

In addition to the sizes of the planets and other bodies in the solar system, their relative distances from the Sun are also important to understand. Before examining planetary distances, some familiarity with the work of the German astronomer Johannes Kepler (1571–1630) may be helpful.

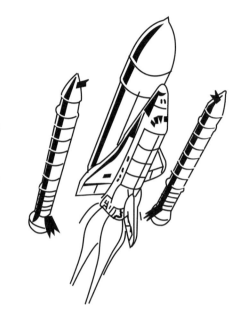

In 1543, before the lifetime of Kepler, the Polish astronomer Nicholas Copernicus published his theory that the planets revolve around the Sun in circular orbits. Kepler, however, had access to a voluminous set of accurate observations of the stars and planets, and by studying those data, he was forced to conclude that the planetary orbits could not be circular. At the time, Kepler's abandonment of the theory of circular orbits was considered radical; nonetheless, he published three laws of planetary motion (the first two in 1609 and the third in 1619) that changed astronomy and physics forever. Kepler's laws state the following:

1. The planets revolve around the Sun in elliptical orbits with the Sun at one focus of the ellipse.

2. A line joining the planet to the Sun will sweep over equal areas in equal periods of time.

3. The square of the period of a planet—that is, the time required for the planet to make one complete orbit—is proportional to the cube of its average distance from the Sun.

A greatly exaggerated diagram of an elliptical orbit is shown in figure 1.1, along with common terminology and symbolism. In this diagram, the eccentricity of the ellipse is about 0.75, giving it an elongated shape. In reality, however, the orbits of the planets are much more circular. Figure 1.2 is a much closer approximation of the shape of Earth's orbit. The accompanying table gives the eccentricities of all the planetary orbits.

**aphelion:** the point on the orbit farthest from the Sun

**perihelion:** the point on the orbit nearest to the Sun

**focal distance ($c$):** the distance from the center to either focus

**semi-major axis ($a$):** half the length of the major axis

**semi-minor axis ($b$):** half the length of the minor axis

**eccentricity ($e$):** the ratio of the focal distance to the semi-major axis ($e = c/a$)

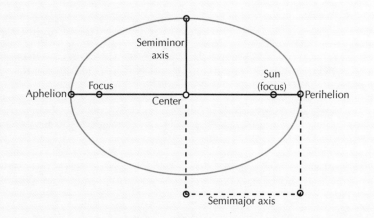

Fig. 1.1

Fig. 1.2. Approximate shape of Earth's orbit

| Body | Eccentricity |
| --- | --- |
| Mercury | .206 |
| Venus | .007 |
| Earth | .017 |
| Mars | .093 |
| Jupiter | .048 |
| Saturn | .056 |
| Uranus | .046 |
| Neptune | .009 |
| Pluto | .248 |
| Moon | .055 |

Planets "in a row"

*The Solar System: Distances*

| Body | Mean Solar Distance (Millions of km) | Mean Solar Distance (Millions of mi) | Mean Solar Distance (AU) | Orbital Period (Earth Years) |
|---|---|---|---|---|
| Mercury | 57.9 | | | 0.24 |
| Venus | 108.2 | | | 0.62 |
| Earth | 149.6 | | 1 | 1.00 |
| Mars | 227.9 | | | 1.88 |
| Jupiter | 778.3 | | | 11.86 |
| Saturn | 1,427 | | | 29.46 |
| Uranus | 2,871 | | | 84.01 |
| Neptune | 4,497 | | | 164.79 |
| Pluto | 5,914 | | | 247.70 |
| Moon (from Earth) | 0.38 | | | |

1. The table above gives the *mean distances* of the planets from the Sun. Copy the information into your spreadsheet. Because you may be more accustomed to thinking about distances in miles, calculate the mean solar distances in millions of miles.

2. An *astronomical unit* (AU) is equal to the mean distance from Earth to the Sun. The Earth–Sun distance is commonly used as a "measuring stick" to express other distances in space. Use your spreadsheet to calculate the distances from the other planets to the Sun in AUs. In other words, find the ratios of the planet–Sun distances to the Earth–Sun distance.

3. Using a large map of North America, measure the distance from Seattle, Washington, to Miami, Florida. Let that distance represent the mean distance from the Sun to Pluto. Assume that you have placed a model of the Sun at Miami (where else?). Draw the orbits of the other planets. Name the cities that you could visit on a "trip" from planet to planet. Identify the scale that you developed in inches to millions of miles and in centimeters to millions of kilometers.

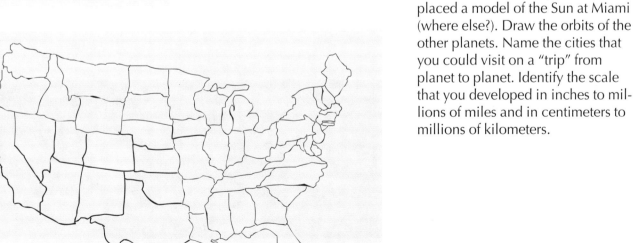

## Investigation 4—Continuing the Mission

Making a scale model of planetary sizes or planetary distances is much easier than making a single model of both planetary sizes and distances. To appreciate the problem of constructing one model for both size and distance, select a single ratio and use it to make a physical model of the solar system that shows both size and distance to the same scale. For example, use the previous scale of a basketball to represent Earth, and determine appropriate sizes for the Sun and the other planets, as well as the distances at which the planets must be placed from the Sun. You might also use one of the geographical models, such as locating 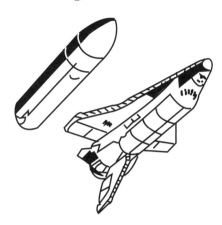 the Sun in Miami and Pluto in Seattle, and determine how big each planet will be and where it will be located in this model.

1. The International Space Station and other manned spacecraft usually orbit about 200 to 250 miles above Earth. Where would such an orbiting spacecraft be located in your model of the solar system?

2. Why does Kepler's second law lead to the conclusion that the planets must be traveling faster in their orbits when they are closer to the Sun and slower when they are farther from the Sun?

3. Use the data in the preceding table and your spreadsheet to demonstrate Kepler's third law. Use mean distances in AUs and orbital periods in years.

4. Write a description of what you have learned about the relative sizes and distances of objects in our solar system. What surprised you the most?

This image of Mars was taken on August 27, 2003 from the Hubble Space Telescope. This image is the most detailed view of Mars ever taken from Earth. Visible features include the south polar cap in white at the image bottom, circular Huygens crater just to the right of the image center, Hellas Impact Basin—the large light circular feature at the lower right, planet-wide light highlands dominated by many smaller craters and large sweeping dark areas dominated by relatively smooth lowlands. Credit: J. Bell (Cornell U.), M. Wolff (SSI) et al., STScI, NASA

The unit "Communicating through Space" considers the problems of transmitting information from planetary probes or other distant objects. Such signals are transmitted at the speed of light, yet the time required to send a signal from a distant spacecraft back to Earth is significant.

Aldrin's footprint in the lunar soil

## Investigation 5—Reaching Out

On 20 July 1969, astronaut Neil Armstrong stepped onto the surface of the moon and became the first human to set foot on another world. The mission, which included a number of orbits of Earth, travel time to and from the moon, and 26 hours on the lunar surface, took a little more than eight days from launch to splashdown. To break out of low Earth orbit (LEO) en route to the moon, the Apollo spacecraft had to achieve a velocity of just over 24,000 miles per hour.

Perhaps because we have become accustomed to science fiction in movies and on television, in which starships are assumed to travel at impossible speeds, we often do not appreciate the magnitude of the time necessary to traverse the enormous distances even within our solar system and certainly those beyond our immediate "neighborhood." We can gain a better understanding of such magnitudes by considering the travel times required to reach other planets.

Think about two planets in orbit around the Sun, and assume for simplicity that they are in circular orbit. As you can tell from the diagram in the margin, the distance between the planets varies considerably depending on whether the planets are on the same side or opposite sides of the Sun. When Earth, the Sun, and a planet are in

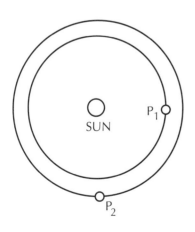

alignment, with the Sun between Earth and the planet (fig. 1.3a), the planet is said to be *in conjunction;* when the three bodies are in alignment with the Sun and planet on opposite sides of Earth (fig. 1.3b), the planet is in *opposition.*

Interplanetary communications and travel are affected by the relative positions of the planets as they orbit the Sun.

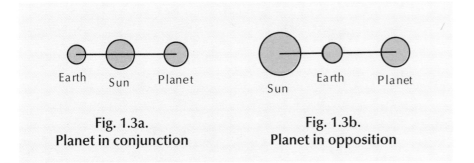

**Fig. 1.3a.**
**Planet in conjunction**

**Fig. 1.3b.**
**Planet in opposition**

Study the diagrams, and for each of the following situations, determine how to calculate the distance from Earth to another planet if the planet's distance from the Sun is known.

(a) The planet's orbit is between Earth and the Sun, and the planet and Earth are on the same side of the Sun.

(b) The planet's orbit is between Earth and the Sun, and the planet and Earth are on opposite sides of the Sun.

(c) Earth's orbit is between the planet and the Sun, and the planet and Earth are on the same side of the Sun.

(d) Earth's orbit is between the planet and the Sun, and the planet and Earth are on opposite sides of the Sun.

1. You can get a good idea of how the distance between planets changes by modeling their motion with software, such as The Geometer's Sketchpad or Cabri Geometry II. To construct such a model, create two or more concentric circles of different radii; these circles represent orbits. Place a point, representing a planet, on each circle, and use the animate or animation command to move the planets around their respective orbits. Vary the speeds of animation to see how the planets move into, and out of, alignment with each other.

2. Using your calculator or spreadsheet and the chart of distances of the planets from the Sun (on the following page), calculate the minimum and maximum distances between Earth and each of the other planets. Note that this problem uses the simplifying assumption that all the planets lie in the same orbital plane. Although this approach affects the calculations somewhat, the results are adequate for the purposes of this investigation.

3. A jet airplane travels at speeds of about 600 miles, or 960 kilometers, per hour; a rocket escaping Earth's gravity might travel at

*Solar System Distances*

| Body | Mean Solar Distance (Millions of km) | Minimum Distance from Earth (Millions of km) | Maximum Distance from Earth (Millions of km) |
|---|---|---|---|
| Mercury | 57.9 | | |
| Venus | 108.2 | | |
| Earth | 149.6 | N/A | N/A |
| Mars | 227.9 | | |
| Jupiter | 778.3 | | |
| Saturn | 1,427 | | |
| Uranus | 2,871 | | |
| Neptune | 4,497 | | |
| Pluto | 5,914 | | |
| Moon (Distance from Earth) | 0.38 | N/A | N/A |

A *light year* is the distance light travels in one year at the rate of 186,000 miles per second; it is a measure of distance, not time—almost $6(10^{12})$ miles.

Here are the distances in light years to some of the brightest stars:

Canopus . . . . . . . . . . . . . 98

Rigel . . . . . . . . . . . . . . . 910

Betelgeuse . . . . . . . . . . 510

Antares . . . . . . . . . . . . . 330

Pollux . . . . . . . . . . . . . . . 36

Deneb . . . . . . . . . . . 1,800

What was happening on Earth when the light that you see tonight left the star on its journey to Earth?

25,000 miles, or 40,000 kilometers, per hour; light travels at 186,000 miles per second. Add columns to your spreadsheet to determine travel times to each of the other planets under the following conditions:

— Traveling by jet
— Traveling by rocket
— Traveling at the speed of light

4. How much time is required for light from the Sun to reach each planet? Why is the following statement accurate: "When you look into the sky, you are looking back in time"?

5. Look up the distances from Earth to several stars or galaxies visible in the sky with either a telescope or the naked eye. What was happening on our planet when the light you see from those bodies left on its journey to Earth? For example, when the light we see now left the Pleiades, Kepler had not yet published his laws of planetary motion!

*Galactic Travel Times from Earth at the Speed of Light*

| Galactic Destination | Travel Time (in Years) |
|---|---|
| Sirius (Dog Star) | 8.4 |
| Pleiades star cluster | 400 |
| Crab Nebula | 4,000 |
| Center of Milky Way | 38,000 |
| Nearest Galaxy, Andromeda (M-31) | 2.2 million |

## Investigation 6—Launch Windows

*The* Mars Observer *spacecraft passed another milestone toward launch when it was moved from the Payload Hazardous Servicing Facility on Kennedy Space Center to Launch Complex 40 on Cape Canaveral Air Force Station and mated to the Martin Marietta Titan III rocket. With the payload atop the launch vehicle, checks of the* Mars Observer *spacecraft and the attached Transfer Orbit Stage (TOS) will begin this weekend.... All activities are currently on schedule to support a launch at the opening of the Mars planetary opportunity on September 16. The launch window extends from 1:02 to 3:05 P.M. EDT.*

Mars Observer *will be the first U.S. mission to Mars since the Viking program in 1975. From a circular Martian polar orbit of 250 miles, it will create a detailed global portrait of the planet. The spacecraft will map the surface and study Mars geology while profiling its atmosphere and weather. The mission is designed to span one Martian year, or 687 Earth days.*

Press release from Kennedy Space Center
August 12, 1992

When NASA plans to launch a mission, all orbital maneuvers are carefully timed and are based on a set of conditions that must be present at the time of launch. If the launch is delayed and conditions have changed enough that the mission cannot continue as designed, NASA must either scrap the mission or wait until the necessary conditions again prevail.

The *Mars Observer* spacecraft was originally scheduled to be launched on 16 September 1992. After a delay caused by contamination on the surface of the spacecraft, *Mars Observer* was successfully launched on 25 September. Had the mission missed its launch window, which would have expired on 13 October, scientists would have had to wait another two years before launch conditions would again be acceptable. One factor in timing launch conditions is the relative positions of the planets in their orbits. Because Earth completes one full revolution of

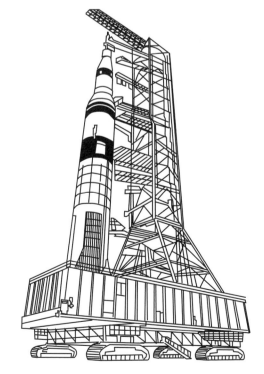

Launch windows are crucial factors whenever two spacecraft are to rendezvous in orbit, such as when the Space Shuttle is on a servicing mission to the Hubble Space Telescope. Such launch windows can be as short as a few minutes in duration.

the Sun in 365 days and Mars completes one full revolution in 687 days, the planets obviously do not maintain the same alignment as they move through their orbital paths around the Sun.

Given the vast distances of space that we saw modeled in earlier activities, we now turn to the question of launch windows, or times when conditions are favorable for placing a satellite in orbit. When launch windows are discussed in the context of sending a mission to Mars, two considerations come into play: First, a daily window occurs, during which a rocket launched from Florida will be on a proper "outward" heading. Suppose such a window exists between 10 A.M. and noon. Obviously, during that same two-hour period, a rocket launched from the opposite side of the globe would be headed in the "wrong" direction. Likewise, because of the rotation of Earth on its axis, after a period of some hours, a rocket launched from Florida will also be headed in the "wrong" direction.

The second type of launch window arises from the relative positions of Earth and Mars in their orbits. As the previous activities have shown, at times, Mars is too far from Earth and in the wrong location relative to the Sun for a successful launch. Launches must be timed to coincide with proper planetary alignment, an opportunity that, for Mars, occurs every 26 months. Planning for these launches requires extensive mathematical calculations. Consider, for example, that the *Galileo* probe was launched from the Space Shuttle on 18 October 1989 and arrived at its destination, Jupiter, precisely as planned on 7 December 1995!

*NASA's Exploration of Mars*

| Spacecraft | Launch Date | Arrival Date | Nature/Outcome of Mission |
|---|---|---|---|
| *Mariner 4* | 11/28/64 | 7/14/65 | Flyby |
| *Mariner 6* | 2/25/69 | 7/31/69 | Flyby |
| *Mariner 7* | 3/27/69 | 8/5/69 | Flyby |
| *Mariner 9* | 5/30/71 | 11/13/71 | Orbit |
| *Viking 1* | 8/20/75 | 6/19/76 | Orbit and landing |
| *Viking 2* | 9/9/75 | 8/7/76 | Orbit and landing |
| *Mars Observer* | 9/25/92 | 8/24/93? | Lost on arrival |
| *Mars Global Surveyor* | 11/7/96 | 9/12/97 | Orbit |
| *Mars Pathfinder* | 12/4/96 | 7/4/97 | Landing and rover exploration |
| *Mars Climate Orbiter* | 12/11/98 | 9/23/99 | Lost on arrival |
| *Mars Polar Lander* | 1/3/99 | 12/3/99 | Lost on arrival |
| *2001 Mars Odyssey* | 4/7/01 | 10/24/01 | Orbit |
| Mars Exploration Rovers | | | Exploration by two rovers |
| "Spirit" | 6/10/03 | 1/4/04 | |
| "Opportunity" | 7/7/03 | 1/25/04 | |
| *Mars Reconnaissance Orbiter* | Planned for 2005 | | Orbit |

The activity outlined below concerns the second type of launch window.

Because travel times to Mars may vary from just over four months to almost a year, when a spacecraft is launched from Earth, it must be placed in a trajectory that will take it not to where Mars is but to where Mars *will be* at the time of arrival. This situation is analogous to a quarterback throwing a long pass to a receiver downfield. The quarterback must anticipate where the receiver will be when the football arrives and aim the pass accordingly.

If you have not already done so, complete the activity on modeling planets traveling in different orbits using a software application such as The Geometer's Sketchpad or Cabri Geometry II (see page 11). This activity will help you visualize Earth in an inner orbit completing one revolution in 365 days and Mars in an outer orbit completing one revolution in 687 days.

You may also set up a two-dimensional Cartesian-coordinate model of the orbits of Earth and Mars around the Sun. For simplicity, assume that the orbital paths are circular and in the same plane. Use the following guidelines to design your model:

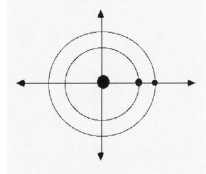

1.  Let the Sun be located at the origin, and construct two concentric circles, with centers at the origin, to represent the orbits of Earth and Mars. Select appropriate radii for these circles proportional to the average distance of each planet from the Sun. (See the chart of distances on page 12.)

2.  Assume initially that launch conditions are such that both planets lie on the positive *x*-axis and that launch occurs on 1 January. Remember that all assumptions are made to simplify the model; once the model is working, the complexities of launching on other dates and from different relative positions can be included.

3.  Create a spreadsheet, such as the one begun below, to calculate the angular motion of Earth and Mars around the Sun through two complete Earth years. Plot the location of each of the planets on

*Positions of Earth and Mars*

| Date | Days Elapsed | Position of Earth (Degrees) | Position of Mars (Degrees) |
|---|---|---|---|
| 1 Jan | 0 | 0 | 0 |
| 1 Feb | 31 | | |
| 1 Mar | 59 | | |
| 1 Apr | | | |
| 1 May | | | |
| 1 Jun | | | |

the first day of each month for the two-year period, then answer these questions.

(a) Through how many degrees does Earth move in one day?

(b) Through how many degrees does Mars move in one day?

(c) Write the equations of the circles that represent the orbital paths of Earth and Mars. Explain how you determined what the radii should be.

(d) Six months after launch, where will each of the planets be?

(e) When Earth crosses the positive y-axis for the first time, where will Mars be? Explain how you identified this location.

(f) How much time is required for Mars to cross the negative x-axis? At that time, where will Earth be?

(g) By the time Earth has completed one full orbit, where will Mars be?

(h) By the time Mars has completed one full orbit, where will Earth be? How many orbits around the Sun will Earth have completed?

(i) We assumed that both planets were initially on the positive x-axis; at that time, their angular separation was 0 degrees. When Mars has completed one orbit, what will be the angular separation of Earth and Mars?

When the *Mars Observer* was launched in September 1992, the two planets, Earth and Mars, were not in a straight-line path from the Sun, as assumed in the previous activity. Rather, a 42-degree *phase angle* existed between them. In other words, the central angle formed by connecting the location of each planet to the Sun was 42 degrees. To provide a reference point from which to model this situation, assume that Earth starts at an angle of 0 degrees and Mars, at an angle of 42 degrees to the positive x-axis, with both planets moving in a counterclockwise direction. Modify your spreadsheet to track the relative positions of the two planets, starting on 25 September 1992, and determine the next two times when the planets would be in the same relative alignment.

4. In creating these simulations, the problem has been oversimplified to make it easier to analyze. Describe at least one factor that this simulation has ignored but that would have to be considered if we were actually trying to predict accurately the next launch-window opportunity.

5. Write a paragraph explaining why launching spacecraft to Mars at "any old time" is not possible. Use charts or diagrams to support your explanation.

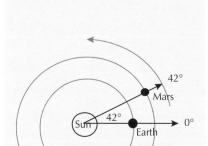

# Solutions and Teacher Commentary

The table below gives relevant solar-system data taken from NASA charts. Values computed by students may vary slightly as a result of rounding.

Measurements in the tables in this chapter are given in units commonly used by NASA scientists and others. Metric or customary units may be used for measurements under different circumstances. Teachers may choose whether to work in one or both systems; experiences with either system should help students develop a sense of the orders of magnitudes of sizes and distances. Teachers should also engage students in discussion about accuracy versus approximation and the reasons that many of the numbers are rounded to thousands or even millions. Students will also encounter some new units that may be unfamiliar, such as an *astronomical unit* (AU) or a *light year;* these units should be recognized as measures of distance, not time.

Discussing the simplifying assumptions that are made in this unit is important. For these activities, planetary orbits are assumed to be circular and co-planar, and average distances from the Sun are used. In a subsequent unit in Mission Mathematics, "Modeling Elliptical Orbits," students construct ellipses to match the eccentricities of some planetary orbits and compare them with the graphs of circles. Because the planetary eccentricities are quite close to zero, students should be able to see why the approximation with circular orbits is a reasonable first step. The orbits unit allows more advanced students to refine their models of orbits to include ellipses.

[High school students] need to become familiar with different ways of representing numbers. As part of their developing technological facility, students should become adept at interpreting numerical answers on calculator or computer displays.

*(NCTM 2000, p. 291)*

Geometry has always been a rich arena in which students can discover patterns and formulate conjectures. The use of interactive geometry software enables students to examine many cases, thus extending their ability to formulate and explore conjectures.

*(NCTM 2000, pp. 309–10)*

## Solar System Data

| Body | Equatorial Diameter (km) | Equatorial Diameter (mi) | Diam. Comp. with Earth | Mean Solar Dist. (M km) | Mean Solar Dist. (M mi) | Mean Solar Dist. (AU) | Orbit Period (Earth Years) | Ecc. | $T^2$ (T in Years) | $R^3$ (R in AU) | $T^2/R^3$ (Kepler's 3rd Law) |
|------|------|------|------|------|------|------|------|------|------|------|------|
| Mercury | 4,880 | 3,026 | 0.38 | 57.9 | 35.9 | 0.39 | 0.2 | 0.206 | 0.06 | 0.06 | 0.98 |
| Venus | 12,100 | 7,502 | 0.95 | 108.2 | 67.1 | 0.72 | 0.6 | 0.007 | 0.38 | 0.37 | 1.01 |
| Earth | 12,756 | 7,909 | 1.00 | 149.6 | 92.8 | 1 | 1.0 | 0.017 | 1.00 | 1.00 | 1.00 |
| Mars | 6,794 | 4,212 | 0.53 | 227.9 | 141.3 | 1.52 | 1.9 | 0.093 | 3.54 | 3.51 | 1.01 |
| Jupiter | 143,200 | 88,784 | 11.23 | 778.3 | 482.5 | 5.2 | 11.9 | 0.048 | 140.66 | 140.61 | 1.00 |
| Saturn | 120,536 | 74,732 | 9.45 | 1,427 | 884.7 | 9.55 | 29.5 | 0.056 | 867.89 | 870.98 | 1.00 |
| Uranus | 51,800 | 32,116 | 4.06 | 2,871 | 1,780.0 | 19.22 | 84.0 | 0.046 | 7,057.68 | 7,100.03 | 0.99 |
| Neptune | 49,528 | 30,707 | 3.88 | 4,497 | 2,788.1 | 31.11 | 164.8 | 0.009 | 27,155.74 | 30,109.26 | 0.90 |
| Pluto | 2,330 | 1,445 | 0.18 | 5,914 | 3,666.7 | 39.44 | 247.7 | 0.248 | 61,355.29 | 61,349.46 | 1.00 |
| Moon | 3,476 | 2,155 | 0.27 | * 0.38 | * 0.2 | | | 0.055 | | | |
| Sun | 1,392,000 | 863,040 | 109.13 | | | | | | | | |

* from Earth

## Investigation 4—Continuing the Mission

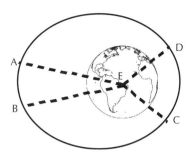

To visualize Kepler's second law, imagine that an orbiting satellite is connected with the center of Earth (point *E* in the diagram at the left) by a long string that sweeps across the orbital plane as the satellite moves. When the satellite travels from *A* to *B,* the area of region *ABE* is "swept" (think of it as being shaded in); when the satellite travels from *C* to *D,* the region swept is *CDE.* Kepler determined that when the areas of two such regions are equal, the times required for the satellite to move along the orbit from one endpoint of the elliptical arc to the other are equal. If the areas of regions *ABE* and *CDE* in the diagram are equal, then the time required to move from *A* to *B* equals the time required to move from *C* to *D.* This representation enables the recognition that the length of arc *AB* is less than the length of arc *CD,* or that the satellite travels slower along arc *AB* than along arc *CD.* In other words, satellites travel fastest at *perigee* and slowest at *apogee.* Thus, as a satellite moves from perigee to apogee, it slows down; as it moves from apogee to perigee, it speeds up.

## Investigation 5—Reaching Out

In these equations, $r(E)$ and $r(P)$ are the mean distances from the Sun to Earth and the planet. Below are approximations of the minimum and

| | Min. Dist. | Max. Dist. |
|---|---|---|
| (a) *P* orbit between *E* & *S;* *P* & *E* same side of *S* | $r(E) - r(P)$ | |
| (b) *P* orbit between *E* & *S;* *P* & *E* opposite sides of *S* | | $r(E) + r(P)$ |
| (c) *E* orbit between *P* & *S;* *P* & *E* same side of *S* | $r(P) - r(E)$ | |
| (d) *E* orbit between *P* & *S;* *P* & *E* opposite sides of *S* | | $r(P) + r(E)$ |

*Distances between Earth and the Other Planets*

| Body | Min. Dist. from Earth | Max. Dist. from Earth |
|---|---|---|
| Mercury | 91.7 | 207.5 |
| Venus | 41.4 | 257.8 |
| Mars | 78.3 | 377.5 |
| Jupiter | 628.7 | 927.9 |
| Saturn | 1,277.4 | 1,576.6 |
| Uranus | 2,721.4 | 3,020.6 |
| Neptune | 4,347.4 | 4,646.6 |
| Pluto | 5,764.4 | 6,063.6 |

Students should be able to decide whether a problem calls for a rough estimate, an approximation to an appropriate degree of precision, or an exact answer. They should select a suitable method of computing from among mental mathematics, paper-and-pencil computations, and the use of calculators and computers and be proficient with each method. Electronic computation technologies provide opportunities for students to work on realistic problems and to perform difficult computations, for example, computing roots and powers of numbers or performing operations with vectors and matrices.

*(NCTM 2000, p. 294)*

maximum distances between Earth and the other planets in millions of kilometers:

Some examples of travel times to these distances under various conditions are shown in the following chart.

| | *TravelTimes from Earch* | | |
|---|---|---|---|
| Destination (from Earth) | By Jet (600 mph) | By Rocket (25,000 mph) | At Light Speed (186,000 mi/sec) |
| Mercury | 10 yr, 10 mo | 3 mo | 5 min |
| Venus | 5 yr, 5 mo | 1.5 mo | 2.5 min |
| Mars | 8 yr, 10 mo | 2.5 mo | 4 min |
| Jupiter | 74 yr, 3 mo | 1 yr, 9 mo | 35 min |
| Saturn | 150 yr, 5 mo | 3 yr, 7 mo | 1 hr, 11 min |
| Uranus | 318 yr, 6 mo | 7 yr, 7 mo | 2 hr, 30 min |
| Neptune | 513 yr, 2 mo | 12 yr, 3 mo | 4 hr, 2 min |
| Pluto | 690 yr, 1 mo | 16 yr, 5 mo | 5 hr, 25 min |
| Moon | 16.5 days | 9.4 hr | 1.2 sec |
| Sun | 17 yr, 8 mo | 4 mo | 8.5 min |
| Alpha Centauri | $4.8(10^6)$ yr | 114,155.2 yr | 4.2 yr |
| Sirius | $9.6(10^6)$ yr | 228,310.4 yr | 8.4 yr |

## Investigation 6—Launch Windows

Given that Earth completes one orbit of 360 degrees around the Sun in one year, the planet moves about 0.99 degree per day; Mars, which orbits the Sun in 1.88 Earth years, or approximately 687 Earth days, advances in its orbit about 0.52 degree per day. The sketch on the next page was created with The Geometer's Sketchpad using data compiled in a spreadsheet. It represents the positions of Earth and Mars after 18, 19, …, 26 months, assuming that both planets were aligned along the positive x-axis at the start of the first month (1 January). The corresponding data from the spreadsheet are shown following the diagram. The spreadsheet and graphic allow us to draw the following conclusions:

✦ About 22.5 months (687 days) after the 1 January "start" (that is, in mid-November), Mars has completed its first orbit and returned to its initial position on the positive x-axis. At the same time, Earth has completed one orbit plus approximately 318 degrees of its second orbit. Earth now "trails" Mars by about 42 degrees.

✦ Two years after the 1 January start, again on 1 January, Earth has completed two orbits and is now back to its initial position on the positive x-axis. Mars has moved forward to a position 22.5 degrees from the positive x-axis. Earth, which is moving faster than Mars, has closed the gap to 22.5 degrees after 24 months.

Investigation 6 can be conducted as a whole-class activity led by the teacher, or students can work independently from the investigation sheet included with this unit.

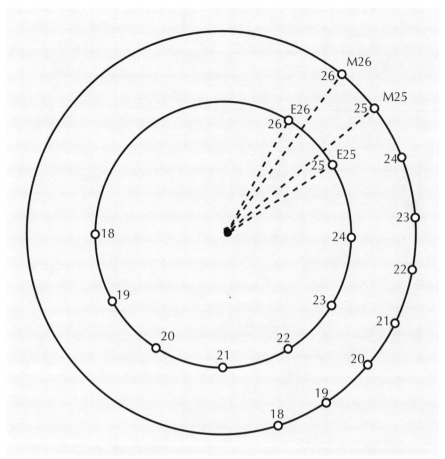

Representation of the relative positions of Earth and Mars after 18, 19, …, 26 months

◆ After 25 months, Earth is about 8 degrees "behind" Mars, and after 26 months, Earth has overtaken and is about 5 degrees "ahead" of Mars. Sometime during that period, the phase angle between the two has again closed to 0 degrees, although at that time, both planets were about 48 degrees beyond the positive *x*-axis. The alignment occurred on approximately 19 February.

Once again, these models have made simplifying assumptions, among them the presumption of circular orbits and constant orbital velocities. In fact, with elliptical orbits, planets travel faster when they are near the Sun (the focus) and more slowly when they are far away. These simplifying assumptions, however, enable us to understand the mathematics of orbits without introducing unnecessary complexity.

High school students' algebra experience should enable them to create and use tabular, symbolic, graphical, and verbal representations and to analyze and understand patterns, relations, and functions with more sophistication than in the middle grades.

*(NCTM 2000, p. 297)*

| Date | Months Elapsed | Days Elapsed | Location of Earth (Degrees) | Location of Mars (Degrees) |
|------|----------------|--------------|------------------------------|-----------------------------|
| 1 Jul | 18 | 546 | 178.5 | 286.1 |
| 1 Aug | 19 | 577 | 209.1 | 302.4 |
| 1 Sep | 20 | 608 | 239.7 | 318.6 |
| 1 Oct | 21 | 638 | 269.3 | 334.3 |
| 1 Nov | 22 | 669 | 299.8 | 350.6 |
| 1 Dec | 23 | 699 | 329.4 | 6.3 |
| 1 Jan | 24 | 730 | 0.0 | 22.5 |
| 1 Feb | 25 | 761 | 30.6 | 38.8 |
| 1 Mar | 26 | 789 | 58.2 | 53.4 |

# Space Debris

## Craters, Craters, Craters

What do the Moon, Arizona, the Space Shuttle, and the International Space Station (ISS) have in common? Think about the Moon's surface. Does it appear to be smooth? Does it appear to have mountains? Can an observer see that the circular features of the Moon are craters, caused by collisions of asteroids with the Moon's surface?

Asteroids are rocks or hunks of metal orbiting the Sun. Many asteroids travel their paths between the orbits of Mars and Jupiter. Thousands of these asteroids—many are large enough to be seen with a medium-sized telescope—have been observed, named, and cataloged by scientists. At times, these asteroids collide, often resulting in pieces that are thrown out of their orbits to begin a collision path with other planets and moons. In this way, many asteroids have collided with the surface of the Moon, resulting in craters that are quite large.

Arizona also has a crater of some significance. Barringer Crater is one of the most visible sites of a collision of an asteroid with the Earth's surface in the United States. Barringer Crater is 1.2 kilometers in diameter and 180 meters deep. Scientists have determined that an iron meteorite—a metallic rock from space—up to 60 meters in diameter and weighing about 900 million kilograms slammed into Earth to form the crater. The force of the explosion caused by the impact may have been equivalent to the explosion of a 15-megaton bomb. Scientists use this crater and one more recently formed in Siberia to estimate the effect that another collision of the same magnitude would have on our planet. Some scientific evidence also points to an earlier collision during the time of the dinosaurs. Although no one is certain how that collision might have been related to the dinosaurs' extinction, the evidence has fueled speculation about the possible catastrophic result of a future impact. Our popular culture has capitalized on such possibilities through feature films, including *Asteroid, Deep Impact,* and *Armageddon.*

Those traveling in the Space Shuttle or living on the ISS are also concerned about another type of material in space, human-made objects that orbit Earth. This "space junk," or orbital debris, comes in many sizes. Some pieces of the debris are only small particles, but even tiny paint flecks can be dangerous because they travel at high speeds. In fact, Space Shuttles have been hit by such particles. For instance, the impact of a fleck of paint resulted in a crater in an orbiter window! Fortunately, the window was thick enough to withstand the blow.

Because orbital debris, even in its smallest form, is a danger in space travel, NASA scientists are working on the problem from many angles. For example, as you might imagine, space junk is a threat to astronauts performing extravehicular activities (EVAs). If a particle should hit an astronaut, it could certainly puncture his or her space suit and cause it to depressurize. Scientists catalog the location of orbital debris to ensure that future satellites, Shuttle missions, and the ISS are not placed in collision paths with the debris.

In some instances, a Shuttle or the ISS has been maneuvered to avoid collisions with orbital debris. Designers of space suits continue to develop better materials and suit designs that will resist punctures. Backup systems are available to help an astronaut return to the orbiter or the Space Station if hit by orbital debris. Scientists at NASA's Hypervelocity Impact Test Facility (HITF) at White Sands, New Mexico, fire small missiles to determine the effects of high-velocity impact on different materials, including those used to make the skin of the Space Shuttle and the ISS.

The success of these projects and other vital NASA laboratory work will continue to improve the margin of safety for space travel.

Earth's moon

# Modeling Orbital Debris Problems

This unit uses the problems caused by human-made debris in orbit as a context for studying mathematical modeling. The investigations in this unit will help students realize that not all problems are solvable with precise measurements, exact answers, and known formulas but that mathematical models enable us to explore trends and make predictions about probable outcomes. The ambiguity associated with the results of these activities may be frustrating to some, yet it reflects the realities with which mathematicians, statisticians, and scientists must work.

## Purpose

The purpose of this unit is to create and compare various mathematical models as a way to investigate some of the questions raised by the pro-liferation of orbital debris. Although the models are greatly simplified to make them more understandable, they offer insight into the process of mathematical modeling and its importance. The investigations assume that students will work with appropriate technology. Depending on availability and teacher preferences, these tools may include graphing calculators, computer graphing utilities, spreadsheets, or nongraphing calculators.

## Introduction

An important outcome for this unit is to develop an appreciation for the power and limitations of mathematical modeling. Students should real-ize that the two most basic expectations of models are (1) the ability to account for or represent known phenomena and (2) the ability to pre-dict future results. Thus, the models developed in this unit should enable students to answer such questions as "What will happen if this trend continues?" or "What will happen if this element is changed?"

Other outcomes anticipated from this unit include the following:

✦ Students will gain a better understanding of the differences among linear, quadratic, and exponential functions (models) and the pat-terns of growth that arise from them.

✦ Students will develop a more concrete realization of the vastness of space and the seeming paradox that large quantities of debris are in orbit in space, yet the probability of encountering any debris is small.

✦ Students will come to appreciate the power of mathematics to help "get a handle on" seemingly unmanageable problems.

Data included in this unit are from various NASA sources and from other space-related Web sites. The following three news items are examples of the sources from which data for the unit were gleaned.

*SPACE CENTER, Houston (CNN). Carrying a crew of seven and the Hubble Telescope, space shuttle Discovery fled to a safer, higher orbit Saturday to avoid a piece of space junk the size of a book. The fragment of an exploded rocket would have come dangerously close to Discovery and the telescope anchored in its cargo bay had the*

High school students should be able to create and interpret models of more-complex phenomena, drawn from a wider range of contexts, by identifying essential features of a situation and by finding representations that capture mathematical relationships among those features.

*(NCTM 2000, p. 361)*

The term *mathematical model,* which is the focus in this context, means a mathematical representation of the elements and relationships in an idealized version of a complex phenomenon. Mathematical models can be used to clarify and interpret the phenomenon and to solve problems.

*(NCTM 2000, p. 70)*

*pilots not steered out of the way. A few hours after Discovery's pilots steered the shuttle and the moored Hubble into a 2-mile-higher orbit to extend the lifetime of the telescope, they were ordered to go up an additional half-mile. An 8-inch-square fragment of an exploded Pegasus rocket was due to pass within a half-mile of the shuttle and telescope, officials said, and Mission Control did not want to take any chances. The speed of the debris: 17,500 mph. The Pegasus was launched in 1994 with a military research satellite, which ended up in the wrong orbit. The rocket fragment was one of 8,014 orbiting objects being tracked by the U.S. Space Command on Saturday, most of it junk. (CNN Interactive, February 1997)*

*KANSAS CITY, MO (AP). Streaks of brilliant light that were spotted from Texas to Nebraska on Saturday night apparently were caused by space debris breaking up, authorities said. A dispatcher at the Kansas Turnpike Authority in Wichita said callers reported the lights from the Oklahoma border to near Kansas City. In Hastings, Neb.,*

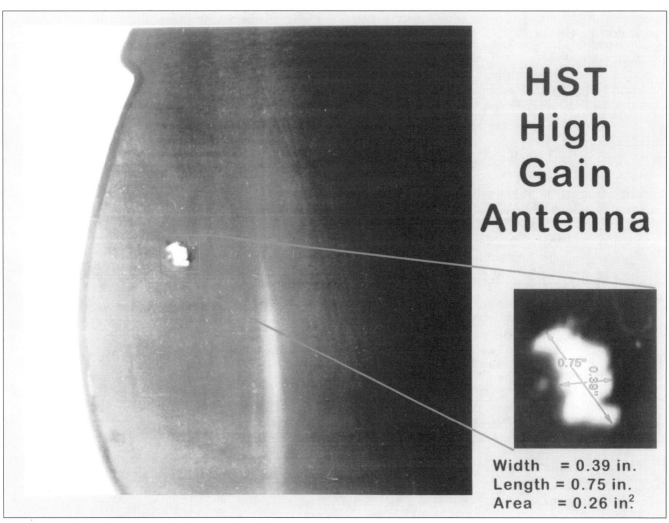

HST
High
Gain
Antenna

Width  = 0.39 in.
Length = 0.75 in.
Area   = 0.26 in.²

Impact caused by a ¼-inch particle (happened in orbit)

*meteorologist Larry Wirth of the National Weather Service said callers described a bright light that crossed the horizon from southwest to northeast and broke. "People said it appeared to break up into about 30 little balls, with tails, more or less like fireworks," Wirth said. Wirth said NORAD—the North American Air Defense Command—reported to the Federal Aviation Administration's regional center in Minneapolis that some kind of space debris had broken up in the atmosphere. NORAD monitors satellites and space debris that re-enters the atmosphere.* (USA Today, 2 December 2001)

*The International Space Station (ISS) has been moved to a higher orbit to avoid the danger of a collision with a floating tool dropped by a spacewalking astronaut. The change was made by the space shuttle Discovery, which is currently docked to the ISS about 380 kilometres (236 miles) above the surface of the Earth. On Wednesday, mission controllers ordered shuttle commander James Wetherbee to fire Discovery's thrusters, moving the two craft about four kilometres (2.5 miles) further up and well clear of the piece of space junk. NASA later admitted that it was a false alarm, saying their readings of the object's path had been wrong. The conjoined platform and orbiter are moving at a speed of about eight kilometres (five miles) per second. Any collision with the shoebox-sized tool could have punched a hole in the space station's walls, leading to a rapid drop in pressure. The errant piece of equipment was lost by astronaut James Voss near the start of a nine-hour spacewalk on Sunday.* (BBC News, 15 March 2001)

Given that this topic involves current events, teachers should be alert for updated information related to the problem. News stories such as the ones provided here help make the concern over the problem of space pollution seem more immediate. Keep in mind, too, that some of the data used in these investigations, such as the amount of debris in orbit, are estimates based on the best technology and information available at a given time. These estimates are continually revised as new information becomes available. Neither students nor teachers should be overly concerned about whether the numbers provided for the amount of debris or the rate of accumulation, for example, are the latest, most precise figures available; rather, the focus should be on patterns of change and on how quantities increase or decrease over time under various conditions, such as linear, quadratic, or exponential growth. If the class finds different estimates of some of these quantities, students might explore how their models can be adjusted to account for this new information.

## Getting Started

In January 1996, two days into a mission, the crew of the Space Shuttle *Endeavour* performed a maneuver to slow its speed by 4 feet per second, thereby steering clear of a 350-pound piece of space junk, a defunct Air Force satellite that would have passed within $4/5$ mile of Endeavour. Although the Shuttle was in no danger of collision, NASA

Good problems give students the chance to solidify and extend what they know and, when well chosen, can stimulate mathematics learning.... In high school, many areas of the curriculum can be introduced through problems from mathematical or applications contexts.

*(NCTM 2000, p. 52)*

flight safety rules call for at least 1.3 miles of separation between the Shuttle and any other orbiting object. The maneuver widened the distance to 6 miles.

The incident, however, called attention to the continuing problem of space debris. The Air Force catalogs almost 9,000 orbiting objects of grapefruit size and larger. On the basis of this tracking of space debris, the Shuttle and the ISS have performed maneuvers to avoid orbiting objects. As humans and their vehicles and probes prepare to spend extended times in space, they must also prepare to confront the growing problem of space debris.

NASA scientists continue to study the repercussions of this space-age form of pollution. Just as pollution creates worsening conditions for us on Earth, so, too, do we experience hazards from space pollution.

Estimates for the year 2002 indicate that approximately 11 million pounds of manufactured materials are in Earth orbit. Of that amount, only a small percentage is operating payloads; the vast majority consists of human-made debris: old rocket parts, non-functioning satellites, discarded or dropped tools, by-products of explosions and collisions, and other odds and ends, as well as countless numbers of smaller objects, such as paint chips and dust-sized particles. On the basis of current launch rates and space-debris accumulation since 1980, researchers estimate that the nations in the space business will contribute an additional 350,000 pounds to 420,000 pounds of debris per year for the foreseeable future.

Rings continue to form around Earth—not the rings of rock, dust, and ice that encircle other planets but rings of human-made orbital debris—and their density is increasing. Don Kessler, a former NASA scientist who made a career of studying space debris, said, "Rings are nature's way of saying it doesn't like things in noncircular orbit out of Earth's equatorial plane. Nature wants to tear these objects apart and reform them into either a ring or a single object ... it is just a question of when."

By the mid-1980s, ground-based telescopes allowed scientists to see marble-sized pieces of orbital debris. An "inventory" published in 2000 by the U.S. Space Command identified 8,927 radar-trackable objects, that is, of baseball size and larger, in space. In addition, the Space Command estimated the presence of 110,000 objects at least 1 centimeter in diameter, including literally trillions of tiny paint flakes and tens to hundreds of trillions of dust-sized particles of aluminum oxide. During hypervelocity, which begins at 3 kilometers per second, particles as small as a paint flake can be damaging or even lethal.

"We get hit regularly on the shuttle," said Joseph Loftus, assistant director of engineering for NASA's Space and Life Science Directorate. "We've replaced more than 80 [Shuttle] windows because of debris impacts." (Weinstock 2000)

The first loss of a spacecraft part directly attributable to human-made orbital debris occurred during the Shuttle mission of STS-7 in 1983. The crew of the *Challenger* reported an impact

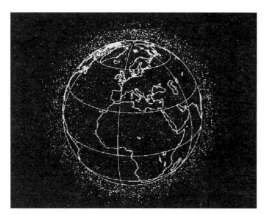

This computer-generated image shows the thousands of satellites, spent rocket stages, and breakup debris in low-Earth orbit.

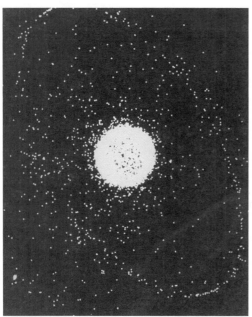

This computer-generated image illustrates Earth's rings formed from human-made orbital debris.

crater on one of the orbiter's windows significant enough to require replacement. This damage occurred despite the fact that the window is $5/8$ inch thick and built to withstand pressures of 8,600 pounds per square inch and temperatures up to 482°C. By studying the traces found in the pitted window, NASA determined that the damage was caused by white paint specks about 0.2 millimeter in diameter traveling between 3 and 5 kilometers per second.

Cosmonauts on the Soviet spacecraft *Salyut 7* reported a similar window incident just weeks later and even heard the impact. The Solar Maximum Mission satellite had been in space for 50 months when the crew of STS-41C repaired it in space and returned to Earth with 15 square feet of the insulation blanket and 10 square feet of aluminum louvers showing thousands of pits and excessive wear and tear. The blanket showed 32 holes per square foot, and the louvers, 6 holes per square foot, many more than NASA scientists expected; analysis revealed that most of the pits were caused by paint flakes.

Collisions and breakups significantly increase the number of particles orbiting Earth, but they differ in fragmentation and the resulting hazards. Collisions produce smaller fragments and increased hazard. If a 10-pound mass hits a 1,000-pound stage at orbital speeds, a tremendous amount of energy is released that could result in 4 million particles and 10,000 larger pieces. Breakups caused by explosions produce fewer small fragments, giving scientists more opportunity to learn about the causes of explosions and, thus, prevent them. For example, when seven second-stage Delta rocket breakups occurred three years after launch, scientists were able to determine that they had been caused by unspent hypergolic fuels; this knowledge resulted in launch changes that corrected the problem.

## What's out there?

Operating payloads . . . . 5%

Payloads no longer operating . . . . . . . . . . . 21%

Spent stages and gear . . . . . . . . . . . 25%

Breakup debris . . . . . . 49%

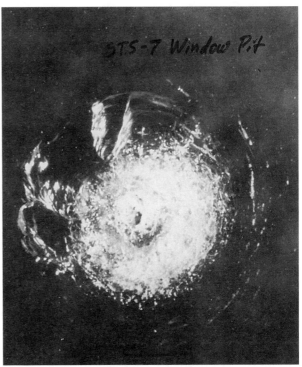

Impact crater on the Space Shuttle *Challenger's* window created by orbital debris

# Modeling Space-Debris Accumulation

Modeling involves identifying and selecting relevant features of a real-world situation, representing those features symbolically, analyzing and reasoning about the model and the characteristics of the situation, and considering the accuracy and limitations of the model.

*(NCTM 2000, p. 303)*

Estimates for the year 2002 indicate that approximately 11 million pounds of manufactured materials are in Earth orbit.

On the basis of current launch rates and space-debris accumulation since 1980, researchers estimate that the nations in the space business will contribute an additional 350,000 pounds to 420,000 pounds of debris per year for the foreseeable future.

The data we read about space debris include such numbers as 11 million pounds and 350,000 pounds per year. We have become accustomed to reading such numbers, but few of us have an intuitive sense of what they represent. How much is 11 million pounds of anything? Have students try to come up with at least three concrete examples that would help someone else get a sense of the mass of millions of pounds of debris. For example, finish the following sentence: "A total of 11 million pounds of pennies would fill …."

The following sections discuss Investigations 1 through 7 (found on pp. 38–43, 48–49). These investigations are used to create, analyze, and compare various mathematical models that help answer some of the questions raised by the proliferation of orbital debris. The models are greatly simplified in their assumptions to enable students to conduct the investigations using calculators, spreadsheet software, and graphing utilities, but they foster insight into the process of mathematical modeling and its importance.

## Investigation 1—Modeling the Problem: Linear Growth

The problem of determining the amount of debris in space and the anticipated rate of increase of such matter is one that cannot be solved directly nor with a high degree of certainty. According to J.-C. Liou of Lockheed Martin Space Operations at NASA's Johnson Space Center, "It is very difficult to predict the future debris environment since some controlling factors are simply unpredictable (for example, future launch traffic, solar activities, etc.)." (Liou 2002)

We cannot locate, count, and weigh all the objects in orbit. Nor can we predict with assurance when two of them will collide. Instead, we must rely on existing data and on mathematical models to help us represent the problem and identify trends and expected outcomes. Again, Liou says,

> What is being done typically (including NASA and ESA's [the European Space Agency's] models) is to assume a "business-as-usual" scenario for future projection. The scenario is based on several simple assumptions, including [the ideas that] (1) future launch traffic can be represented by repeating the launch traffic from the past 8 or 10 years, (2) the future breakup mechanisms/rates are identical to those from the same cycle, (3) the future solar activities can be represented/predicted using the previous two solar cycles. (Liou 2002)

Predictions about future accumulation of space debris afford an excellent opportunity for students to create and analyze simple mathematical models. Mathematicians strive to find the simplest model that will adequately represent the problem. For this reason, Investigation 1 on page 38 is a good starting point for students to create linear models to predict the amount of accumulated space debris on the basis of the number of pounds of debris being added each year. In so doing, students will look at an estimated 2002 accumulation rate of 350,000 pounds per year (rate of increase) and an initial amount of 11 million pounds. If the year is represented by $t$ (with $t = 1$ in 2002) and the total amount of debris is represented by $y$ (in units of millions of pounds), the linear model is $y = 0.35 t + 11$. Similarly, by using the rate of 420,000 pounds per year, the model is $y = 0.42 t + 11$.

The linear models are analogous to models of constant velocity. Because students are familiar with distance-rate-time problems, they should be able to see that increasing the amount of debris at a constant rate is equivalent to increasing the distance traveled when moving at a constant speed.

The linear model of debris accumulation is analogous to moving at constant velocity.

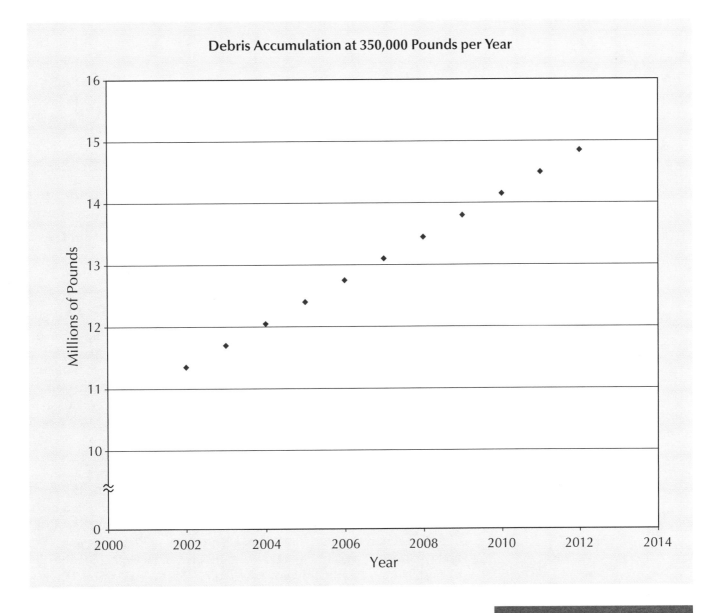

Debris Accumulation at 350,000 Pounds per Year

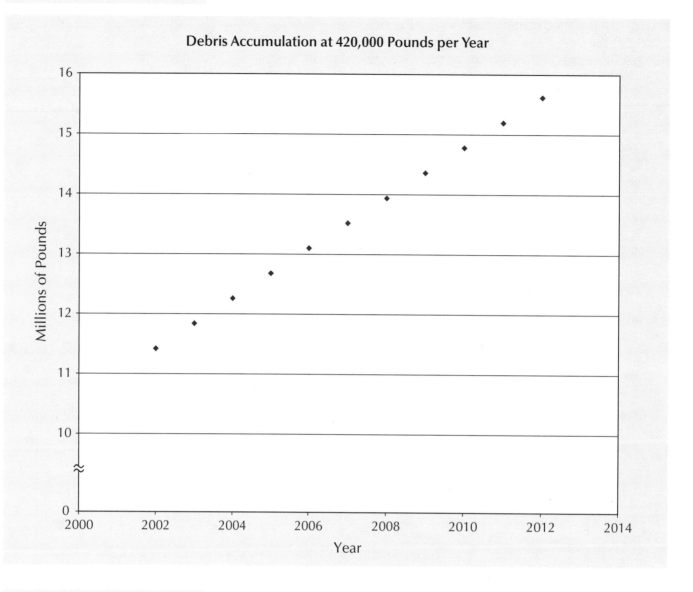

**Debris Accumulation at 420,000 Pounds per Year**

*The quadratic model of debris accumulation is analogous to moving with constant acceleration.*

## Investigation 2—Refining the Model: Quadratic Growth

Investigation 1 suggests a new question: Does either linear model realistically describe the situation? Does either rate, 350,000 pounds per year or 420,000 pounds per year, tell us how much debris will build up between 2002 and 2012? Which rate of increase should we use over this ten-year time period? Most certainly, the amount being added each year is changing during this period, but by how much each year? When students realize the limitations inherent in their original attempts to find a linear model, they should try to adjust the model to account for the fact that neither the rate of 350,000 pounds per year nor the rate of 420,000 pounds per year remains constant throughout the period. The problem becomes one of acceleration, not constant velocity. Students who have studied motion in a physics class should make the connection between examples of uniformly accelerated motion, such as a body in free fall, a ball rolling down an incline, or a car accelerating at a constant rate, and the uniform acceleration of space dumping.

Mathematicians prefer to start with a simple model, then add complexities to refine it as needed. Here, we make the simplest of assumptions: Debris is accumulating in space at a constant rate from 350,000 pounds per year in 2002 to 420,000 pounds per year in 2012. This adjustment means that over the ten-year period from the end of 2002 through 2012, the rate ("velocity") of littering will increase by 0.07 million pounds per year (420,000 – 350,000 = 70,000 pounds, or 0.07 million pounds). We are making the assumption that this increase is achieved in equal annual increments of 0.007 million pounds (7,000 pounds) per year in each year of the ten-year period. Have students complete Investigation 2 on pages 39–40 to show the amount of debris added each year and the total amount in orbit at the end of the year. Then use the information in the chart to explore the remaining questions.

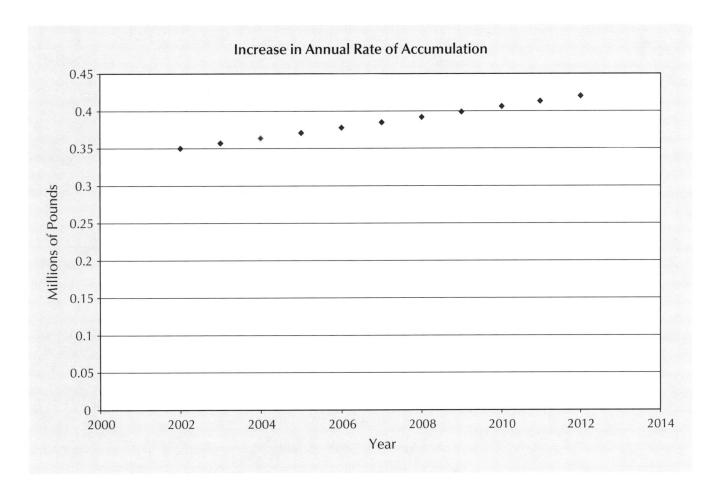

## End-of-Year Accumulation, Quadratic Model

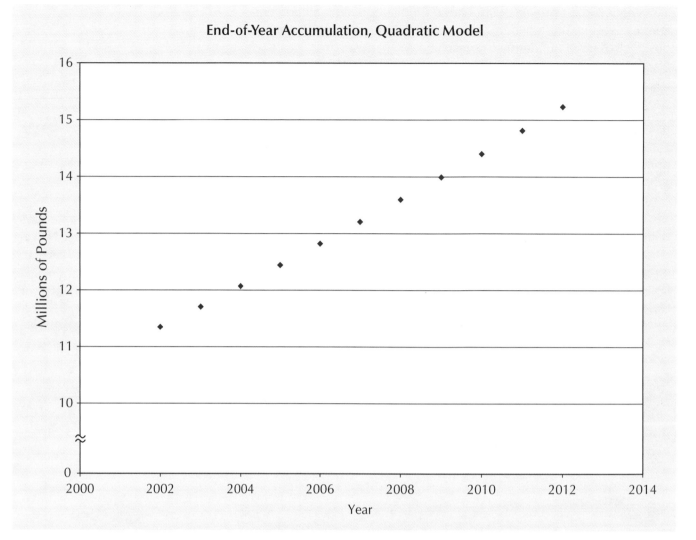

A number of important concepts emerge from this investigation. Although the plots generated in Investigation 2, and those that your students generate, may appear to be linear over the ten-year range of the initial data, extending the domain to twenty or thirty or fifty years, as suggested in Investigation 2, reveals that the graph of the end-of-year total accumulation is, indeed, not linear. Students can verify the fact that the accumulation is quadratic by—

✦ attempting to align a straightedge or piece of paper along the graph;

✦ manually creating a best-fit line and checking its predictions against those generated by the chart patterns;

✦ generating linear- and quadratic-regression equations on a graphing calculator and overlaying both the linear-regression graph and the quadratic-regression graph on the scatterplot of the data; or

✦ using the method of constant differences and the data from the charts to generate a quadratic equation. This method is summarized in the following paragraphs.

## Quadratic Model after Thirty Years

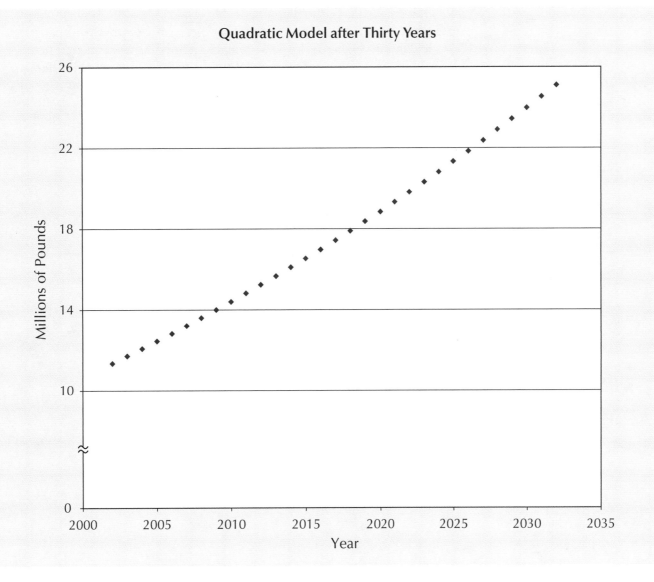

Many methods exist for determining or verifying that a particular set of data can be appropriately modeled by a particular function. For instance, a best-fit line can be created manually; that model's predicted outcomes can then be compared with the actual outcomes. A graphing calculator will also generate regression equations that can be compared with actual outcomes. In either method, a plot of the suggested model can be superimposed over a scatterplot of the data set, again to compare predicted and actual outcomes in judging goodness of fit. Another method for generating polynomial models relies on patterns that emerge in polynomial data. This method, the method of constant differences, can also be applied to the orbital debris information used in Investigations 1 and 2.

First, recall that for all linear functions $y = f(x)$, the differences between successive values of $f(x)$ are constant when $x$ is an integer. We refer to these differences as *first differences*. First differences correspond to the slope of the line. In quadratic functions, such first differences are

As high school students study several classes of functions and become familiar with the properties of each, they should begin to see that classifying functions as linear, quadratic, or exponential makes sense because the functions in each of these classes share important attributes. Many of these attributes are global characteristics of the functions.

*(NCTM 2000, p. 300)*

not constant, but the differences calculated for successive first differences, aptly called the *second differences*, are constant. This pattern extends to higher-order polynomial functions, as well: cubic functions do not have constant differences until we look at the set of third differences; quartic functions first have constant differences when we look at the fourth differences; and so on. The chart below shows the pattern of constant differences for the general linear and quadratic cases and for two specific examples from our orbital-debris explorations.

## The Method of Constant Differences:
*Pattern for General Linear and Quadratic Cases with Orbital-Debris Examples*

| Linear Function: $f(x) = ax + b$ | | | | | Quadratic Function: $f(x) = ax^2 + bx + c$ | | | | | | |
| --- | --- | --- | --- | --- | --- | --- | --- | --- | --- | --- | --- |
| General Case | | | $f(x) = 0.35x + 11$ | | General Case | | | | Debris Example | | |
| $x$ | $f(x)$ | 1st dif | $f(x)$ | 1st dif | $x$ | $f(x)$ | 1st dif | 2nd dif | $f(x)$ | 1st dif | 2nd dif |
| 1 | $a + b$ | | 11.35 | | 1 | $a + b + c$ | | | 11.35 | | |
| | | $a$ | | 0.35 | | | $3a + b$ | | | 0.357 | |
| 2 | $2a + b$ | | 11.70 | | 2 | $4a + 2b + c$ | | $2a$ | 11.707 | | 0.007 |
| | | $a$ | | 0.35 | | | $5a + b$ | | | 0.364 | |
| 3 | $3a + b$ | | 12.05 | | 3 | $9a + 3b + c$ | | $2a$ | 12.071 | | 0.007 |
| | | $a$ | | 0.35 | | | $7a + b$ | | | 0.371 | |
| 4 | $4a + b$ | | 12.40 | | 4 | $16a + 4b + c$ | | | 12.442 | | |

Using the quadratic data in the chart, students can generate the following equations and solve them for *a*, *b*, and *c*.

$$a + b + c = 11.35 \qquad c = 11$$
$$3a + b = 0.357 \qquad b = 0.3465$$
$$2a = 0.007 \qquad a = 0.0035$$

The resulting quadratic function, based on the values of *a*, *b*, and *c* just determined, is $f(x) = 0.0035x^2 + 0.3465x + 11$, where $f(x)$ gives the amount of debris in orbit at the end of year *x* and $x = 1$ in 2002. Superimpose this quadratic model over the scatterplot of the data created in Investigation 2 to compare the model with the data. Ask students how they would describe the goodness of fit between the model and the data.

## Investigation 3—One More Perspective: Exponential Growth

So far, students have looked at two models. One was a "constant velocity" linear model, and the other, a "uniformly accelerated" quadratic model. In this investigation, students explore a third model.

Suppose that the amount of litter accumulating each year in space grew not by a fixed number of pounds but by a fixed percent of the amount already in space—a situation analogous to an investment of money with interest compounded annually. For example, what would happen to the original 11 million pounds if the litter added each year was 5 percent of the amount already in orbit? Have students complete Investigation 3 on pages 40–41 to determine the amount of debris that would accumulate over the period from 2002 to 2012. Use of a spreadsheet is recommended for students to perform the calculations required to complete the chart. With a spreadsheet, students can hypothesize different rates of increase and explore what would happen if debris were added at those rates. The findings can then be compared with the patterns of linear and quadratic growth. The major objective for this investigation is to help students appreciate the impact of exponential growth.

## Investigation 4—What Goes Up Might Come Down: Extending the Models

The models developed thus far assume that the additional debris added each year stays in orbit and accumulates there, but most students know that not everything in orbit stays there forever. In fact, every year, some of the debris slows down enough to reenter the atmosphere, where it burns up or, on rare occasions, returns to Earth. Investigation 4 on page 42 offers an opportunity for students to explore the implications of assumptions about debris returning to Earth or burning up on return to our atmosphere. This investigation is a natural extension of the modeling process as it evolves. To be realistic, the models that students develop should take into account both the addition to, and the destruction of, orbital debris. The models simultaneously become more complex and represent reality more closely.

The exponential model of debris accumulation is analogous to investing money with interest compounded annually.

The expanded class of functions available to high school students for mathematical modeling should provide them with a versatile and powerful means for analyzing and describing their world. With utilities for symbol manipulation, graphing, and curve fitting and with programmable software and spreadsheets to represent iterative processes, students can model and analyze a wide range of phenomena. These mathematical tools can help students develop a deeper understanding of real-world phenomena.

*(NCTM 2000, p. 297)*

## Comparison of Four Models

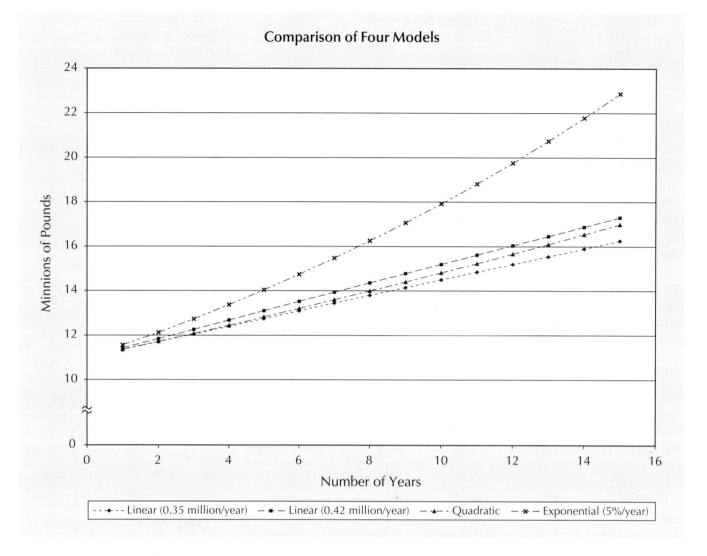

--•-- Linear (0.35 million/year)　—■— Linear (0.42 million/year)　—▲-- Quadratic　—✕— Exponential (5%/year)

## Investigation 5—Putting the Models to Work

The power of mathematical models derives from their ability to enable us to ask "What if?" questions. A previously posed question is a good example: What if we could increase the rate at which orbital debris is destroyed? Other such questions include the following:

✦ What if we decrease the rate at which we are adding debris?

✦ What if we decrease the rate at which we are adding debris and, at the same time, find a way to increase the rate at which existing debris is destroyed?

Such questions lead to open-ended investigations using mathematical models. Investigation 5 on page 43 is designed to encourage students to pose and explore such questions. To give students the opportunity to form and test hypotheses of their own, no data are provided for this investigation. Students should try modifications that assume destruction at a fixed rate per year (linear), as well as at a fixed percent (exponential

High school students should study modeling in greater depth, generating or using data and exploring which kinds of functions best fit or model those data.

*(NCTM 2000, p. 303)*

decay). Students should look for models that might predict an eventual decrease in the amount of orbital debris even though we assume that NASA and others will continue to launch payloads and, thereby, continue to add to the orbital debris. These open-ended investigations are designed to let students experience the search for models that might lead to desirable consequences—although, in reality, we may need to invent the necessary technology to implement the model.

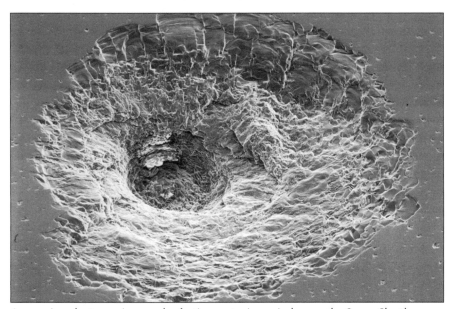

A scanning electron micrograph of a tiny crater in a window on the Space Shuttle *Challenger* in June 1983

Students should have frequent opportunities to formulate, grapple with, and solve complex problems that require a significant amount of effort and should then be encouraged to reflect on their thinking.

*(NCTM 2000, p. 52)*

Students can discuss the suitability of linear, quadratic, exponential, and rational functions by arguing from their data or from the physics of the situation.

*(NCTM 2000, p. 303)*

## Investigation 1—Modeling the Problem: Linear Growth

NASA scientists realize the enormity of the problems caused by a space-age form of pollution: human-made debris in orbit around Earth. Estimates for the year 2002 indicate that approximately 11 million pounds of manufactured materials are in Earth orbit, including old rocket parts, nonfunctioning satellites, discarded or dropped tools, by-products of explosions and collisions, and other odds and ends, as well as countless numbers of smaller objects, such as paint chips and dust-sized particles. On the basis of current launch rates and space-debris accumulation since 1980, researchers estimate that the nations in the space business will contribute an additional 350,000 pounds to 420,000 pounds of debris per year for the foreseeable future. The problem of determining the amount of debris in space and the anticipated rate of increase of such matter is one that cannot be solved directly nor with a high degree of certainty. We cannot locate, count, and weigh all the objects in orbit, nor can we predict with assurance when two of them will collide. Instead, we must rely on existing data and mathematical models to help us represent the problem and identify trends and expected outcomes.

1. Using an estimated rate of increase of 350,000 pounds per year in the year 2002 and for the next ten years, and assuming 11 million pounds of existing debris at the beginning of 2002, write a linear model to predict the number of pounds of orbital debris at the end of any given year, $t$. Assume that $t = 1$ represents 2002.

2. Write a second linear model using an estimated rate of increase of 420,000 pounds per year in the year 2002 and for the next ten years, and assuming 11 million pounds of existing debris at the beginning of 2002.

3. Evaluate the models you wrote for tasks 1 and 2 for several different years to determine the year in which the amount of accumulated debris will reach 15 million pounds. Find a solution using (a) the first model and (b) the second model.

4. When a vehicle travels at a constant rate, $r$, for a length of time, $t$, the distance traveled by the vehicle is modeled by a linear function. Compare the familiar linear model for distance-rate-time with your linear models for accumulating space debris. Why can we refer to your linear models as constant-velocity models for amassing space debris?

5. Do you think that either of your linear models accurately represents the situation of increasing amounts of space debris as described in the introduction to this problem? Why or why not?

## Investigation 2—Refining the Model: Quadratic Growth

Investigation 1 suggests a new question: Does either linear model realistically describe the situation of orbital-debris accumulation? Does either rate, 350,000 pounds per year or 420,000 pounds per year, tell us how much debris will build up between 2002 and 2012? Which rate of increase should we use over this ten-year period? Most certainly, the amount of debris accumulating each year is changing during this period, but by how much each year?

1. Complete the following chart to show the amount of debris added each year and the total amount in orbit at the end of the year calculated on the basis of the following assumptions:

    — Debris is accumulating in space at a constant rate from 350,000 pounds per year in 2002 to 420,000 pounds per year in 2012. Thus, over the ten-year period from the end of 2002 through 2012, the rate ("velocity") of littering will increase by 0.07 million pounds per year.

    — The increase is in equal annual increments of 0.007 million pounds (7,000 pounds) per year in each year of the ten-year period.

2. Working from the assumption that the increase in the velocity of littering was achieved in equal annual increments, write a linear equation to describe the increase in the amount of debris being added each year (that is, the increase in the annual velocity of littering) as a function of the number of years since 2002. Here, let $a = 0$ in 2002 because the 2002 rate of 0.35 million pounds per year is

| Year | Amount Added during Year (Millions of Pounds) | Total in Orbit at End of Year (Millions of Pounds) |
|------|-----------------------------------------------|----------------------------------------------------|
| 2002 | 0.350 | 11.35 |
| 2003 | 0.357 | |
| 2004 | | |
| 2005 | | |
| 2006 | | |
| 2007 | | |
| 2008 | | |
| 2009 | | |
| 2010 | | |
| 2011 | | |
| 2012 | 0.420 | |

assumed to be the baseline rate. Use $d = f(a)$ to represent the rate of littering $a$ years after 2002.

3. The situation described in the equation from task 2, where the rate of increase of litter is itself increasing at a constant rate, is analogous to the situation of a vehicle that accelerates at a constant rate from an initial velocity, $v_0$, to a final velocity, $v_f$. Use the data generated in the chart from task 1 to create a scatterplot of the total number of pounds of orbital debris that has accumulated relative to the year. Your graph should cover the period from 2002 through 2012.

4. Fit a line to the scatterplot you created in task 3, and use it to decide whether the accumulation of debris appears to be linear. Record your linear equation, write your conclusion, and describe the evidence on which you based your decision.

5. Using a graphing calculator or a computer graphing program, calculate the linear-regression equation for the data in task 1. Do your calculations support a linear relationship? Explain. How does this line compare with the line that you fitted manually in task 4?

6. Generate a quadratic-regression equation for the same data. Record the quadratic-regression model. How well does your quadratic equation fit the data compared with the linear approximations you made in tasks 4 and 5?

7. Compare your quadratic-regression equation with the two linear-regression equations that you developed in tasks 4 and 5. Use your models to predict the accumulation of debris after twenty years, thirty years, and fifty years. Describe the behavior of the linear-regression model versus the quadratic model over time.

8. For the period from 2002 to 2012, the graph of the quadratic model lies between the graphs of the two linear models. Explain why this result is reasonable. Will the quadratic graph always lie between the two linear graphs? Explain.

9. Explain why the quadratic model for the debris problem can be described as a "uniform acceleration" model.

## Investigation 3—One More Perspective: Exponential Growth

What if the amount of space litter added each year grew not by a fixed number of pounds but by a fixed percent of the amount already in space? For example, what would happen to the original 11 million pounds if the litter added each year was 5 percent of the amount already in orbit?

1. Suppose that the original 11 million pounds of space debris present in 2002 increases so that each year, 5 percent of the amount already in orbit is added to what is already there. Complete the following chart to determine the amount of debris that would

accumulate under this condition over the period from 2002 to 2012. If possible, use a spreadsheet to carry out the calculations and organize your results.

| Year | Amount Added Each Year Equivalent to 5% of Previous Amount (Millions of Pounds) | Total in Orbit at End of Year (Millions of Pounds) |
|---|---|---|
| 2002 | 0.55 | 11.55 |
| 2003 | 0.5775 | 12.1275 |
| 2004 | 0.606375 | 12.733875 |
| 2005 | | |
| 2006 | | |
| 2007 | | |
| 2008 | | |
| 2009 | | |
| 2010 | | |
| 2011 | | |
| 2012 | | |

2. Write an exponential model to describe the growth of the original 11 million pounds of debris over the years according to the data in the chart just completed. Use your model to predict the amount of debris that would accumulate in twenty years, thirty years, and fifty years when debris is added at the rate of 5 percent per year.

3. Economists use what is referred to as the *rule of 72* to predict how much time is needed for an amount of money to double if it is invested at a rate of $R$ percent compounded annually. According to the rule of 72, the doubling time, $D$, is given by the equation $D = 72/R$. Use the rule of 72 to predict when the amount of debris will double if littering compounds at the rate of 5 percent per year. When will the original 11 million pounds increase to 88 million pounds? Do the data in your chart agree with those calculations?

4. If the growth of space debris was following an exponential model and concern arose that the amount of debris would double in only ten years, what must the annual percent increase in debris have been to result in this doubling time?

## Investigation 4—What Goes Up Might Come Down: Extending the Models

The models you have developed so far assume that the additional debris added each year stays in orbit and accumulates there, but not everything in orbit stays there forever. In fact, every year, some of the debris slows down enough to reenter the atmosphere, where it burns up or, on rare occasions, returns to Earth.

1. Assume that 2 percent of the debris in orbit at the beginning of any year will be destroyed during that year. Modify the linear, quadratic, and exponential models you developed in Investigations 1, 2, and 3 to account for the situation in which additional debris is being added each year while 2 percent of what was already in orbit is being destroyed. Create tables, charts, plots, and written descriptions to account for your work.

2. In which case—linear, quadratic, or exponential—does the assumption of a 2 percent reentry rate have the greatest effect? Explain how you determined your answer.

3. Assume the same rates of adding debris as you did when you generated the models for Investigations 1, 2, and 3, but try different rates of annual destruction of orbital debris. For each of the three models, does a reasonable destruction rate exist that will result in a net decrease in orbital debris despite the fact that additional debris is accumulating? What might be some advantages of knowing whether such a rate is possible?

## Investigation 5—Putting the Models to Work

The power of mathematical models derives from their ability to enable us to ask "What if?" questions, such as the following:

✦ What if we decrease the rate at which we are adding debris?

✦ What if we decrease the rate at which we are adding debris and, at the same time, find a way to increase the rate at which existing debris is destroyed?

Work with a partner or a small group to generate at least three specific questions that you would like to investigate regarding the build-up of orbital debris.

✦ What if …?

✦ What if …?

✦ What if …?

1. Describe a plan for investigating each of your questions using spreadsheets, graphing utilities, or other appropriate technology.

2. Carry out each plan to generate data, then analyze your data in light of each "What if?" question.

3. For each question, describe the models you used. Organize your data, and include commentary that describes what the data represent and what you concluded from your investigation.

4. Use your data, models, analyses, and any other information you have collected to prepare a presentation that helps your audience think about steps we might take to manage the problem of orbital debris and the likely consequences of not doing so.

# Modeling Collision Effects

*Hypervelocity* refers to speeds in excess of 3 kilometers, or nearly 2 miles, per second.

In this system, mass is measured in kilograms (kg), velocity is measured in meters per second (m/s), and energy is measured in units called joules (J), where

$$1J = \frac{1\,kg \cdot m^2}{sec^2}.$$

This investigation addresses a problem of major significance to the aerospace community: the consequences of impact at hypervelocity. Tests done in NASA laboratories, as well as evidence from returned spacecraft, confirm the extensive damage that can result when even small particles strike at orbital speeds.

An inventory published in 2000 by the U.S. Space Command identified 8,927 radar-trackable objects, that is, objects of baseball size and larger, in space. In addition, the Space Command estimated the presence of 110,000 objects at least 1 cm in diameter, along with trillions of tiny paint flakes and tens to hundreds of trillions of dust-sized particles of aluminum oxide. When objects, even very small ones, travel at hypervelocity (defined to be in excess of 3 kilometers per second), the effects of a collision can be devastating. For example, an orbiting particle 0.3 millimeter in diameter, just slightly larger than a grain of salt, can puncture a space suit with a hole large enough to force an astronaut to return quickly to the spacecraft or risk depressurization.

An object in motion possesses kinetic energy, a term that comes from the Greek word *kinetos,* meaning "moving." Physicists have determined that the kinetic energy (*KE*) of a body of mass m traveling at a velocity v is given by the relationship $KE = (\frac{1}{2})mv^2$. Kinetic energy is measured in units that may not be immediately familiar, so this discussion uses metric units consistently to minimize confusion. In this system, mass is measured in kilograms (kg), velocity is measured in meters per second (m/s), and energy is measured in units called joules (J), where

$$1J = \frac{1\,kg \cdot m^2}{sec^2}.$$

To get a better sense of what 1 joule of energy represents, guide students in calculating the kinetic energy for the situations listed below. Use the following conversions where needed: 1 mile = 1.61 kilometers, 1 kilometer = 0.62 mile, 1 pound = 0.45 kilogram, and 1 kilogram = 2.20 pounds.

✦ a 3,500-pound truck traveling at 60 miles per hour:

$$3500\,lbs \times 0.45\frac{kg}{lb} \times \left(60\frac{mi}{hr} \times \frac{1}{60}\frac{hr}{min} \times \frac{1}{60}\frac{min}{sec} \times 1.61\frac{km}{mi} \times 1000\frac{m}{km}\right)^2$$

$$= 1,134,043.75\,J$$

✦ a 350-pound satellite orbiting at 17,500 miles per hour:

$$350\,\text{lbs}\times0.45\frac{\text{kg}}{\text{lb}}\times\left(17500\,\frac{\text{mi}}{\text{hr}}\times\frac{1}{60}\frac{\text{hr}}{\text{min}}\times\frac{1}{60}\frac{\text{min}}{\text{sec}}\times1.61\frac{\text{km}}{\text{mi}}\times1000\,\frac{\text{m}}{\text{km}}\right)^2$$

$$= 9{,}647{,}247{,}178.82\,\text{J}$$

✦ a 1-gram paint chip orbiting at 17,500 miles per hour:

$$1\text{g}\times\frac{1}{1000}\frac{\text{kg}}{\text{g}}\times\left(17500\,\frac{\text{mi}}{\text{hr}}\times\frac{1}{60}\frac{\text{hr}}{\text{min}}\times\frac{1}{60}\frac{\text{min}}{\text{sec}}\times1.61\frac{\text{km}}{\text{mi}}\times1000\,\frac{\text{m}}{\text{km}}\right)^2$$

$$= 61{,}252{,}363\,\text{J}$$

Given these examples, what might be the kinetic energy of a hard-hit baseball or a well-served tennis ball?

NASA studies the effects of high-velocity collisions in its HITF. The HITF uses light-gas "guns" to accelerate particles that range in diameter from 100 microns (0.1 mm) to 10 millimeters. Particles are fired into samples of various materials in different configurations at velocities in

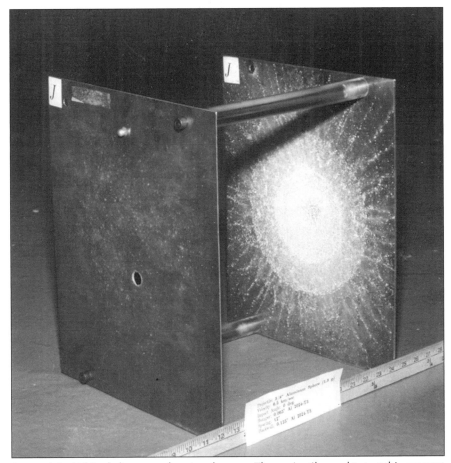

A test of the Whipple bumper, showing damage. The projectile used to test this concept is a small aluminum ball. The function of the bumper is to break up the projectile, disperse the fragments, and reduce their velocity below that of the original projectile, thereby eliminating the projectile's ability to penetrate a second layer.

School mathematics experiences at all levels should include opportunities to learn about mathematics by working on problems arising in contexts outside of mathematics.... [I]n grades 9–12 students should be confidently using mathematics to explain complex applications in the outside world.

*(NCTM 2000, pp. 65–66)*

the range of 2 kilometers per second to 7 kilometers per second to study impact effects. Each gun fires particles of different masses: one fires particles with masses from 0.0015 milligram to 5.8 milligrams; another gun shoots particles with masses from 0.091 milligram to 46 milligrams; a third propels particles whose masses range from 46 milligrams to 1.45 grams.

The highest velocities achieved in the laboratory, about 7 kilometers per second, correspond to speeds of nearly 16,000 miles per hour; nevertheless, NASA estimates that only about 25 percent of the orbital-debris collisions occur at speeds of 8 kilometers per second or less. Thus, scientists must rely on mathematical modeling to scale the experimental results observed in the laboratory to higher velocities.

## Investigation 6—Modeling Collision Effects

The open-ended exploration and questions in Investigation 6 on page 48 introduce the concept of kinetic energy. Students who are studying physics or physical science should be familiar with this form of energy. The joule may be less familiar because it is a "hybrid" unit and not something for which we have everyday references. By calculating the kinetic energy involved in some everyday situations, such as a truck traveling at highway speeds or a hard-hit baseball, students can then relate other energies, such as the kinetic energy of impact from a paint flake in orbit, as some multiple or fraction of the more familiar examples. Students may be surprised to discover that a 1-gram paint chip traveling at orbital speed has nearly $\frac{1}{10}$ the kinetic energy of a 3,500-pound truck moving at 60 miles per hour or that a 350-pound satellite at orbital speed has 10,000 times the kinetic energy of the truck.

Spreadsheets and calculators should be used throughout this investigation. The most important purpose of Investigation 6 is to foster open-ended exploration and discussion of the relative effects of the linear factor (mass) compared with the quadratic component (velocity). Teachers should be less concerned that students come up with precise answers to particular questions than that they understand the larger concept of how the functions behave.

## Investigation 7—Modeling Collision Probability

Throughout this unit, students have worked with enormous quantities—millions of pounds—of debris, but they may not relate those quantities to the vastness of space, even the relatively "close-fitting" sphere in which payloads orbit Earth. Most manned spacecraft fly in low-Earth orbit, at about 200 to 250 miles (or 320 to 400 kilometers) above Earth. What is the likelihood that such an orbiting vehicle will encounter a particle of orbital debris? Students can use a geometrical model to estimate collision probabilities.

Investigation 7 on page 49 asks students to calculate the volume of a "shell" 200 kilometers thick extending from an altitude of 200 to 400 kilometers above Earth—a volume of just over $1.1(10^{11})$ cubic kilometers. Assuming that 5.5 million pounds (2.5 million kilograms) of debris is evenly distributed throughout this volume, the density of debris is on the order of $2.3(10^{-5})$ kilogram, or 0.023 gram, per cubic kilometer.

Further assuming that the debris has the density of aluminum, 2.7 grams per cubic centimeter, we can estimate that the measurement of 0.023 gram per cubic kilometer represents approximately 0.0084 cubic centimeter of debris per cubic kilometer of the shell. The probability of hitting any of that debris is the ratio of the volume of debris to the volume of the shell; hence, the probability of hitting the debris is approximately $8.5(10^{-12})$. Although the amount of debris in orbit around Earth is considerable, the probability of encountering any of it appears to be very small, but the consequences of an encounter, should one occur, can be devastating.

The situations associated with space debris are significant and real, and they provide a context in which to demonstrate the necessity of employing mathematical models to tackle otherwise inaccessible problems.

## Investigation 6—Modeling Collision Effects

Tests done in NASA laboratories, as well as evidence from returned spacecraft, confirm that enormous damage can be done when even small particles strike at orbital speeds.

An object in motion possesses kinetic energy, a term that comes from the Greek word *kinetos,* meaning "moving." Physicists have determined that the kinetic energy (*KE*) of a body of mass *m* traveling at a velocity *v* is given by the relationship $KE = (\frac{1}{2}) mv^2$. Kinetic energy is measured in units that may not be immediately familiar, so this discussion uses metric units consistently to minimize confusion. In this system, mass is measured in kilograms (*kg*), velocity is measured in meters per second (*m/s*), and energy is measured in units called *joules* (J), where

$$1J = \frac{1\,\text{kg} \cdot \text{m}^2}{\text{sec}^2}.$$

Use a computer spreadsheet or the table function of your graphing calculator to create a model that allows you to calculate the kinetic energies of various objects, from microscopic particles moving at orbital or near-orbital speeds to familiar objects moving at realistic Earth-bound speeds. Use your model and your calculations to address the following questions:

1. What effect does the mass have on the kinetic energy of a moving body? For example, if two objects, one with 10 times the mass of the other, travel at the same speed, how do their kinetic energies compare?

2. What effect does velocity have on the kinetic energy of a moving body? For example, if two objects of equal mass are moving, one with 10 times the velocity of the other, how do their kinetic energies compare?

3. Which factor, mass or velocity, makes the greater contribution to the total amount of kinetic energy? Why?

4. NASA scientists have stated that trackable objects pose a relatively small hazard to spacecraft but that the vast number of smaller breakup-debris particles present a hazard disproportionate to their size. Why do you suppose that statement is true?

## Investigation 7—Modeling Collision Probability

The various models you have constructed for debris accumulation have involved enormous quantities—millions of pounds—of debris. But we have not yet related those quantities to the vastness of space, even the relatively "close-fitting" sphere in which payloads orbit Earth. Most manned spacecraft fly in low-Earth orbit, at about 200 to 250 miles (or about 320 to 400 kilometers) above Earth. What is the likelihood that such an orbiting vehicle will encounter a particle of orbital debris? We can use a geometrical model to estimate collision probabilities.

Consider the cross section of Earth shown in the figure below. Earth's radius is about 6,400 kilometers. Although the figure is not drawn to scale, you can see that the region in which spacecraft orbit is very close to Earth in terms of astronomical distances. Use the distances from the figure and the series of questions posed here to estimate the likelihood of a collision involving orbital debris.

1. First, envision a series of spherical "shells" surrounding Earth. The shell closest to Earth includes the atmosphere and is below the surrounding sphere, within which orbital flight takes place. As a first approximation to simplify the calculations, assume that each of the shells is 200 kilometers in thickness. What is the volume of the shell that lies between the two spheres of radius 6,600 kilometers and 6,800 kilometers?

2. Suppose that 5.5 million pounds of orbital debris in low-Earth orbit is randomly distributed within this shell. If the average density of this debris is that of aluminum (2.7 grams per cubic centimeter), how much debris would you expect to encounter in each cubic kilometer of space?

3. Use the models that you developed previously in this unit to study how the probability of encountering space debris changes as the total amount of debris escalates.

4. If we remove one of our simplifying assumptions and let the "shell of orbital flight" be from 160 to 320 kilometers, a more realistic range, will the conclusions you have drawn thus far change appreciably? In other words, are we justified in making the simplifying assumptions? Prepare a written or oral report of your findings.

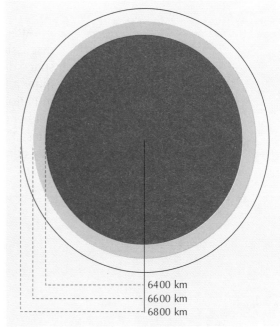

6400 km
6600 km
6800 km

A "shell" 200 kilometers thick extending from an altitude of 200 to 400 kilometers above Earth

# Solutions and Teacher Commentary

## Investigation 1—Modeling the Problem: Linear Growth

Using the two linear equations or a chart, students can calculate the increased accumulations over time (see chart).

*Accumulation of Orbital Debris*

| Amount Added (Millions of Pounds) | End-of-Year Accumulation (Millions of Pounds) | Year | Amount Added (Millions of Pounds) | End-of-Year Accumulation (Millions of Pounds) |
|---|---|---|---|---|
| 0.35 | 11.35 | 2002 | 0.42 | 11.42 |
| 0.35 | 11.70 | 2003 | 0.42 | 11.84 |
| 0.35 | 12.05 | 2004 | 0.42 | 12.26 |
| 0.35 | 12.40 | 2005 | 0.42 | 12.68 |
| 0.35 | 12.75 | 2006 | 0.42 | 13.10 |
| 0.35 | 13.10 | 2007 | 0.42 | 13.52 |
| 0.35 | 13.45 | 2008 | 0.42 | 13.94 |
| 0.35 | 13.80 | 2009 | 0.42 | 14.36 |
| 0.35 | 14.15 | 2010 | 0.42 | 14.78 |
| 0.35 | 14.50 | 2011 | 0.42 | 15.20 |

After studying the accumulation calculations in the chart, a fruitful discussion should result regarding the differences in the accumulated space debris after ten years. How do the estimated accumulation values differ after each year? What assumptions are being made about accumulation rates under these calculations? Students should realize that neither model is likely to be accurate because neither of the estimated rates, 350,000 pounds per year or 420,000 pounds per year, is likely to stay constant over a multiyear period.

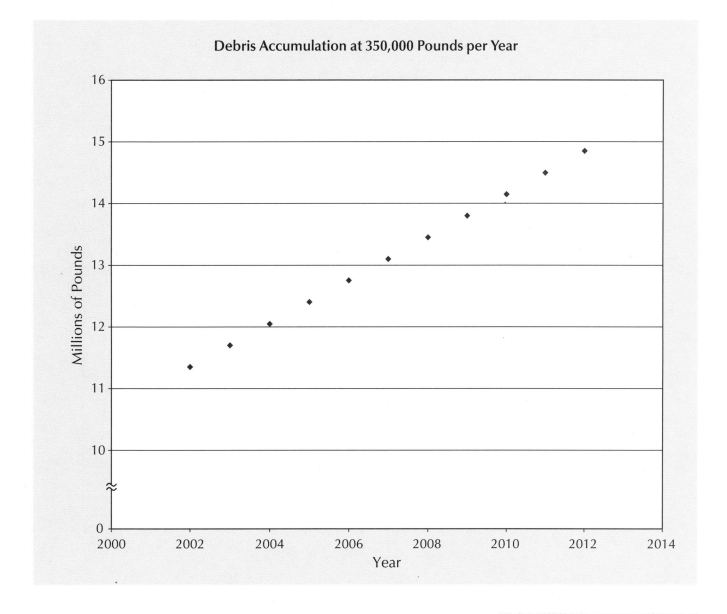

Debris Accumulation at 350,000 Pounds per Year

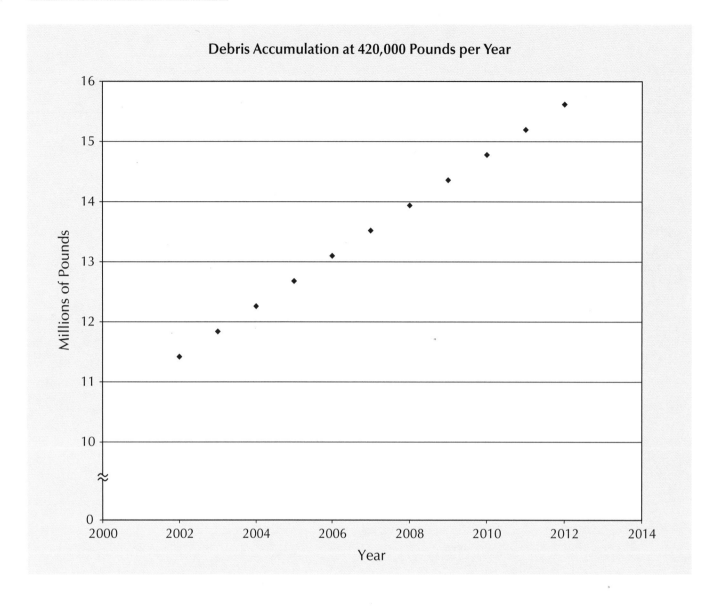

## Investigation 2—Refining the Model: Quadratic Growth

When students realize the limitations inherent in their initial models, they should try to adjust the model to account for the fact that neither the rate of 350,000 pounds per year nor the rate of 420,000 pounds per year remains constant throughout the period. Scientists and mathematicians prefer to start with a simple model, then add complexities to refine it as needed. For this reason, in Investigation 2, we make the simplest assumption to account for the changing rate of increase over the period: Debris is accumulating at a constant rate from 350,000 pounds per year in 2002 to 420,000 pounds per year in 2012. That is, the rate (velocity) of littering increases by 70,000 pounds per year, achieved in equal increments of 7,000 pounds per year each year over a ten-year period. Students can then create a chart and a graph of the rate of "dumping" versus the year by using the data points (0, 0.35) and (10, 0.42). This rate of change for dumping is given by the equation $d = 0.007a + 0.35$, where $a = 0$ in 2002. The increases in both the dumping rate and the total accumulation are shown in the chart and the graphs that follow.

   Although both plots shown here and those that your students generate may appear to be linear over the ten-year range of the initial data, extending the domain to twenty or thirty or fifty years, as suggested in Investigation 2, reveals that the graph of the end-of-year total accumulation is, indeed, not linear.

   Investigation 2 compares the quadratic model for debris with the more familiar case of constant acceleration. Students who have studied motion in a physics class should make the connection between examples of uniformly accelerated motion, such as a body in free fall, a ball rolling down an incline, or a car accelerating at a constant rate, and the "uniform acceleration of space dumping." More advanced mathematics students may pursue the fact that the linear equation $d = 0.007x + 0.35$,

*Rate of Dumping and Total Accumulation*

| Year | Amount Added in Year (Millions of Pounds) | Total in Orbit at End of Year (Millions of Pounds) |
|------|-------------------------------------------|----------------------------------------------------|
| 2002 | 0.35 | 11.35 |
| 2003 | 0.357 | 11.707 |
| 2004 | 0.364 | 12.071 |
| 2005 | 0.371 | 12.442 |
| 2006 | 0.378 | 12.82 |
| 2007 | 0.385 | 13.205 |
| 2008 | 0.392 | 13.597 |
| 2009 | 0.399 | 13.996 |
| 2010 | 0.406 | 14.402 |
| 2011 | 0.413 | 14.815 |
| 2012 | 0.420 | 15.235 |

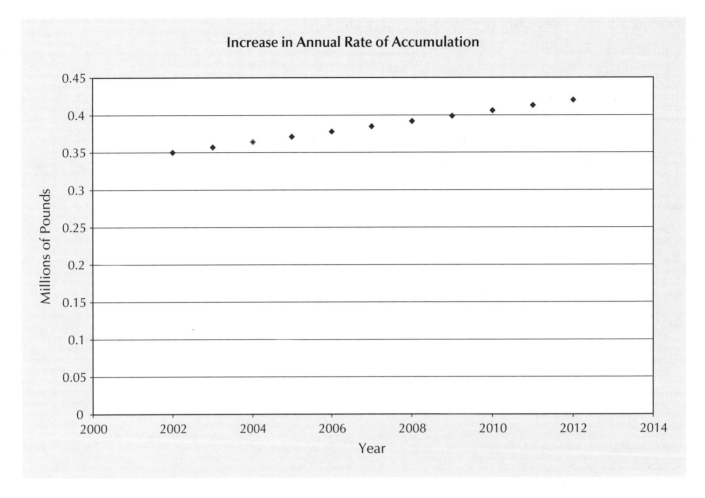

**Increase in Annual Rate of Accumulation**

where $x$ is the number of years since 2002, is the equation of the tangent to the curve $y = 0.0035x^2 + 0.3465x + 11$, the equation previously derived. That is, the first equation is the derivative of the second.

In this investigation, students are likely to have the greatest difficulty differentiating among the rate ('velocity') of littering (e.g., 350,000 pounds per year in 2002), the total change in the littering rate over ten years (i.e., an increase of 70,000 pounds per year between the 2002 rate of 350,000 pounds per year and the 2012 rate of 420,000 pounds per year), and the rate of change (acceleration) of littering velocity (an increase of 7,000 pounds per year each year). Teachers should pay special attention to these concepts.

In comparing the quadratic model, $y = 0.0035x^2 + 0.3465x + 11$, with the two linear models, $y = 0.35x + 11$ and $y = 0.42x + 11$, students will find that the graph of the quadratic model lies between the two lines. They should be able to interpret this result in terms of what would happen if the rate of adding debris stayed at 350,000 pounds per year, was always 420,000 pounds per year, or gradually changed from 350,000 to 420,000 pounds per year. They should also determine when the output of the quadratic model will surpass the second linear model and realize that thereafter, the quadratic model will always produce greater values.

### End-of-Year Accumulation, Quadratic Model

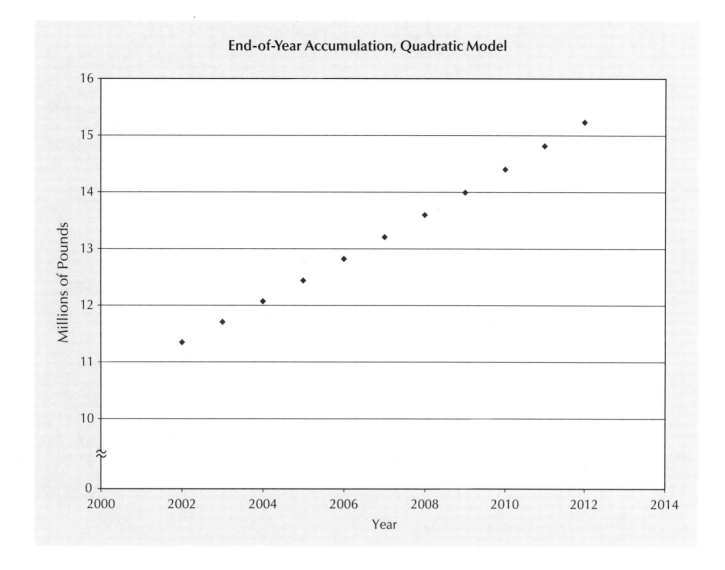

## Investigation 3—One More Perspective: Exponential Growth

The major objective of Investigation 3 is to help students realize the impact of exponential growth. With a spreadsheet, they can hypothesize different rates of increase and explore what would happen if debris were added at those rates. The findings can be compared with the patterns of linear and quadratic growth. Some examples are shown in the chart below and the graph on the following page; the amounts are in millions of pounds.

*Examples of Linear, Quadratic, and Exponential Growth*

| (Number of Years | Linear Growth at $0.35(10^6)$ per Year | Linear Growth at $0.42(10^6)$ per Year | Quadratic Growth | Exponential Growth at 5% per Year | Exponential Growth at 10% per Year |
|---|---|---|---|---|---|
| 1 | 11.35 | 11.42 | 11.35 | 11.55 | 12.1 |
| 2 | 11.70 | 11.84 | 11.707 | 12.1275 | 13.31 |
| 3 | 12.05 | 12.26 | 12.071 | 12.733875 | 14.641 |
| 4 | 12.40 | 12.68 | 12.442 | 13.37056875 | 16.1051 |
| 5 | 12.75 | 13.1 | 12.82 | 14.0390971075 | 17.71561 |
| 10 | 14.5 | 15.2 | 14.815 | 17.9178408946 | 28.5311670611 |
| 20 | 18.0 | 19.4 | 19.33 | 29.1862747566 | 74.0024994426 |
| 30 | 21.5 | 23.6 | 24.545 | 47.5413661267 | 191.943424958 |
| 50 | 28.5 | 32.0 | 37.075 | 126.141397643 | 1291.29938168 |

## Comparison of Four Models

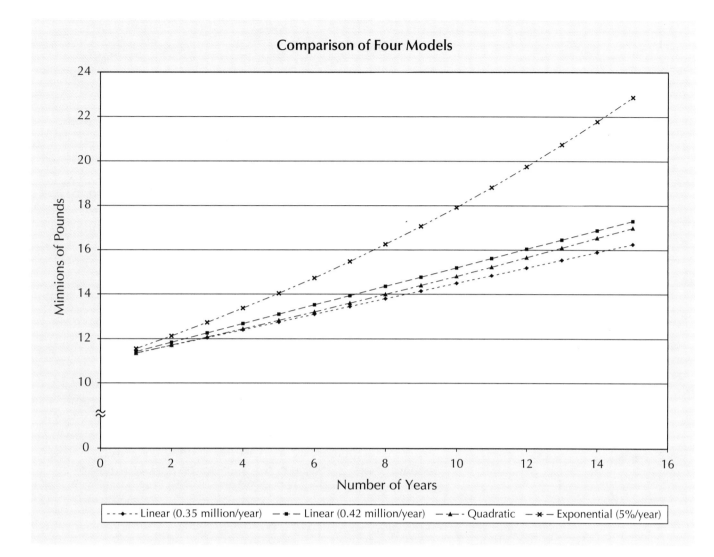

## Investigation 4—What Goes Up Might Come Down: Extending the Models

Investigation 4 provides no data so that students have the opportunity to form and test hypotheses of their own. They should try modifications that assume destruction at a fixed rate per year (linear) and at a fixed percent (exponential decay). Students should look for models that might predict an eventual decrease in the amount of orbital debris, even though we assume that NASA and others will continue to launch payloads and, thereby, continue to add to the orbital debris. These open-ended investigations are designed to let students experience the search for models that might lead to desirable consequences— although, in reality, we may need to invent the necessary technology to implement the model.

## Investigation 5—Putting the Models to Work

In Investigation 5, students are encouraged to generate "What if?" questions and to use their models to discover answers. Before you ask students to formulate their questions, you might want to pose some of your own. The following are examples:

✦ What if, at the end of 2007, we stopped adding to the debris in space and were able to decrease the amount of existing debris at a rate of 300,000 pounds per year for the next three years? What would be the total poundage remaining at the end of 2010? What would be the percent of decrease? Note that the answers will vary depending on what assumptions are made about the rate of increase during the years 2002–2007.

✦ In addition, what if, at the beginning of 2010, new technology would allow us to improve the rate of decrease to 500,000 pounds per year for a two-year period? What would be the total debris remaining at the beginning of 2012?

Again, this investigation does not provide data so that students have the opportunity to form and test hypotheses of their own.

## Investigation 6—Modeling Collision Effects

This investigation introduces the concept of kinetic energy. If your students are studying physics or physical science, they should be familiar with this form of energy. The joule may be less familiar because it is a "hybrid" unit and not something for which we have everyday references. To get a better sense of what 1 joule of energy represents, students might calculate the kinetic energy involved in some everyday situations, such as a truck traveling at highway speeds or a hard-hit baseball, then relate other energies, such as the kinetic energy of impact from a paint flake in orbit, as some multiple or fraction of the more familiar examples.

In this investigation, students must pay close attention to the units of measure used. They should realize that their calculations of such quantities as mass, velocity, and energy must be expressed in appropriate units to be meaningful. Note that the units used in the activity are mixed, including pounds, kilograms, grams, miles per hour, kilometers per second, and so on, because different units may commonly be used in measuring the associated phenomena. This situation is realistic, and with spreadsheets and calculators, making conversions should pose no problems. Further, some measurements, such as the mass of a baseball or the velocity at which it may be hit, are left for students to find or approximate for themselves. Sports enthusiasts sometimes carry this sort of information in their heads; others may prefer to use data from their own sports experiences; still others will look up the data in a book or on a Web site focusing on sports statistics.

Again, the purpose of Investigation 6 is to foster open-ended exploration and discussion of the relative effects of the linear factor (mass) compared with the quadratic component (velocity). Teachers should be less concerned with eliciting precise answers to particular questions than with fostering students' understanding of how these functions behave.

## Investigation 7—Modeling Collision Probability

This activity asks students to calculate the volume of a "shell" 200 kilometers thick extending from an altitude of 200 to 400 kilometers above Earth—a volume of just over $1.1(10^{11})$ cubic kilometers. Assuming that 5.5 million pounds (2.5 million kilograms) of debris is evenly distributed throughout this volume, the density of debris is on the order of $2.3(10^{-5})$ kilogram, or 0.023 gram, per cubic kilometer.

These questions assume that the debris has the density of aluminum, 2.7 grams per cubic centimeter. By making this assumption, we can estimate that the measurement of 0.023 gram per cubic kilometer represents approximately 0.0084 cubic centimeter of debris per cubic kilometer of the shell. The probability of hitting any of that debris is the ratio of the volume of debris to the volume of the shell; hence, the probability of hitting the debris is approximately $8.5(10^{-12})$. These calculations are outlined below.

Volume of a "shell" 200 kilometers thick extending from an altitude of 200 to 400 kilometers above Earth:

$$V = \frac{4}{3}\pi(6800^3 - 6600^3)\,\text{km}^3$$
$$V = 1.1(10^{11})\,\text{km}^3$$

If we assume 5.5 million pounds (2.5 million kilograms) of debris is evenly distributed throughout this volume, the density of debris is

$$\frac{2.5(10^6)\,\text{kg}}{1.1(10^{11})\,\text{km}^3} = 2.27(10^{-5})\,\frac{\text{kg}}{\text{km}^3} = 0.023\,\frac{\text{gm}}{\text{km}^3}.$$

If the debris has the density of AL,

$$2.7\,\frac{\text{gm}}{\text{cm}^3},$$

then the 0.023 gram of debris in each cubic kilometer of space represents

$$\frac{0.023 \text{ gm}}{2.7 \frac{\text{gm}}{\text{cm}^3}} = 0.0085 \text{ cm}^3$$

of debris per cubic kilometer of shell. The probability of hitting debris is the ratio of the volume of debris to the volume of the shell, or

$$\frac{8.5 \left(10^{-3}\right) \text{cm}^3}{\text{km}^3} \cdot \frac{1 \text{ km}^3}{10^9 \text{ cm}^3} = 8.5 \left(10^{-12}\right).$$

Removing the simplifying assumption of a 200-kilometer-thick shell does not change the order of magnitude of the probability.

# Orbits

## What Is Orbiting Out There?

In a previous chapter, we explored models for the proliferation of space junk in Earth orbit. What is being done to monitor this orbital debris that is growing around Earth?

NASA and other space agencies have already made tremendous efforts to curb space-junk encounters. At the most rudimentary level, the U.S. Space Command keeps track of many of the objects orbiting Earth, including debris. As of June 2000, the total number of trackable space objects—including 90 space probes, 2,671 satellites and 6,096 pieces of space junk—was a whopping 8,927.

If any of the more than 6,000 space-junk objects gets too close for comfort to a satellite or inhabited spacecraft, the Space Command sends out a warning. Already, the ISS has had to move out of the way of an oncoming piece of space debris; in October 1999, ground controllers successfully maneuvered the ISS out of the way of a piece of debris that was headed right for the station. The space shuttle has also had to make way for a number of pieces of space junk. (Weinstock 2000)

Just how does the Space Command know where these objects are? The answer is that the agency models the paths of space-junk orbits using mathematics. In this unit, students will learn what we mean by an orbiting object, study several mathematical models used to describe orbital paths, and apply their knowledge to orbits involving spacecraft, planets, comets, and more.

What do we know about orbiting bodies in our solar system? The fact that Earth and other planets of the solar system orbit the Sun is common knowledge. However, details about the orbits of asteroids, comets, satellites of the planets, and other bodies in the solar system are less well known. NASA's solar-system exploration is providing more data about the many entities that orbit larger celestial bodies or the Sun; thus, this information is becoming available to the general population.

More than one hundred satellites orbit planets in our solar system. The inner planets—Mercury, Venus, Earth, and Mars—have only three satellites. The Moon orbits Earth, and two irregularly shaped bodies orbit Mars. The Martian satellites are probably asteroids that were captured by the gravitational field of that planet. The outer planets—Jupiter, Saturn, Uranus, Neptune, and Pluto—have numerous satellites, and more are being discovered. By 2003, NASA reported that Jupiter has more than sixty, Saturn has more than thirty, Uranus has more than twenty, Neptune has more than ten, and Pluto has one.

In addition to the planets, other celestial bodies orbit the Sun. Asteroids generally orbit the Sun in an area called the asteroid belt, which is between the orbits of Mars and Jupiter. More than 5,000 asteroids have been named and cataloged. Although the belt of asteroids is generally between Mars and Jupiter, the orbits are not always aligned with the orbital planes of these planets. Thus, the orbits of the asteroids intersect the orbits of the planets. As a result, asteroids may pass close to a planet and even be "caught" by the planet's gravitational field and crash onto its surface. Some asteroids have Earth-orbit intersections. In 1989, asteroid 4581 Asclepius passed within 500,000 miles of Earth, a relatively small distance in solar-system terms.

Comets, too, orbit the Sun. Less is known about comets because their large orbits cause them to appear infrequently. These orbits pass close to the Sun and extend deep into the solar system. Some comets have their point of greatest distance from the Sun, or *aphelion,* in the region of the outer planets; for example, seventy-five comets are at their farthest distance from the Sun somewhere near Jupiter. Because comet orbits have varying aphelion distances, the periods on Earth between each observation of a specific comet vary from 3.3 years, for Encke's comet, to thousands of years.

Given that comets have predictable orbits—orbits that can be modeled with mathematics—space scientists have been able to collect data about them from space probes. In 1985, the *Interplanetary Sun-Earth Explorer 3* was maneuvered into an encounter with comet P/Giacobini-Zinner. Perhaps one of the most famous comets because it appears every 76 years, Halley's comet was the target of flybys by spacecraft from three other space agencies during its 1986 pass by Earth.

The work of NASA scientists has shown without a doubt that space in the solar system is not empty. Many natural orbiting bodies, as well as rings of interplanetary dust, exist in the solar system. A knowledge of orbital mechanics not only allows us to monitor space junk orbiting the Earth but also helps scientists launch satellites into Earth orbit and into orbit around other planets. The data returned from such probes have allowed humanity to learn about Earth and the entire solar system.

# Modeling Orbits

Throughout history, humans have been fascinated by the motions of the planets, comets, and other celestial bodies. Accounts of early observations of the heavens and theories proposed to explain motion in space form a rich chapter in the history of mathematical and scientific thought. Two fundamental questions arise from the study of celestial motion: (1) Why do objects orbit? (2) What paths do orbiting objects follow? This unit examines those questions and their mathematical answers.

## What Keeps a Satellite in Orbit?

The path of a body that moves around another object in space is known as an *orbit,* and all orbiting objects, including the planets orbiting the Sun, the many moons in the solar system orbiting their respective planets, and the man-made objects that we have placed into orbit around Earth, obey the same mathematical laws of motion. However, we cannot take aerial photographs of orbits as we can a network of highways or canals; for this reason, conceptualizing orbits is challenging, especially when dealing with the scale of distances in space.

Through his work on universal gravitation, Isaac Newton (1642–1727) provided answers to the question of how satellites orbit. In particular, he explained that the natural path of a planet is a straight line, but the planet is forced into a curved path by the gravitational pull of the Sun. To understand, consider the following simpler situation:

*When a ball rolls across a table, it has velocity, a vector quantity, in the forward, horizontal direction. At the moment the ball leaves the table, gravity accelerates it in the downward, vertical direction. The combination of the constant-speed horizontal velocity with the downward acceleration of gravity causes the ball to move in a trajectory that carries it beyond the edge of the table, as shown (path a). If the ball is made to roll across the table at greater and greater speeds, as it moves over the table's edge, it will continue to hit the floor in the same amount of time but at greater and greater distances from the table (paths b, c). If the floor is an infinite horizontal plane, the ball will always hit the floor somewhere.*

*In a similar manner, if the ball is thrown in a horizontal direction from the top of a tall tower or hill, gravity pulls it in a trajectory back to Earth, and the greater the horizontal velocity, the farther it will travel before hitting the ground. Because of the*

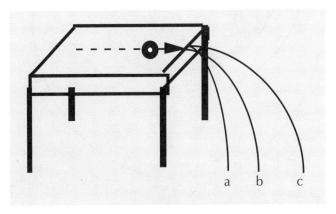

a    b    c

Ground Control to the crew of *Apollo 8:* "Who's driving up there?"

*Apollo 8:* "I think Isaac Newton is doing most of the driving right now."

*curvature of the Earth, however, different results are possible. When the ball's horizontal velocity is slow, the curvature of the ball's path is greater than the curvature of Earth, and the ball falls back to the ground (paths a, b, and c). When the ball's forward motion is fast enough, it is pulled into a path whose curvature matches the curvature of Earth, and the ball enters into a circular orbit (path d). In this situation, the ball is continuously falling toward Earth, but because the curvatures match, the ball never hits the ground. If the ball is thrown with even greater initial horizontal velocity, Earth's curvature will be greater than the trajectory of the ball and the resulting orbit will be elliptical (path e). In the latter two situations, the orbiting ball is in a state of continuously falling toward the center of Earth. If gravity were suddenly to disappear, the ball would fly away in a straight line just as an object tied to the end of a string and twirled overhead does if the string is suddenly released.*

The description above is, of course, greatly simplified. It does not, for example, take into account the effects of Earth's atmosphere, and it gives no indication of the amount of thrust required to achieve orbital velocity. We are dealing with models, however, and in modeling, we begin with simple, familiar representations and later move to more accurate but more complex representations.

In his study of universal gravitation, Newton noted that the gravitational attraction between two bodies is directly proportional to the product of their masses and inversely proportional to the square of the distance between their centers: $F_{grav} \propto \dfrac{m_1 m_2}{r^2}$, or $F_{grav} = G\dfrac{m_1 m_2}{r^2}$,

where $G$ is known as the *constant of universal gravitation.* Thus, an object orbiting closer to Earth than another object of equal mass experiences a greater gravitational pull and must travel with a greater forward velocity to maintain orbital motion. For example, to orbit at an altitude of 400 kilometers (250 miles), the vicinity in which the Space Shuttle flies, requires a velocity in excess of 17,000 miles per hour, whereas an orbit with an altitude of 10,000 kilometers (6,200 miles) requires a velocity of "only" 11,000 miles per hour. The Moon, which orbits Earth at an altitude of nearly 240,000 miles, travels at a "mere" 2,000 miles per hour.

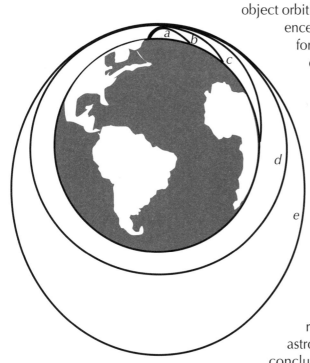

## What Do Orbits "Look Like"?

We know that NASA launches satellites into orbit somewhere "up there," but just where, exactly, is "up there"? And what do the orbits "look like"? We get some of our answers from the work of astronomer Johannes Kepler (1571–1630).

Kepler studied a large set of data compiled from accurate observations of the stars and planets by the Danish astronomer Tycho Brahe (1546–1601); from these data, Kepler concluded that planetary orbits were elliptical, not circular.

Although his abandonment of the prevailing theory that planets moved in circular orbits was considered radical at the time, Kepler nonetheless published three laws of planetary motion (the first two in 1609 and the third in 1619) that changed astronomy and physics forever. Kepler's laws state the following:

1. The planets revolve around the Sun in elliptical orbits with the Sun at one focus of the ellipse.

2. A line joining the planet to the Sun will sweep over equal areas in equal periods of time.

3. The square of the period of a planet (the time required to make one complete orbit) is proportional to the cube of its average distance from the Sun.

Kepler's laws apply not only to the motion of planets around the Sun but to all orbiting bodies. When applied to objects in Earth orbit, Kepler's first law states that satellites and spacecraft orbit Earth in elliptical paths with the center of Earth at one focus of the ellipse. The following paragraphs offer a closer look at elliptical orbits.

*The Ellipse: A Review*

The standard form for the equation of an ellipse centered at $(h, k)$ in the Cartesian plane is

$$\frac{(x-h)^2}{a^2} + \frac{(y-k)^2}{b^2} = 1,$$

with the semimajor axis having length $a$ and semiminor axis having length $b$. When the center is at the origin, the equation becomes

$$\frac{x^2}{a^2} + \frac{y^2}{b^2} = 1.$$

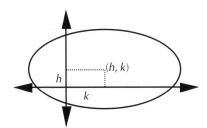 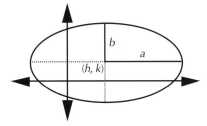

Recall the locus definition of this conic: a set of points in the plane such that the sum of the distances from two fixed points, called *foci*, remains constant. One way to sketch an ellipse using string and two pins is shown on the following page. This device can be used to reveal meaningful relationships among the crucial elements $a$ (the *semimajor axis*), $b$ (the *semiminor axis*), and $c$ (the *center-focus distance*) of the ellipse.

Provide students with a representation of Earth drawn on a piece of paper, and ask them to sketch a representation of where they think the orbiting ISS might be relative to Earth. Many will probably locate the ISS quite far from Earth, perhaps in an exaggerated egg-shaped orbit. Encourage class discussion to reveal students' expectations about the size and shape of satellite orbits.

Modeling elliptical orbits is a natural extension of the units on scaling the solar system and modeling orbital-debris problems.

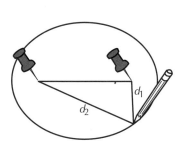
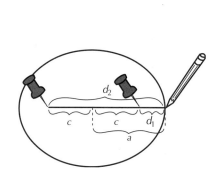
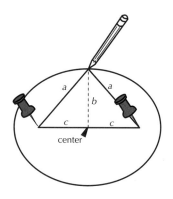

To draw an ellipse, use a pencil to stretch a string around two push-pins, as shown above. Because the length of the string does not change, the distances $d_1$ and $d_2$ have a constant sum; therefore, the path traced by the pencil will be an ellipse with foci at $F_1$ and $F_2$, the locations of the pins. The sum is represented as $d_1 + d_2 = k$.

To determine the value of $k$, move the pencil to one end of the major axis. You can see that $d_1 = a - c$ and $d_2 = a + c$; therefore, $d_1 + d_2 = 2a$ and, thus, $k = 2a$. Further, this constant sum, $2a$, is the length of the major axis.

### The "a, b, c Connection"

Position the pencil on the endpoint of the minor axis, as shown in the third figure above. Now the string forms an isosceles triangle, and the two pencil-pin distances are equal. The sum of the distances is known to be $2a$; therefore, each distance equals $a$. Using the Pythagorean

Using a graphing utility, have students construct a representation of Earth in three dimensions by graphing ellipses with the following parameters:

Ellipse:

$$\frac{x^2}{a^2} + \frac{y^2}{b^2} = 1$$

1) $a = 4, b = 4$ (Earth outline)
2) $a = 4, b = 1$ (equator)
3) $a = 3, b = 4$ ⎫
4) $a = 2, b = 4$ ⎬ (lines of longitude)
5) $a = 1, b = 4$ ⎭

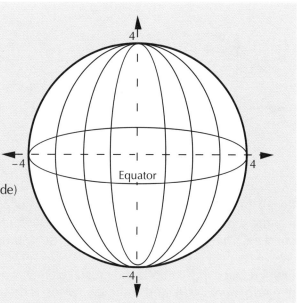

relationship, we find that $a^2 = b^2 + c^2$. We call this relationship the "a, b, c connection."

## Investigation 1—The Ellipse Game: "Find My Foci"

To play the game called "find my foci," each student should draw an accurate ellipse using the string method, a graphing utility, a template, or any other precise method. Be sure that the foci are not visible when the ellipse is shown to another player. The object of the game is to locate precisely both foci of the ellipse. Students should play the game several times and describe a strategy for finding the foci.

*Eccentricity*
Given time to explore the string construction of ellipses, students will observe how the shapes change as the foci (pins) are moved closer together and farther apart. The amount of deviation from the circle is called the *eccentricity* of the ellipse and is defined by the ratio $\frac{c}{a}$. The extremes for this ratio are 0 and 1; therefore, for any ellipse $0 < \frac{c}{a} < 1$ or $0 < e < 1$, where *e* stands for eccentricity. Note that the letter *e* is often used in print to stand for eccentricity, but students should make sure that their calculators or graphing devices do not interpret *e* as Euler's constant, approximately 2.718281828459045….

Take a close look at the ellipse for the extreme values of e (0 and 1). If the pins are separated so far that they lie at the ends of the major axis (hence, $c = a$ and $e = 1$), the pencil will run along the major axis, and the "ellipse" will degenerate into a line segment. At the other extreme, if the pins are moved closer together until they are at the same point

The Geometer's Sketchpad or other geometry software can be used to explore the shape of ellipses dynamically.

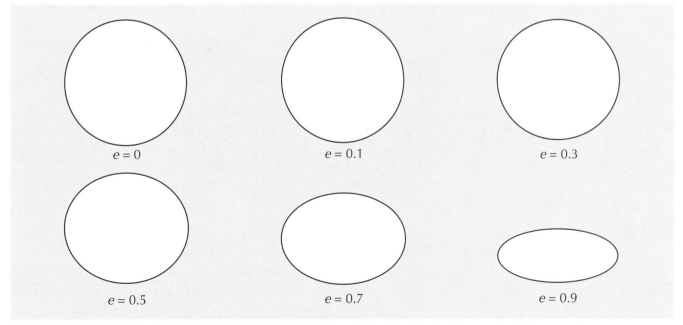

These figures show the approximate shapes of ellipses with different eccentricities.

Mathematics is one of humankind's greatest cultural achievements. It is the "language of science," providing a means by which the world around us can be represented and understood. The mathematical representations that high school students learn afford them the opportunity to understand the power and beauty of mathematics and equip them to use representations in their personal lives, in the workplace, and in further study.

*(NCTM 2000, p. 364)*

(that is, only one pin is used), then $c = 0$, and the trace becomes a circle. Between those two extremes, ellipses of varying degrees of elongation can be constructed.

*Orbits of Earth and Other Planets*

In books and models, diagrams of planetary orbits are usually shown as quite elongated, as seen in the figure below.

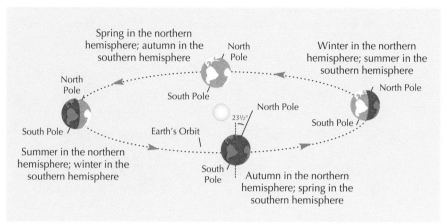

Typical textbook illustration of Earth's orbit depicting seasonal changes at different times of the year

Are such representations accurate? What shapes do the planetary orbits really have? Answering these questions presents some interesting challenges. How can we plot the orbit of Earth when we are "riding around" on it? How can we plot the orbits of other planets when those planets and Earth are millions of miles apart and both are constantly moving in different orbits? Investigations 2, 3, and 4 allow students to plot the orbits of Earth, Mars (an outer planet), and Mercury (an inner planet). The investigations use strategies involving different mathematical principles, as described.

## Investigation 2—Plotting the Oribt of Earth

To plot the orbit of Earth, students begin with the observation that objects that are nearer to us appear larger than same-sized objects that are farther away. Students use that relationship, along with data about the apparent size of the Sun, which seems to vary through the year, to determine the changing distance between the Sun and Earth. (Investigation 2 is found on pages 77–79.)

## Investigation 3—Plotting the Orbit of Mars

To plot the orbit of Mars, which is farther from the Sun than we are, students use a method called *parallax*. Because Mars and Earth orbit the Sun at different speeds, when we observe Mars at the same location on two successive Martian orbits, we are sighting from two different points in Earth's orbit. The angular differences between such pairs of sightings allow us to locate positions in the orbit of Mars. (Investigation 3 is found on pages 79–81.)

## Investigation 4—Plotting the Orbit of Mercury

To plot the orbit of Mercury, which is much closer to the Sun than we are and orbits the Sun in a much shorter period, students observe the maximum separation between Mercury and the Sun as the planet orbits and use those observations to plot tangents to Mercury's orbit. (Investigation 4 is found on pages 82–84.)

Students may be surprised at the shapes of the orbits plotted in these investigations. The orbits will probably look more circular than expected. The eccentricities of the planets in the solar system are all relatively small, as shown in the table below.

| Planet | Semimajor axis in AU* | Eccentricity |
|---|---|---|
| Mercury | 0.3871 | 0.2056 |
| Venus | 0.7233 | 0.0068 |
| Earth | 1.000 | 0.0167 |
| Mars | 1.524 | 0.0934 |
| Jupiter | 5.203 | 0.0484 |
| Saturn | 9.539 | 0.0543 |
| Neptune | 19.18 | 0.046 |
| Uranus | 30.06 | 0.0082 |
| Pluto | 39.44 | 0.2481 |

* An astronomical unit (AU) is equal to the average distance between Earth and the Sun, about 93 million miles.

Even Mercury and Pluto, with their relatively large eccentricities compared with those of the other planets, do not approach the exaggerated elliptical orbits usually seen in textbook drawings. Not until students plot orbits of comets do they begin to encounter truly elongated elliptical orbits. For example, Comet Hyakutake, which was visible from Earth in 1996, had an orbital eccentricity of 0.9997; Comet Hale-Bopp, which appeared in 1997, had an eccentricity of 0.995. Later in this unit, students will learn techniques for plotting orbits using a graphing utility. At that time, they should plot several orbits of planets, comets, and artificial satellites to get a better sense of their shapes. First, however, they must develop a vocabulary for talking about orbits.

### An Earth-Centered Coordinate System

The diagram on the following page represents Earth situated in the *geocentric M-50 coordinate system.* This system is commonly used to locate points on or near Earth, and it allows us to precisely locate orbiting objects. In the M-50 coordinate system—

✦ the center (origin) of the coordinate system is at the center of the Earth;

✦ the *x*-axis points to stars in the constellation Aries;

✦ the *z*-axis points to the North Pole; and

✦ the *y*-axis lies in Earth's equatorial plane and is mutually perpendicular to the other two axes.

The M-50 system derives its name from the fact that the coordinates described above correspond to conditions in the year 1950. Actually, the rotation of Earth, the gravitational attraction of the Moon, and the movement of the stars through the universe all cause changes to occur. For instance, today, the *x*-axis points to the location where Aries was in the year 1950; the North Pole and the *z*-axis are in slightly different positions; and the equator no longer lies exactly in the *x*-*y* plane. These changes are slight, but when precise orbital calculations are required, certain modifications to the coordinate system must be made. Never-

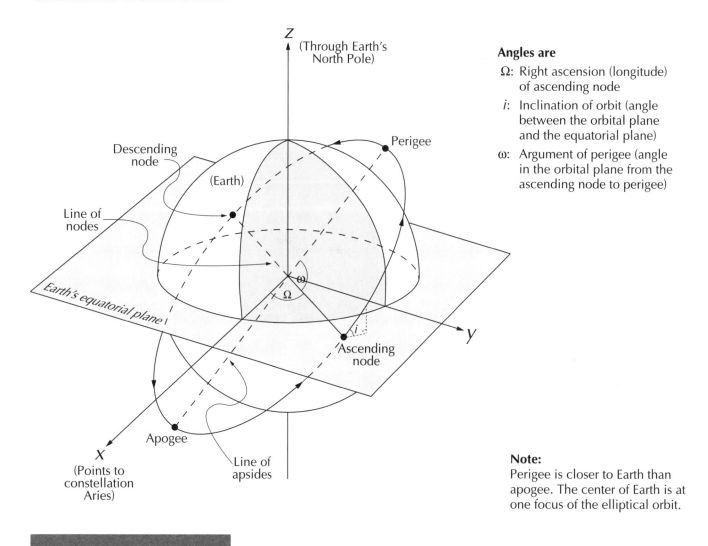

Angles are

Ω: Right ascension (longitude) of ascending node

*i*: Inclination of orbit (angle between the orbital plane and the equatorial plane)

ω: Argument of perigee (angle in the orbital plane from the ascending node to perigee)

**Note:**
Perigee is closer to Earth than apogee. The center of Earth is at one focus of the elliptical orbit.

theless, this coordinate system continues to be useful; one of its major advantages is that axes remain stationary even though Earth rotates. Thus, the M-50 coordinates of points on Earth constantly change because of Earth's rotation, but the coordinates of points above Earth remain constant. This fact enables us to locate objects in orbit by describing certain important parameters.

*The Mathematical Vocabulary of Orbits*

The following terms are used in discussing orbits:

**Apsides:** The endpoints of the major axis of an elliptical orbit. Thus, the major axis is also known as the *line of apsides.*

**Periapsis:** The point in the elliptical orbit closest to the focus. For Earth-centered orbits, this point is also known as *perigee;* for Sun-centered orbits, it is called *perihelion.*

**Apoapsis:** The point in the elliptical orbit farthest from the focus. For Earth-centered orbits, this point is also known as *apogee;* for Sun-centered orbits, it is called *aphelion.*

**Ascending node:** Point where the satellite moves from below to above the equatorial plane.

**Descending node:** Point where the satellite moves from above to below the equatorial plane.

**Line of nodes:** Line through the center of the Earth that connects the ascending and descending nodes.

**Posigrade direction:** Eastward, or counterclockwise as seen looking down from the North Pole. The Moon and most satellites move in the posigrade direction.

**Retrograde direction:** Westward, or clockwise as seen looking down from the North Pole.

**Right ascension:** Angular measurement eastward or westward from the *x*-axis; analogous to longitude on Earth.

**Inclination:** The angle between the orbital plane and the equatorial plane.

**Ground track:** The locus of points on Earth directly below the orbital path.

*Orbital Elements*

Six parameters make up the set of classical *orbital elements.* These elements, which completely and uniquely describe the size, shape, and position of any orbit, are the following:

$a$  The length of the semimajor axis

$e$  The orbital eccentricity ($e = \dfrac{c}{a}$, where $c$ is the distance from the center of the ellipse to the focus)

i   The angle of inclination of the orbit

Ω   The right ascension (longitude) of the ascending node

ω   The argument of perigee (angle in the orbital plane between the ascending node and perigee)

t   Time of perigee passage (a precise time when the satellite passed through perigee)

The orbital elements allow us to analyze and plot elliptical orbits, as we will see in the next sections.

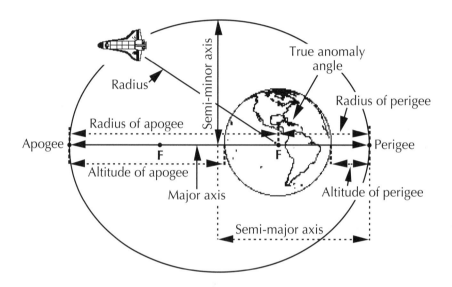

## Investigation 5—Orbital Motion: How Far? How Fast?

Isaac Newton discovered three laws that describe the motion of objects. Newton's laws can be summarized as follows:

1.   Every object at rest remains at rest, and every object in motion continues in uniform, straight-line motion unless acted on by an external force.

2.   The acceleration of an object is directly proportional to, and in the same direction as, the net (unbalanced) force acting on it, and it is inversely proportional to the mass of the object. This relationship is given in the equation

$$a = \frac{F_{net}}{m} \text{, or } f_{net} = m \cdot a \text{ .}$$

3.   For every action, there is always an equal and opposite reaction.

The first of these laws, the *law of inertia,* states that an object in motion will travel in a straight line at a constant velocity unless it is acted on by an external force. If you tie a key to the end of a string, for example, and twirl the key in a circle above your head, your hand provides the force that keeps the key moving in a circle, but the instant you let go of the string, the key flies away in a straight line. The key obeys Newton's first law.

By the same token, the planets, the Moon, and other objects moving in space should travel in straight lines. The fact that the Moon orbits Earth and the planets orbit the Sun in what appear to be circular paths led Newton to observe that a net force must be acting on all those objects; he concluded that that force was the same force that caused an apple to fall to the ground—the force of gravity. We can use Newton's laws, together with his law of universal gravitation, to determine how fast objects must travel to maintain orbit at various altitudes.

First, consider an object traveling clockwise in a circular orbit just above the surface of Earth. At point $P$, the object has forward velocity $v$ "to the right." In a small time interval $\Delta t$, the object will travel distance $d$, given by $d = v \cdot \Delta t$. During that same time, $\Delta t$, the object is accelerated toward the center of Earth and falls a distance $h$, given by

$$h = \frac{1}{2} a_g (\Delta t)^2 \, ,$$

where $a_g$ is the acceleration of gravity. Applying the Pythagorean theorem, we see that

$$(R + h)^2 = R^2 + d^2,$$

$$R^2 + 2Rh + h^2 = R^2 + d^2,$$

$$2Rh + h^2 = d^2.$$

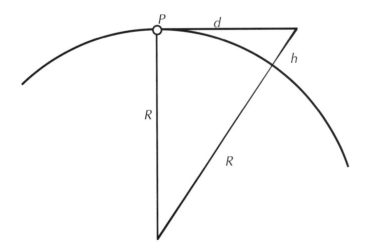

However, $h$ is very small compared with $R$, the radius of Earth; therefore, $h^2$ is very small compared with $Rh$. Also, as $\Delta t$ becomes very, very small, $h$ approaches zero. For this reason, we can neglect the $h^2$ term and simplify the foregoing expression to $2Rh = d^2$. Finally, we can substitute for $d$ and $h$ to get

$$2R \cdot \frac{1}{2} a_g (\Delta t)^2 = (v \cdot \Delta t)^2,$$

$$R \cdot a_g (\Delta t)^2 = v^2 \Delta t^2,$$

$$a_g = \frac{v^2}{R}.$$

An object traveling with forward velocity $v$ in a circular path of radius $R$ is accelerated toward the center with acceleration equal to

$$\frac{v^2}{R}.$$

We can use this result to examine orbital velocities.

If a satellite of mass $m_s$ orbits Earth at an altitude $r'$ above the surface of Earth, Newton's law of universal gravitation tells us that the gravitational force between the satellite and Earth is $F_g = G \frac{m_E m_s}{r^2}.$

Here $r$ is the distance to the center of Earth, or $r = R + r'$ (the radius of Earth plus the altitude of the satellite). Newton's second law of motion also tells us that $f = m \cdot a$, where $m$ is the mass of the satellite, $m_s$, and $a$ is the $a_g$ derived above. This force acts on the satellite to cause uniform circular motion.

To keep a satellite in a circular orbit, these two forces must be equal. Thus,

$$m_s \cdot a_g = G \frac{m_e m_s}{r^2},$$

$$\frac{v^2}{r} = G \frac{m_e}{r^2},$$

$$v^2 = G \frac{m_e}{r},$$

$$v = \sqrt{G \frac{m_e}{r}}.$$

To maintain circular orbit at distance $r$ from the center of Earth, a satellite must travel with velocity

$$v = \sqrt{\frac{Gm_e}{r}}.$$

Notice that this relationship is independent of the mass of the satellite. Thus, the Space Shuttle, the ISS, and the smallest bit of orbital debris all travel at the same velocity when in an orbit of fixed radius.

## How Do Satellites Change Orbits?

We saw above that the closer to Earth a satellite or space vehicle orbits, the greater the velocity required to maintain orbit. But how do satellites move from one orbit to another?

Satellites change orbits with the help of rocket engines, or *thrusters,* that operate according to the principle of Newton's third law of motion. When the thrusters expel gas at high speed in one direction, the escaping gas pushes back on the rocket in the opposite direction. Thus, the thrusters are fired in the direction opposite of the desired velocity change. To see how satellites change orbits, consider a satellite in circular orbit around Earth.

A *horizontal burn* occurs when the thrusters are fired in the direction of the orbital motion; horizontal burns increase or decrease the satellite's forward velocity. A *posigrade horizontal burn* fires the thrusters in the direction opposite the direction of motion, causing the satellite to be pushed forward at greater speed. A *retrograde horizontal burn* fires the thrusters in line with the direction of motion, thus slowing the satellite by pushing back against it from the front.

Increasing the satellite's forward velocity in this manner has the same effect as rolling a ball off a table or throwing it from a high hill with greater and greater speeds, as discussed previously. With greater forward velocity, the satellite falls farther from Earth, allowing it to achieve a higher altitude. The burn raises every point on the orbit except the burn point, thus placing the satellite into an elliptical orbit; the burn point becomes the perigee of the new orbit. The altitude of the new orbit depends on the magnitude of the velocity change resulting from the burn.

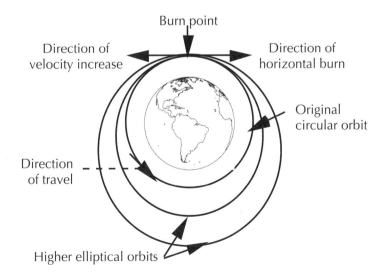

A similar result occurs when a posigrade burn takes place at perigee of an elliptical orbit: the burn raises every point on the orbit except the burn point; thus, the burn point becomes perigee of both orbits. The resulting orbit is more eccentric than the original. If a posigrade burn (velocity increase) occurs at apogee of an elliptical orbit, the burn raises every point on the orbit except the burn point; thus, the resulting orbit has a higher perigee altitude but the same apogee as the original orbit, and the resulting orbit is less eccentric than the original. Retrograde horizontal burns (velocity decrease) have the opposite effect: the retrograde burn lowers every point on the orbit except the burn point. A retrograde burn in a circular orbit or at the apogee of an elliptical orbit produces a new orbit that is lower and more eccentric than the original; a retrograde burn at the perigee of an elliptical orbit results in a lower, less eccentric orbit.

These examples of orbital changes as a result of a single burn all produce orbits that intersect in a common point. To move a satellite between two orbits that do not intersect requires at lease two rocket burns. In 1925, more than three decades before the first satellite was launched into space, Dr. Walter Hohmann, a German engineer, derived a method for transferring spacecraft between two circular orbits with the same inclination but different radii. The transfer that bears his name is the most energy-efficient method for moving between two such circular orbits. In short, the Hohmann transfer places the satellite into an elliptical orbit with its perigee on the lower circular orbit and its apogee on the higher circular orbit; it can be used to move from the lower to the higher orbit, or vice versa.

The diagram below shows a satellite moving from a lower to a higher orbit. A posigrade burn increases the velocity of the satellite and places it into an elliptical transfer orbit having the burn point as perigee and apogee on the desired higher orbit. As the satellite coasts from perigee to apogee, it slows down. At apogee, a second posigrade burn takes place, again increasing the velocity of the satellite and raising the orbit to match the desired higher circular orbit. Of course, precise mathematical calculations are required to determine the exact amount of thrust needed to achieve the desired orbital changes.

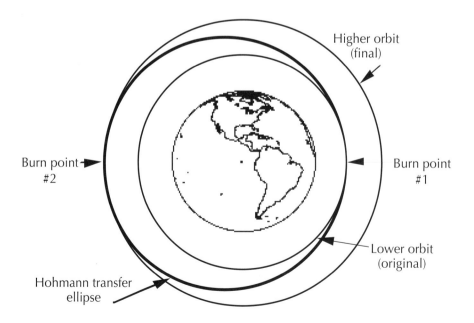

## Investigation 2—Plotting the Orbit of Earth

You know from everyday experience that objects appear smaller the farther away they are. If you construct a sighting device (fig. 3.1a) by attaching a vertical scale to a dowel or meterstick at a fixed distance $d$ from your eye, then an object of height $h$ placed next to the scale will read $h$ units in height (fig. 3.1b). (For the vertical scale, you can use a small centimeter ruler, or you can make your own scale on an index card.) However, if you focus on more distant objects, an object of height $2h$ at a distance $2d$ from your eye will also appear to be h units tall because, in your line of sight, the top of the distant object will align with the $h$ mark on the scale of your sighting device (fig. 3.1c). The apparent height ($h$) of the object at distance $2d$ will be only half its true height. Likewise, objects of height $3h$ at distance $3d$ or of height $4h$ at distance $4d$ (figs. 3.1d and 3.1e) will also appear to you to be of height $h$. That is, their apparent size is inversely proportional to their distance from you. We can use similar triangles to verify this relationship.

You can use this inverse relationship between apparent size and distance to plot the orbit of Earth. This procedure is described in the following paragraphs.

**Fig. 3.1a  Sighting device**

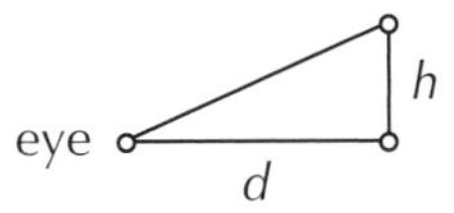

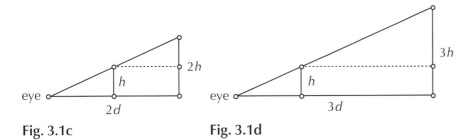

**Fig. 3.1b**

**Fig. 3.1c**

**Fig. 3.1d**

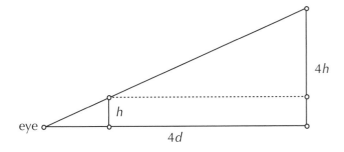

**Fig. 3.1e**

The starting point is to determine a coordinate system. Conventionally, 0 degrees (the positive *x*-axis) is assigned to the direction from Earth to the Sun on the vernal equinox (March 21). All measurements are made counterclockwise from that reference point. This system gives us the geocentric (Earth-centered) longitude of the Sun. To plot the orbit of Earth around the Sun, however, we will need the heliocentric (Sun-centered) longitude of Earth. Because the direction from the Sun to Earth is just the opposite of the Earth-Sun direction (that is, 180-degree difference), one can easily make the conversion.

Earth     Sun     Vernal equinox

Zero degrees denotes the direction to the vernal equinox.

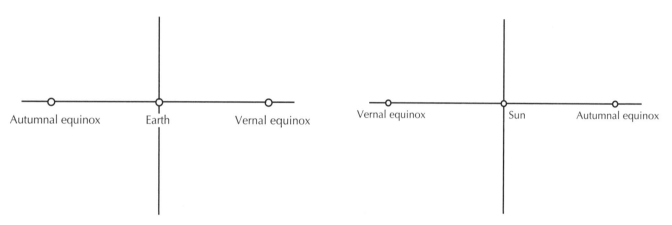

In geocentric coordinates, 0 degrees represents the direction to the Sun at the vernal equinox; 180 degrees marks the direction to the autumnal equinox.

In heliocentric coordinates (that is, looking back at Earth from the Sun), the vernal equinox is at 180 degrees and the autumnal equinox is at 0 degrees.

The table on the facing page gives the geocentric longitude of the Sun on various dates. Convert these measurements to heliocentric longitudes, and plot the direction from the Sun to Earth on each date.

Pictures of the Sun were taken from the same observatory on each of the given dates. Measurements of the size of the Sun in each picture showed variations throughout the year. One possible explanation for this phenomenon could be a periodic change in the volume of the Sun, but astronomers have sufficient reason to rule out that alternative. The best theoretical explanation for the changes in the Sun's size is the assumption that the distance from Earth to the Sun changes throughout the year.

Use your knowledge about the inverse relationship between apparent size and distance and the data in the table to determine the distance between the Sun and Earth on each given day. Plot Earth's orbit. Does

| Date | Geocentric Longitude of the Sun (Degrees) | Apparent Size of the Sun (cm) |
|---|---|---|
| March 21 | 0 | |
| April 6 | 15.7 | 48.7 |
| May 6 | 45.0 | 48.7 |
| June 5 | 73.9 | 48.5 |
| July 5 | 102.5 | 48.1 |
| August 5 | 132.1 | 48.6 |
| September 4 | 162.0 | 49.0 |
| October 4 | 191.3 | 49.5 |
| November 3 | 220.1 | 49.7 |
| December 4 | 250.4 | 49.9 |
| January 4 | 283.2 | 50.0 |
| February 4 | 314.7 | 49.6 |
| March 7 | 346.0 | 49.5 |

your orbit appear to be consistent with Kepler's three laws? Are we justified in approximating Earth's orbit by a circle?

## Investigation 3—Plotting the Orbit of Mars

The method of parallax measurement can be used to determine many inaccessible distances, including the distance to another planet. In this activity, we consider the problem of measuring the distance and direction from Earth to the planet Mars.

To understand the concept of parallax, extend one arm straight out in front of you with your thumb pointed upward. Close your left eye, and look with your right eye at your thumb against the background of objects across the room. Next close your right eye, and again look at your thumb, this time with your left eye. Holding your arm stationary, alternately sight on your thumb with one eye, then the other. Notice how your thumb appears to move from right to left against the background of distant objects as you alternate eyes. This apparent motion of a near object (your thumb, in this instance) against more distant background objects is known as parallax. Because of the distance between your eyes, the line of sight from your left eye to your thumb intersects the line of sight from your right eye at the point where your thumb is located.

We apply this phenomenon to plot the orbit of Mars using an approach developed by the seventeenth-century mathematician-astronomer Johannes Kepler, who is credited with determining that the orbits of the planets are elliptical, not circular. Kepler knew that if he could determine the distance and direction from Earth to Mars at a sufficient number of points, he could plot the orbit of Mars. Determining the direction to Mars was a direct measurement that posed no serious problem. However, the only way to measure the distance was by using parallax. The problem with this approach, though, was that observations were not possible from two points far enough apart on Earth to observe a parallax effect.

Kepler had another possible method for making the measurement. If it were true that Earth moves around the Sun, then observations of Mars could be taken at two places in Earth's orbit that were far enough apart to notice a parallax shift. This method would work well except for one obstacle: Mars, too, is moving; thus, by the time Earth moved from one position to the next, Mars would also have moved to a new position. Parallax measurements depend on the object's remaining in the same position while the observer moves.

Kepler had two other sources of useful information, however: The orbit of Earth could be plotted, and thus its position on any given date could be determined. Also, Copernicus had already determined that the Martian year was 687 Earth-days long, meaning that every 687 days, Mars completed one revolution around the Sun. In that same time, Earth completed slightly less than two revolutions (because two Earth years equals 730 days). Thus, if Mars was observed when Earth was at a position $E_1$, then 687 days later, Mars would be back to the same place in its orbit, but Earth would be at a position $E_2$, 43 days short of returning to its initial position at $E_1$. That distance was enough to reveal a parallax shift. By noting the position of Mars against the background of the fixed stars, Kepler could determine the direction to Mars, and by calculating the position of Earth in its orbit, he could diagram the directions from Earth to Mars. The intersection of the two sight lines located the position of Mars in its orbit. You can apply Kepler's methods to plot your own orbit of Mars by carrying out the following steps:

1. Before you can plot the orbit of Mars, you first must plot the orbit of Earth. You can plot Earth's orbit from observations of the Sun, as described in Investigation 2. You might also simplify the activity in this investigation by approximating Earth's orbit by a circle with the Sun at the center. Recall that Kepler's first law states that the orbits of the planets are ellipses with the Sun at one focus. For Earth, however, the eccentricity of the elliptical orbit is 0.017, which means that the orbit is nearly circular, and its approximation as a circle is reasonable. A circle of radius 10 centimeters is recommended.

2. Locate Earth in its orbit around the Sun (heliocentric longitude) on each of the recorded dates shown in the table on the following page. Use the convention that assigns 0 degrees (the positive *x*-axis) to the direction from Earth to the Sun on the vernal equinox (March 21). All measurements are made counterclockwise from that reference point. (See Investigation 2 for a discussion of this coordinate system.)

3. The table gives ten pairs of observations taken 687 days apart. For each date, the position of Mars is recorded. The data are given as geocentric longitudes, that is, as directions from Earth to Mars. From Earth's position at 1a and 1b, draw the direction to Mars on each date. (To determine the direction to Mars, draw a line from

Earth's position parallel to the x-axis to locate the 0-degree direction. The direction to Mars is measured counterclockwise from that reference.) The intersection of the two lines locates one point on the orbit of Mars.

4.  Repeat step 3 for the other pairs of data to locate ten points on the orbit. Connect the points with a smooth curve. Use your plot of the orbit of Mars to answer the following questions:

    a.  Does the orbit that you plotted seem to support Kepler's conclusion that the planetary orbits are ellipses?

    b.  If the distance from Earth to the Sun is taken to be 1 AU, what is the distance from Mars to the Sun at each of the ten points?

    c.  What is the average Mars-to-Sun distance?

    d.  What is the closest distance (perihelion) and farthest distance (aphelion) of Mars from the Sun?

    e.  What is the approximate eccentricity of Mars's orbit?

    f.  During what months of Earth's year is Earth closest to the orbit of Mars?

    g.  What is the minimum distance from Earth to Mars for the data you plotted?

| Position | Date | Day of Year | Geocentric Longitude of Mars (Degrees) | Heliocentric Longitude of Earth (Degrees) |
|---|---|---|---|---|
| 1a | 3/21/31 | 0 | 119.0 | 180 |
| 1b | 2/5/33 | 321 | 169.0 | 137.6 |
| 2a | 4/20/33 | 30 | 151.5 | 210.6 |
| 2b | 3/8/35 | 352 | 204.5 | 168.2 |
| 3a | 5/26/35 | 66 | 186.5 | 246.1 |
| 3b | 4/12/37 | 22 | 245.5 | 203.7 |
| 4a | 9/16/39 | 179 | 297.5 | 358.5 |
| 4b | 8/4/41 | 136 | 16.5 | 317.1 |
| 5a | 11/22/41 | 246 | 12.0 | 65.6 |
| 5b | 10/11/43 | 204 | 80.0 | 24.2 |
| 6a | 1/21/44 | 306 | 66.0 | 124.8 |
| 6b | 12/9/45 | 263 | 123.0 | 83.3 |
| 7a | 3/19/46 | 363 | 107.5 | 182.0 |
| 7b | 2/3/48 | 319 | 153.5 | 138.6 |
| 8a | 4/4/48 | 14 | 138.0 | 198.7 |
| 8b | 2/21/50 | 337 | 190.5 | 157.3 |
| 9a | 9/11/56 | 174 | 345.0 | 348.1 |
| 9b | 7/30/58 | 174 | 35.0 | 306.2 |
| 10a | 10/30/56 | 223 | 340.0 | 36.5 |
| 10b | 9/17/58 | 180 | 60.0 | 353.5 |

## Investigation 4—Plotting the Orbit of Mercury

The inner planets, Mercury and Venus, are always closer to the Sun than is Earth. Mercury, the innermost planet, is seen close to the horizon only just after sunset (east of the Sun) or just before sunrise (west of the Sun), and viewing Mercury is difficult because of the glare of the Sun. Mercury also has the second most eccentric orbit of any of the planets ($e = 0.206$).

We can plot the orbit of Mercury by observing its maximum angular separation east or west of the Sun as seen from Earth on various dates. This angle between the Earth-Sun sight line and the Earth-Mercury sight line is called the *angle of elongation* (see fig. 3.2a). When the angle of elongation is at its maximum, the Earth-Mercury sight line is tangent to Mercury's orbit (see fig. 3.2b). Because both Mercury and Earth are moving in elliptical orbits, the maximum elongation angle varies from one

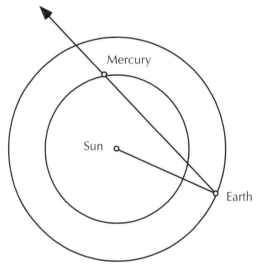

**Fig. 3.2a. The angle between the Earth-Sun sight line and the Earth-Mercury sight line is called the *angle of elongation*.**

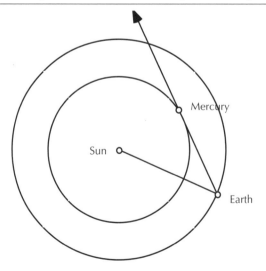

**Fig. 3.2b. When the angle of elongation is at its maximum, the Earth-Mercury sight line is tangent to Mercury's orbit.**

orbital revolution to another. The table below gives the maximum elongation of Mercury during the years 2000 through 2003.

The angle between the Earth-Sun sight line and the Earth-Mercury sight line is called the angle of elongation. When the angle of elongation is at its maximum, the Earth-Mercury sight line is tangent to Mercury's orbit.

For this activity, you can use the orbit of Earth that you plotted previously, or you can approximate Earth's orbit with a circle of radius 10 centimeters with the Sun at the center. Locate the 0-degree reference line and the positions of Earth at the vernal (March) and autumnal (September) equinoxes. Also locate Earth in its orbit on each of twelve successive dates (two years) from the table, and lightly draw the radius connecting Earth to the Sun at each of the twelve positions. Remember that Earth moves through 360 degrees in 365 days. A spreadsheet is a useful tool for calculating the angular positions of Earth in its orbit on the selected dates.

| Points on Mercury's Orbit | Date | Earth to Mercury (Degrees/Direction) |
|---|---|---|
| A | Equinox | Reference point(s) |
| B | 2/15/00 | 18 E |
| C | 3/28/00 | 28 W |
| D | 6/9/00 | 24 E |
| E | 7/27/00 | 20 W |
| F | 10/6/00 | 26 E |
| G | 11/15/00 | 19 W |
| H | 1/28/01 | 18 E |
| I | 3/11/01 | 27 W |
| J | 5/22/01 | 22 E |
| K | 7/9/01 | 21 W |
| L | 9/18/01 | 27 E |
| M | 10/29/01 | 19 W |
| N | 1/11/02 | 19 E |
| O | 2/21/02 | 27 W |
| P | 5/4/02 | 21 E |
| Q | 6/21/02 | 23 W |
| R | 9/1/02 | 27 E |
| S | 10/13/02 | 18 W |
| T | 12/26/02 | 20 E |
| U | 2/4/03 | 25 W |
| V | 4/16/03 | 20 E |
| W | 6/3/03 | 24 W |
| X | 8/14/03 | 27 E |
| Y | 9/27/03 | 18 W |
| Z | 12/9/03 | 21 E |

Next draw the sight lines from Earth to Mercury for the given elongation angles. Remember that in our coordinate system, we are looking down from the North Pole; thus, an eastern elongation is to the left of the Sun, and western elongation is to the right. (Note: This activity can be done effectively with an interactive geometry program, such as The Geometer's Sketchpad.)

In each instance, we know that Mercury is somewhere along the sight line, but we do not know where. We also know that the sight line is tangent to the orbit. A reasonable assumption is that Mercury is at the point on the tangent closest to the Sun, that is, at the point of tangency. Locate those points, and sketch the orbit of Mercury; then complete the tasks below. (Hint: Remember that the radius of a circle is perpendicular to the tangent at the point of tangency.)

✦ Try to locate perihelion (the point closest to the Sun) and aphelion (the point farthest from the Sun) for the orbit of Mercury. Because those points are the endpoints of the major axis, you can draw the major axis of Mercury's orbit.

✦ We let 10 cm = 1 AU (the semimajor axis of Earth's orbit). Use your plotted Mercury orbit to find the length of the semimajor axis (average solar distance) of Mercury in AUs. How does your result compare with the known value?

✦ Given that

$$e = \frac{c}{a},$$

we know that aphelion distance is $(a + c) = (a + a \cdot e) = a(1 + e)$. Use your orbit to determine the eccentricity ($e$) for Mercury. How does your result compare with the known value?

## Investigation 5—Orbital Motion: How Far? How Fast?

Calculate the orbital velocities in the following scenarios using these values and known constants: $G = 6.67(10^{-11})\dfrac{\text{N}\cdot\text{m}^2}{\text{kg}^2}$, $m_e = 6(10^{24})\,\text{kg}$,

and $r_e = 6400\,\text{km}$. Note: A *newton* (abbreviated N) is defined to be the force required to accelerate a mass of 1 kilogram at a rate of 1 meter per second per second, that is,

$$1\text{N} = 1\frac{\text{kg}\cdot\text{m}}{\text{sec}^2}.$$

1. The ISS and the Space Shuttle orbit in the range of 200 to 250 miles (320 to 400 km) above Earth. What velocity is required to keep the ISS in orbit at an altitude of 400 km?

2. At that speed, how much time does the ISS need to make one orbit of Earth?

3. A *geostationary* or *geosynchronous* satellite is one that appears to observers on Earth to always remain over the same point on the surface of Earth. To achieve a synchronous orbit, the satellite must be placed in a west-to-east orbit above the equator at an altitude that will make the orbital period match the rotation of Earth. What must the altitude be for the satellite to complete one orbit in 24 hours? At that altitude, what is the velocity of the satellite?

4. When the Apollo missions visited the Moon, two astronauts descended to the Moon's surface in the lunar module while the third crew member remained in lunar orbit in the command module at an altitude of about 110 km. What was the velocity of the command module during its "parking orbit" around the Moon? Note that the mass of the Moon is about $7.3(10^{22})\,\text{kg}$, or 0.012 times the mass of Earth, and its diameter is about 3,480 km. How much time did the command module require to orbit the Moon?

The picture on this page is a historic one. It is the first picture of a natural satellite, or moon, of an asteroid. The *Galileo* spacecraft took the picture of asteroid 243 Ida and its tiny moon. The moon orbiting Ida at a distance of about 60 miles is only about 1 mile across.

# Modeling Orbital Paths

## Investigation 6—Cartesian Coordinate Models for Elliptical Orbits

How can we apply our knowledge of orbits to represent the orbital paths of familiar satellites and other objects? We begin by using Cartesian coordinates to represent the orbital path of the ISS around Earth.

From Kepler's first law, we know that the ISS must move in an elliptical path with the Earth as one focus of the ellipse. Such an ellipse, drawn out of proportion to emphasize its component parts, is shown below.

The ISS has an apogee of approximately 275 miles (437 km) and a perigee of approximately 225 miles (361 km) (www.spacenet.on.ca/ curriculum/iss2a/observing_tea.htm). If we locate one focus of our ellipse at the center of Earth, it will have Cartesian coordinates (0, 0). Knowing that Earth's radius is approximately 4,000 miles, we can generate the information needed to write an elliptical equation for the path of the ISS, as follows:

♦ The length of the major axis of our ellipse is the sum of the apogee distance, the perigee distance, and twice the radius of Earth:

$$275 + 225 + 4{,}000 + 4{,}000 = 8{,}500 \text{ miles}$$

We represent the length of the major axis of an ellipse as $2a$. For our ellipse, then, $a = 4{,}250$ miles is the length of the semimajor axis.

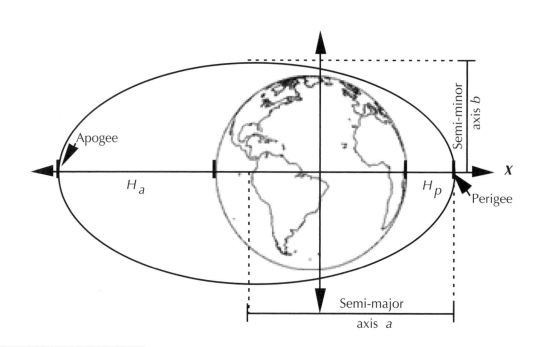

✦ The midpoint of the major axis represents the center of the ellipse. Because it is 4,250 miles from either endpoint of the major axis, its coordinates are (–25, 0). The distance from the center of the ellipse to the focus is the value $c$; thus, for our ellipse, $c = 25$ miles. Although it is greatly distorted, the figure below shows these distances in relation to the parameters of the orbit.

✦ This calculation immediately leads to the coordinates of the other focus as (–50, 0) because the two foci are $2c$ units apart along the major axis.

✦ Using the "a, b, c connection," we now can determine the value $b$:

$$b = \sqrt{a^2 - c^2} = 4{,}249.93 \text{ miles}$$

✦ The eccentricity of the ellipse is $e = c/a = 25/4{,}250 = 0.0059$. As expected, our ellipse is very close to circular!

✦ Using a scale where 1 unit represents 1000 miles, we can now represent the ellipse as follows:

$$\frac{(x - (-0.025))^2}{4.25^2} + \frac{y^2}{\left(\sqrt{4.25^2 - 0.025^2}\right)^2} = 1$$

We can use this representation for the ellipse with a graphing utility to generate a picture of the elliptical orbit of the ISS around Earth. With a typical graphing calculator, we must enter the representation as a function $y = f(x)$. Solving the equation above for $y$ yields two functions:

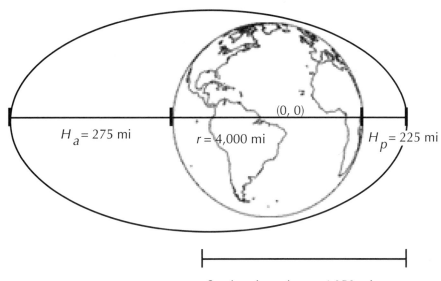

$H_a = 275$ mi    $r = 4{,}000$ mi    (0, 0)    $H_p = 225$ mi

Semi-major axis $a = 4{,}250$ mi

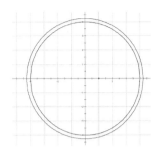

$$y_1(x) = \frac{\sqrt{4.25^2 - 0.025^2}}{4.25}\sqrt{4.25^2 - (x+0.025)^2}$$

$$y_2(x) = -\frac{\sqrt{4.25^2 - 0.025^2}}{4.25}\sqrt{4.25^2 - (x+0.025)^2}$$

In the margin are two graphs that show the elliptical orbit using these two functions. Superimposed on each is a graph representing Earth (radius length, 4,000 miles, or 4 units) using the functions

$$y = f(x) = \pm\sqrt{4^2 - x^2}.$$

Notice how tight fitting is the ISS elliptical orbit.

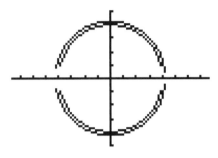

The graph on the top was generated by using the current version of The Geometer's Sketchpad; the graph on the bottom, by using a graphing calculator. A portion of each graph, near the x-axis, appears to be missing on the calculator graph. Most graphing calculators have this limitation because they use a finite number of points—pixels—to represent an infinite number of points on a continuous function. Because of this same limitation, a calculator's trace feature is limited in actually moving along the curve as a representation of the ISS in orbit.

The general layout for an ellipse with semimajor axis length a and each focus c units from the center of the ellipse is shown in the figure below. Students may use this figure as a reference as the class explores problems involving satellite orbits. Investigation 6 on page 93 poses several problems that offer additional opportunities to model orbital paths using Cartesian coordinates and calculators or computers and to analyze the results of such technology-generated models.

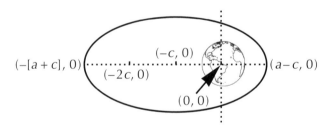

## Investigation 7—Models for Elliptical Orbits: Parametric Equations

Although both teachers and students are usually quite familiar with the Cartesian system, some aspects of orbits modeled in a Cartesian system are not well portrayed. For instance, a calculator's trace function does not model well the movement of an object, such as the ISS, along its path. As previously mentioned, the calculator's display will likely show a gap near the x-axis in most Cartesian plots of orbital paths. These gaps result from the use of a finite device—a graphing utility—to approximate a continuous function. For these and other reasons, those who frequently work with orbits use other models.

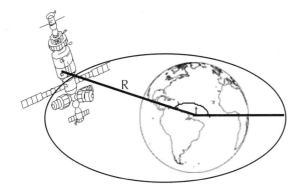

In grades 9–12 students should also explore problems for which using other coordinate systems is helpful. They should have some familiarity with spherical and simple polar coordinate systems, as well as with systems used in navigation.

*(NCTM 2000, p. 314)*

One alternative is a parametric model. It uses the radius *R*, which is the distance between the orbiting object and the center of the Earth, and an angle measure—typically expressed as *q* or *t*—called the *true anomaly*. True anomaly measures the angle between two lines, one connecting the center of Earth to the perigee point and another (the radius) connecting the center of the Earth to the satellite's position. Here, we use *t* to represent true anomaly.

Students may have previous experiences with parametric models, such as in representing circles. Trigonometry offers a straightforward means to show that the Cartesian coordinates (*x*, *y*) for any point on a circle with radius *r* can be represented using the parameter *t*, as follows:

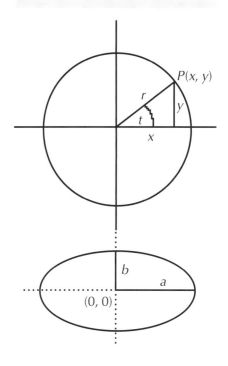

$$x = r \cos(t) \text{ and } y = r \sin(t)$$

We describe these expressions as parametric equations for a circle whose center is at (0, 0) and whose radius has length *r*. For an ellipse centered at (0, 0) with semimajor axis length *a* and semiminor axis length *b*, we know that the Cartesian equation is

$$\frac{x^2}{a^2} + \frac{y^2}{b^2} = 1.$$

Parametric equations for the ellipse shown here are

$$x = a\cos(t) \text{ and } y = b\sin(t).$$

This result can be verified using a graphing utility or symbolically, as shown below, by employing a well-known trigonometric identity to eliminate the parameter *t*.

$$x = a\cos(t) \qquad y = b\sin(t)$$

$$\frac{x}{a} = \cos(t) \qquad \frac{y}{b} = \sin(t)$$

$$\frac{x^2}{a^2} = \cos^2(t) \qquad \frac{y^2}{b^2} = \sin^2(t)$$

$$\cos^2(t) + \sin^2(t) = 1$$

$$\frac{x^2}{a^2} + \frac{y^2}{b^2} = 1$$

Applied problems can furnish both rich contexts for using geometric ideas and practice in modeling and problem solving.

*(NCTM 2000, p. 313)*

High school students should develop facility with a broad range of ways of representing geometric ideas ... that allow multiple approaches to geometric problems and that connect geometric interpretations to other contexts.... This ability to use different representations advantageously is part of students' developing geometric sophistication.

*(NCTM 2000, p. 309)*

For an object in orbit around Earth, however, the center of the elliptical orbit is at $(-c, 0)$, not at $(0, 0)$. Therefore, the $x$-coordinate of the desired parametric equation is translated by the distance $-c$. The resulting parametric equations are

$$x = a\cos(t) - c \quad \text{and} \quad y = b\sin(t).$$

Investigation 7 on page 94 presents opportunities to explore parametric equations and to create and use them to model orbital paths.

## Investigation 8—Connecting the Models

Here, students are given the opportunity to connect the Cartesian and polar representations of a circle centered at the origin. From the equations relating polar and Cartesian coordinates, the class can also derive equations that will be used in subsequent activities to model orbits using a graphing utility.

## Investigation 9—Modeling Low Earth Orbits with Polar Models

A third model for representing orbital paths uses polar coordinates. This model is commonly used in navigation and has advantages over other models for orbital paths. One way to begin making connections to polar coordinates is to use them to represent aircraft location.

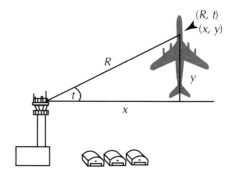

The distance, $R$, from the tower to the aircraft is a function of $t$, the angle of elevation from the tower to the aircraft. The connection between this way to identify location, through the polar coordinate $(R, t)$, and the Cartesian location $(x, y)$ can be made using right-triangle trigonometry:

$$\frac{x}{R} = \cos(t) \qquad \frac{y}{R} = \sin(t) \qquad \frac{y}{x} = \tan(t)$$
$$x = R\cos(t) \qquad y = R\sin(t)$$

Thus,

$$x^2 + y^2 = R^2\cos^2(t) + R^2\sin^2(t) = R^2\left(\cos^2(t) + \sin^2(t)\right) = R^2;$$

therefore,

$$R = \sqrt{x^2 + y^2}.$$

Cartesian and polar coordinates have a significant difference: The Cartesian coordinates for a given point in the plane are unique, whereas an infinite number of polar-coordinate representations are possible for the same point. For example, the point with unique Cartesian coordinates $(1, 1)$ has the following polar-coordinate representations:

$$\left(\sqrt{2}, 45°\right)\left(\sqrt{2}, 405°\right)\left(\sqrt{2}, 765°\right)..., \left(\sqrt{2}, 45° + n \cdot 360°\right),$$

where $n = 0, 1, 2,....$ This characteristic of polar coordinates is useful in modeling situations in which spacecraft remain in one elliptical orbit for more than one revolution, then move into another orbit, such as when completing a rendezvous.

Students might gain an intuitive appreciation for polar-coordinate graphing by exploring one or more of the following connections:

✦ A graphing utility may have built-in software that can be used to display simultaneous polar and Cartesian graphs.

✦ Weather radar on local television can be a useful visual tool when the sweep of the radar is shown.

✦ A Spirograph toy can be used to promote an understanding of complex polar graphs.

✦ Microphone-sensitivity plots can be studied to reveal a direct application of polar graphing.

✦ An engineer at a local radio station may be able to provide copies of antenna patterns, which are polar charts that the station must file with the Federal Communications Commission.

## Investigation 10—Applying the Polar Model: The Graphing Utility as a Space Navigator

Given this discussion of the mathematics of polar equations, students may wonder why a polar model has been proposed as the most useful for representing orbital paths. After all, when given apogee-perigee data, we have found other models that are straightforward to use. Space scientists and astronomers, however, often use the orbital elements, or Keplerian elements, $a$ and $e$. In fact, on the NASA Shuttle Web page during a mission, the first two Keplerian elements listed will be $a$ and $e$. Tasks 5 through 9 in Investigation 9 (pages 98–99) illustrate how polar equations and a graphing utility can be used to model low-Earth orbits (LEOs). Students can complete one or more of the projects described in Investigation 10 (pages 99–102) to reinforce and extend what they have learned about modeling orbital paths.

## Conclusion

Orbital mechanics provides a rich context in which students can explore important mathematics in a realistic and interesting setting. This field of study embodies the goals of using representations set forth in NCTM's *Principles and Standards for School Mathematics*:

*Students' use of representations to model physical, social, and mathematical phenomena should grow through the years.... High school students create and interpret models of phenomena drawn from a wider range of contexts—including physical and social environments—by identifying essential elements of the context and by*

Instructional programs from prekindergarten through grade 12 should enable all students to—

✦ create and use representations to organize, record, and communicate mathematical ideas;

✦ select, apply, and translate among mathematical representations to solve problems;

✦ Use representations to model and interpret physical, social, and mathematical phenomena.

*(NCTM 2000, p. 67)*

Before entering any polar models into a graphing utility, be alert for the following anomalies:

✦ When entering the eccentricity, $e$, be sure that your graphing utility does not interpret this variable as the natural-logarithm base $e$, or 2.718.... If necessary, use another letter to represent eccentricity.

✦ The angle setting for $t$, the true anomaly, should be in radians or degrees. For a complete elliptical orbit, $0 < t < 2\pi$ radians or $0 < t < 360$ degrees. Students should try modeling in both modes, then change the calculator's angle mode accordingly.

*devising representations that capture mathematical relationships among those elements. With electronic technologies, students can use representations for problems and methods that until recently were difficult to explore meaningfully in high school.*

(NCTM 2000, p. 71)

Mission Control Center

## Investigation 6—Cartesian Coordinate Models for Elliptical Orbits

1. The first successful launch of a navigation satellite occurred on April 13, 1960. The satellite, called Transit, orbited Earth with an apogee of 745 km and a perigee of 373 km (Graham 1995).

   — Create an equation to represent the orbital path of this navigation satellite.

   — Plot the orbital path superimposed on a graph representing Earth, where Earth has a radius of 4,000 miles (or 6,400 km).

2. Here is an Internet summary about a Japanese satellite launched in 1998 (National Space Development Agency of Japan 1998):

   *COMETS, dubbed Kakehashi, was launched from the Tanegashima Space Center by the H-II Launch Vehicle Flight No. 5 on February 21, 1998 at 4:55 p.m. Unfortunately, COMETS was not placed in its planned geostationary transfer orbit because the duration of the second firing of the launch vehicle's second-stage engine was shorter than planned. This mishap made it difficult for NASDA to conduct orbital experiments as originally planned on COMETS. NASDA therefore studied the possibility of orbit change by firing [the] satellite's apogee engine with the cooperation of the Communications Research Laboratory (CRL) and other related institutions in order to conduct as many of the planned space experiments as possible. As a result, it was found possible to place the satellite into an elliptical orbit at a perigee of about 500 km and apogee of 17,700 km.*

   — Create an equation for the path of satellite COMETS, and plot that path using a graphing utility.

   — Briefly describe what your plot reveals. What surprises did you observe in your plot? Does your plot have any shortcomings? Explain.

3. The table at the right shows orbital data for several comets that orbit the Sun. Note the units of measure described at the bottom of the table.

   — Identify three comets from the list that you perceive will have distinctive yet different orbital paths around the Sun. Plot those paths, and write a brief description of the plots. Did the plots turn out as you expected?

   — Calculate the eccentricities of the comets in the table.

| Comet | Orbital Period | Perihelion Date | Perigee | Apogee |
|---|---|---|---|---|
| Halley | 76.10 | 02-09-1998 | 0.587 | 17.94 |
| Encke | 3.30 | 06-11-1997 | 0.339 | 2.21 |
| Giacobini-Zinner | 6.52 | 11-21-1998 | 0.996 | 3.52 |
| Grigg-Skjellerup | 5.09 | 07-22-1992 | 0.989 | 2.96 |
| Crommelin | 27.89 | 01-09-1984 | 0.743 | 9.20 |
| Honda-Mrkos-Pajdusakova | 5.29 | 01-17-1996 | 0.581 | 3.02 |
| Wirtanen | 5.46 | 03-14-1997 | 1.063 | 3.12 |
| Temple-Tuttle | 32.92 | 02-27-1998 | 0.982 | 10.33 |
| Kohoutek | 6.24 | 12-28-1973 | 1.571 | 3.40 |
| West-Kohoutek-Ikemura | 6.46 | 01-06-2000 | 1.596 | 3.45 |
| Wild 2 | 6.17 | 05-06-1997 | 1.583 | 3.44 |
| Chiron | 50.70 | 02-14-1996 | 8.460 | 13.70 |
| Hale-Bopp | 4000.00 | 03-31-1997 | 0.914 | 250.00 |
| Hyakutake | 65000.00 | 01-05-1996 | 0.230 | 1600.00 |

Notes: Orbital period is in years. Units for Perigee and Apogee are A.U. (1 A.U. = 93 million miles)

## Investigation 7—Models for Elliptical Orbits: Parametric Equations

1.  Check to see that your graphing calculator is in parametric mode. Then verify that the parametric equations $x = r\cos(t)$ and $y = r\sin(t)$ will generate circles for various positive values of $r$.

2.  Use the parametric equations $x = a\cos(t) - c$ and $y = b\sin(t)$ to graph a parametric model for the orbital path of the ISS. Recall that the ISS has apogee approximately 275 miles and perigee approximately 225 miles. In your model, represent the center of Earth (radius of 4,000 miles) with coordinates (0, 0).

3.  Activate your calculator's trace feature to simulate the movement of the ISS on its orbital path. Verify the coordinates of the apogee and perigee of the ISS. How do the coordinates you found compare with the stated apogee and perigee?

4.  Write a few sentences to describe possible advantages of the parametric model compared with the Cartesian model for graphing low-Earth orbits on a graphing utility.

5.  Return to the setting for task 1 from Investigation 6:

    *The first successful launch of a navigation satellite occurred on April 13, 1960. The satellite, called Transit, orbited Earth with an apogee of 745 km and a perigee of 373 km (Graham 1995).*

    Model Transit's orbital path using a parametric model.

## Investigation 8—Connecting the Models

To more fully examine the connection between the Cartesian and polar models, consider these two ways for representing a circle centered at (0, 0) with radius 4:

$$\text{Cartesian: } x^2 + y^2 = 4^2 \qquad \text{Polar: } R(t) = 4$$

Below are four pairs of representations for identical elements in Cartesian and polar form. For each pair—

✦ supply the missing element and

✦ plot the graphs in both polar and Cartesian coordinates to verify your work. The first pair has been completed for you. Be sure to plot each graph!

$$\text{Cartesian: the line } y = 5 \qquad \text{Polar: } \begin{cases} R(t) \cdot \sin(t) = 5 \\ R(t) = \dfrac{5}{\sin(t)} \\ R(t) = 5 \cdot \csc(t) \end{cases}$$

Cartesian: ?     Polar: $\begin{cases} R(t) \cdot \cos(t) = 2 \\ \qquad \text{or} \\ R(t) = 2 \cdot \sec(t) \end{cases}$

Cartesian: $y^2 = 4x$     Polar: ?

Cartesian: $\dfrac{x^2}{9} + \dfrac{y^2}{4} = 1$     Polar: ?

The connection between polar and parametric forms can also be derived from the equations relating polar and Cartesian coordinates. Here, we use the fact that

$$x = R\cos(t) \quad y = R\sin(t),$$

and we make the "R replacement." For example, if the polar form is

$$R(t) = 6\tan(t),$$

then the parametric form is

$$x = R\cos(t) = R(t)\cos(t) = (6\tan(t))\cos(t),$$
$$y = R\sin(t) = R(t)\sin(t) = (6\tan(t))\sin(t).$$

Take time to verify several similar plots before you continue. If your graphing utility does not include the capacity to graph polar coordinates directly, you can use this parametric representation to produce polar-coordinate graphs.

*Polar-Coordinate Model for Any Ellipse*
In the Cartesian/polar conversion activity, your last conversion was an ellipse with semimajor axis of length 3 and semiminor axis of length 2. Your polar equation should have looked like this:

$$R(t) = \frac{6}{\sqrt{4\cos^2(t) + 9\sin^2(t)}}$$

Although we could use this type of polar equation for an ellipse, a much more useful representation can be derived. For space science and astronomy, the most useful model is the following:

$$R(t) = \frac{a(1 - e^2)}{1 + e\cos(t)}$$

Here, $a$ is the length of the semimajor axis, $e = c/a$ is the eccentricity, and $t$ is the true-anomaly angle.

To derive this model, we need another definition of eccentricity. To this point, we have defined eccentricity only as it applies to the shape of an ellipse. Our alternative definition involves the classic focus-directrix definition of conic sections. The equation we derive next yields a model for plotting any conic section with a graphing utility.

Therefore, it can be used to model suborbital flight and parabolic or hyperbolic flyby trajectories, as well as elliptical orbital paths.

*The Focus-Directrix Polar Model*

Cartesian models for conic sections—parabolas, hyperbolas, ellipses, and circles—are quite straightforward when the center of the conic section is at the origin of the Cartesian plane. In modeling orbits, however, placing a focus of the conic section at the origin is more convenient. Polar models of conic sections have the advantage of taking on a simple form if one of the foci lies at the point $(R, t) = (0, 0)$. This point is called the *pole* in polar coordinates; it corresponds to the origin in the Cartesian plane.

The focus-directrix definition of eccentricity provides a means to classify all conic sections:

> *A set of points in the plane is a conic section if, for any point P = (x, y) in that set, a constant ratio exists between the distance from P to a fixed point (called the* focus) *and the distance from P to a fixed line (called the* directrix). *This constant ratio, labeled e, is the eccentricity of the conic section. If e > 1, the conic is a hyperbola; if e = 1, the conic is a parabola; if 0 < e < 1, the conic is an ellipse; and if e = 0, it is a circle.*

In the polar graph shown at the left, the focus $F$ is located at the pole $(0, 0)$. $P$ is any point on the conic with coordinates $(R, t)$. The directrix is located a distance $d$ units from the focus. We seek to show that the polar equation of any conic section is

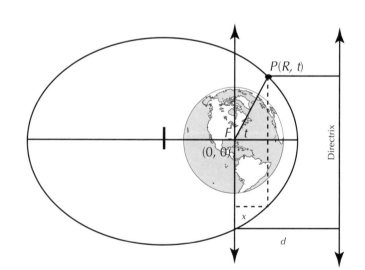

$$(1) \qquad R(t) = \frac{ed}{1 + e\cos(t)}.$$

The eccentricity, or constant ratio, is

$$(2) \qquad e = \frac{|PF|}{|PD|}.$$

where $|PF|$ is equal to the value $R$ and $|PD| = d - x$.

We know, however, that $\frac{x}{R} = \cos(t)$ or $x = R\cos(t)$;

thus, $|PD| = d - R\cos(t)$. Substituting into (2) above gives us

$$(3) \qquad e = \frac{R}{d - R\cos(t)}.$$

Solving (3) for $R$ yields the desired equation (1). Use tasks 1 through 4 from Investigation 9 (pages 98–99) to explore polar representations for orbits.

*The Polar Model for Elliptical Orbits*

Recall the polar model for an ellipse that we stated previously:

(4)
$$R(t) = \frac{a(1 - e^2)}{1 + e\cos(t)}$$

Before we apply the results of our work to orbital models, we want to show that the polar model for conic sections that we just derived,

(5)
$$R(t) = \frac{ed}{1 + e\cos(t)},$$

results in equation (4) for an ellipse.

Consider a general ellipse with semi-major axis of length $a$, one focus located at $(0, 0)$, its directrix $d$ units right of the focus, and its eccentricity $e$ (see figure). We have

$$|PF| = a - c$$

and

$$e = \frac{c}{a} \text{ or } c = a \cdot e,$$

meaning that

(6)
$$|PF| = a - ae = a(1 - e).$$

With $|PF| = R(t)$, when $t = 0$ and $\cos(0) = 1$, the polar equation becomes

(7)
$$|PF| = R(0) = \frac{e \cdot d}{1 + e}.$$

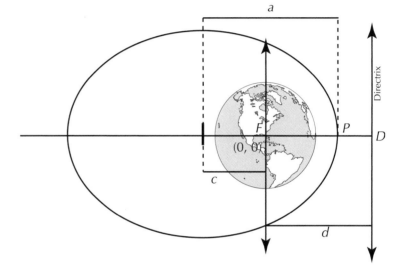

Equations (6) and (7) provide two expressions for $|PF|$ so that

$$\frac{e \cdot d}{1 + e} = a(1 - e) \Rightarrow ed = a(1 - e)(1 + e) = a(1 - e^2).$$

This result shows that the numerators on the right sides of expressions (4) and (5) are equivalent; thus, the two representations for $R(t)$ are equivalent for an ellipse with focus at $(0, 0)$.

## Investigation 9—Modeling Low-Earth Orbits with Polar Models

1. Enter the polar equation for conics, $R(t) = \dfrac{e \cdot d}{1 + e \cos(t)}$, into your graphing utility. Keep the focus-directrix distance constant (let $d = 1$, for example), and change the value of $e$, the eccentricity. Verify the claim that the value of $e$ determines whether the graph is a hyperbola, parabola, or ellipse.

2. Write a brief summary of your exploration in task 1. Explain what to expect when you change the value of $e$.

3. Complete a similar exploration as in task 1, holding e constant and changing the value of $d$ for two or more different conic sections.

4. Write a report to explain how we might apply hyperbolic, parabolic, and elliptical paths to model space flight, comet paths, and other trajectories.

5. Use the polar model to graph the ISS orbit again. Recall the specifications for this orbit: perigee at 225 miles and apogee at 275 miles.

   — Compute $a$ and $e$.

   — Graph the orbit on your graphing utility.

   — Carry out a trace to check the orbit.

6. Keplerian elements for a noted NASA Space Shuttle mission (STS-73, October 1995) were $a = 6{,}644{,}100.18$ meters and $e = 0.0002952$. With your graphing utility, simultaneously graph this orbit and an outline of Earth. Because the NASA data are so precise, use 3,960 miles for the radius of Earth. Note that you will need to convert $a$ to miles or Earth's radius to meters.

7. NASA's World Wide Web site for Shuttle mission STS-73 reported the altitudes at apogee and perigee as 144.658 nautical miles and 142.540 nautical miles, respectively. Examine your plot in task 6, and discuss the accuracy of your orbit plot in light of the NASA data. How many significant digits did you use in operations with the data? Did that condition have any effect on the accuracy of your plot? Explain.

   (Note: A *nautical mile,* the unit of distance commonly used in air and sea navigation, is equal to 6,076 feet, or 1.852 km. A *statute mile,* the common distance unit for land-based measurements, equals 5,280 feet, or 1.609 km.)

8. This task calls for you to model a rendezvous with the Hubble Space Telescope. Assume that you are orbiting in the Space Shuttle. For ease in calculating, also assume that your altitudes of perigee and apogee are 200 miles and 400 miles, respectively. You are in the second orbit of your mission when you receive this transmission from Mission Control: "This is Houston. Please prepare for a posi-

grade burn to change your orbit and rendezvous with the Hubble. Apogee for the Hubble orbit is 800 miles." Assume that your posi-grade burn will take place at perigee in your orbit. At that instant, the burn point will become perigee of your new orbit because we assume that the burn raises every point on the old orbit except the burn point. Next perform the following tasks:

— Plot Earth on your graphing utility using $r = 4{,}000$ miles.

— Superimpose your Shuttle orbit on the outline of Earth. You should be able to calculate $a$ and $c$ from the data given; use a polar model, and recall that $e = c/a$.

— With the information from Houston, calculate the orbital elements for your new orbit. It must have a perigee of 200 miles and an apogee of 800 miles.

— Use your polar model to superimpose the new orbit on the first plot you created.

9. Return to the previous question. Modify your work for plotting the two orbits in such a way that a trace of your polar model on your graphing utility will remain in the initial orbit (perigee 200 miles, apogee 400 miles) for three complete orbits. Then, simulating the burn at perigee, the trace will move into the new orbit (perigee 200 miles, apogee 800 miles) for five complete orbits. Hint: Pay close attention to the $a$, $c$, $e$ connections, and recall how to define a function that changes over different parts of its domain. In this example, the domain for $t$ has two parts.

10. Use print or Internet reference materials to determine the Keplerian elements for several of the comets listed in Investigation 6. Use that information, together with a graphing utility, to plot orbital paths for those comets using polar coordinates.

## Investigation 10—Applications of Polar Models for Orbital Paths

### 1. Eccentric—or Not?

In the mid-1960s, U.S. astronauts flew on a mission that used an orbit with a perigee altitude of 200 miles and an apogee altitude of 800 miles. A television analyst covering the mission commented, "Wow, what an eccentric orbit!" At first glance, that orbit seemed very eccentric, with apogee four times the distance of perigee. However, the analyst failed to recall that orbital calculations depend primarily on the radius $r$, the distance of the spacecraft from the center of Earth. Evaluate the reporter's claim by completing these tasks:

— Approximate the radius of Earth as 4,000 miles, and compare the values of $r$ at apogee and perigee.

— Compute the eccentricity of the orbit.

— Plot Earth and the orbit of the mission to a correct scale on your graphing device, and observe the eccentricity.

— Write an evaluation of the reporter's comment on the basis of your observations.

2. *Modeling the Rendezvous with* Mir

The World Wide Web provides historical data from many space explorations. A NASA Web site that originated in October 1995 provides data for the docking between the Space Shuttle *Atlantis* and the Russian space station *Mir*. The following Keplerian elements were reported:

| | Orbital Element | |
|---|---|---|
| | Semimajor Axis *a* | Eccentricity *e* |
| *Atlantis* | 6,718,397.21 m | 0.0003878 |
| *Mir* | 6,774,825.37 m | 0.0012407 |

Convert the measure of the semimajor axes to miles. Using the polar-coordinate equation for orbits, with 3,960 miles as Earth's radius, plot the following orbits on a graphing utility:

— Earth

— *Atlantis*

— *Mir*

On your graphing utility, call up a small viewing window that allows you to investigate the distance between *Atlantis* and *Mir*. Using your set of equations, carry out calculations of the distance separating *Atlantis* and *Mir*. Compare your results with news reports on such important items as altitude for each spacecraft and time for a complete orbit.

3. *Modeling the Orbit of the Moon*

The orbital elements for the Moon's path around Earth are as follows: length of semimajor axis: 244,900 miles; eccentricity: 0.0549. Using 4,000 miles for the radius of Earth, attempt to superimpose the Moon's orbit on an outline of Earth. As you can surmise, the scale of your window is essential for this plot. You may want to start with a scale of 1 unit = 1,000 miles. Trace the orbit of the Moon to determine the orbit's perigee and apogee. Compare these perigee and apogee readings with values you find in an astronomy table or other resource.

4. *Exploring the Solar System*

Use the polar equation for an elliptical orbit and your graphing device to plot the orbits of the planets around the Sun. Use the information from the table here or from any similar chart of solar-system data.

| Planet | Semimajor axis in AU* | Eccentricity |
|---|---|---|
| Mercury | 0.3871 | 0.2056 |
| Venus | 0.7233 | 0.0068 |
| Earth | 1.000 | 0.0167 |
| Mars | 1.524 | 0.0934 |
| Jupiter | 5.203 | 0.0484 |
| Saturn | 9.539 | 0.0543 |
| Neptune | 19.18 | 0.046 |
| Uranus | 30.06 | 0.0082 |
| Pluto | 39.44 | 0.2481 |

* An astronomical unit (AU) is equal to the average distance between Earth and the Sun, about 93 million miles.

Your choices for scales on the graphing windows of your calculator are important. You might begin with the inner planets and determine how far you can go in plotting orbits until the inner orbits seem to disappear. What is the minimum number of windows needed to get an appropriate display of the planets' orbits?

Use a special window to study only the orbits of Neptune and Pluto. Part of your viewing window should suggest an astronomical event that occurred on January 21, 1979, and March 14, 1999, and will not occur again until September 2226. The behavior that better identifies the event may be hidden. Make a guess about what the event is, then zoom in to decide whether the event is, indeed, possible. You may also want to investigate the perihelion and aphelion for both planets. Remember that perihelion and aphelion are the points in a planet's orbit nearest and farthest from the Sun (from the Greek helios); they are analogous to perigee and apogee in an orbit around Earth.

5. *A Final Challenge*

The models we have looked at throughout this chapter simplify the actual orbits of the objects. Depending on the orientation of Earth, all orbits plotted thus far appear to be passing over the poles. Because U.S. spacecraft are launched from the Kennedy Space Center in Florida, we know that our satellite orbits are inclined at an angle.

— Alter your parametric or polar equations to graph an orbit inclined at an angle of 28 degrees.

— The ground track for such an orbit is sinusoidal. Suppose that the x-axis of this sine curve is a horizontal line through Cape Canaveral, Florida, and that the greatest displacement of the ground track from this line is 1000 miles. Write an equation to model the ground track of a spacecraft that makes a complete orbit every 90 minutes, and plot it on your graphing utility.

— Superimpose your sine wave on a Mercator projection map of the world to produce a plot similar to the one shown in the picture below.

— Plot sine waves on a Mercator projection map of the world to model the ground tracks of orbits over a full twenty-four-hour day or for a complete NASA mission.

— Compare your plot with the big-screen image we often see in pictures from Mission Control in Houston.

# Solutions and Teacher Commentary

## Investigation 2—Plotting the Orbit of Earth

Locate the direction from the Sun to Earth on each given date. Select a convenient ratio, such as 10 cm, to represent the distance from the Sun to Earth on January 4 (the closest distance, because the apparent size of the Sun was greatest on that day). Use the inverse relationship between size and distance to calculate the distance from the Sun to Earth on each of the remaining dates.

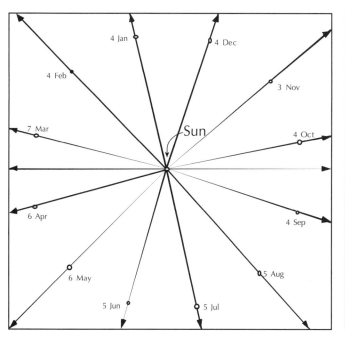

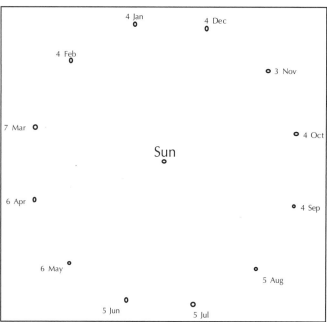

The plot below shows how close Earth's orbit (represented by a solid line) is to a circle (represented by a dashed line). For an elliptical orbit with semimajor axis (a) scaled to equal 10 cm, the distance from the center of the ellipse to the focus (Sun) is 1.7 mm. In reality, the focal distance is about 1.6 million miles.

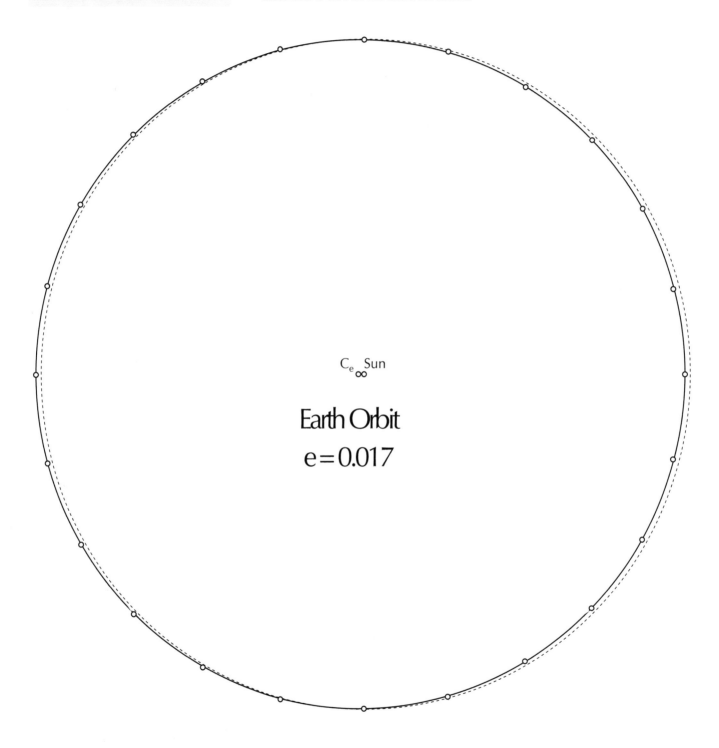

$C_e$  Sun

**Earth Orbit**

**e = 0.017**

## Investigation 3 — Plotting the Orbit of Mars

The plot shown below was made with The Geometer's Sketchpad using a circle to approximate the orbit of Earth. The radius of the Earth-orbit circle represents 1 AU.

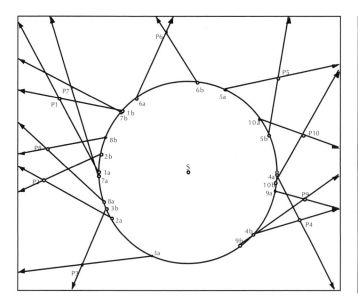 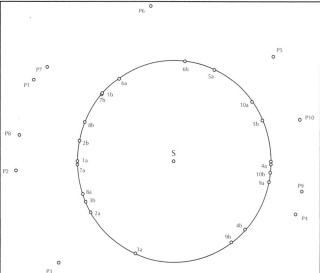

a–b. The orbit of Mars appears to be elliptical, as shown by the varying distance of the planet from the Sun at different points in its orbit.

| Point on Mars's Orbit | Distance from Sun (in AUs) |
| --- | --- |
| P1 | 1.66 |
| P2 | 1.63 |
| P3 | 1.56 |
| P4 | 1.36 |
| P5 | 1.46 |
| P6 | 1.56 |
| P7 | 1.61 |
| P8 | 1.62 |
| P9 | 1.35 |
| P10 | 1.36 |

c. The average Mars-Sun distance for these points is 1.52 AU. This value compares well with the average orbital radius of Mars reported in the table in this chapter.

d. For Mars, perihelion (its closest approach to the Sun) appears to be about 1.35 AU, occurring in the vicinity of points P4, P9, and P10.

Aphelion (the planet's greatest distance from the Sun) occurs near points P1, P8, and P2 and is approximately 1.66 AU.

e. Using the measured values for aphelion and perihelion from our plot, we calculate the semimajor axis of Mars to be

$$\frac{1.66 \text{ AU} + 1.35 \text{ AU}}{2} = 1.51 \text{ AU}.$$

Given that aphelion distance = $(a + c) = (a + a \cdot e) = a(1 + e)$, and that $a = 1.66$ AU, we calculate

$$1.66 \text{ AU} = (1.51 \text{ AU})(1 + e),$$

$$1.10 = 1 + e,$$

$$0.10 = e.$$

This value is very close to the accepted value of 0.093 for the eccentricity of Mars.

f. The orbit of Earth is closest to the orbit of Mars around August, and the orbits are farthest apart around February.

g. For these data, the minimum distance from Earth to Mars occurred on 9/11/56 (point 9a), a distance of about 0.35 AU, or approximately 33 million miles. Recall that these values are approximations and are influenced by our use of a circle, rather than an ellipse, to represent the orbit of Earth. See the note below for more precise data about the closest approach of the planets. Despite this information, the approximations made in this activity are within reasonable limits.

Note: On August 27, 2003, Mars and Earth were at their closest approach in more than 57,000 years. At that time, the separation was 0.37271 AU, or 34,649,589 miles. The next time the two planets will come close to this distance again will be on August 30, 2082, when they will pass within 0.37356 AU (34,724,502 miles). On August 22, 1924, they were separated by 0.37284 AU (34,661,675 miles).

## Investigation 4—Plotting the Orbit of Mercury

Figure 3.3 shows a plot (made with Geometer's Sketchpad) for locating Mercury from the data given for the years 2000–2001. Figure 3.4 represents the plotted points on Mercury's orbit.

Let the radius of the circle used to represent Earth's orbit be 1 AU. For the points plotted, aphelion (Mercury's greatest distance from the Sun) occurred on or about March 28, 2000 (point C′), at a distance of approximately 0.47 AU. Perihelion occurred twice, on or about February 15, 2000, and again on or about January 28, 2001 (points B′ and H′), at a distance of approximately 0.31 AU.

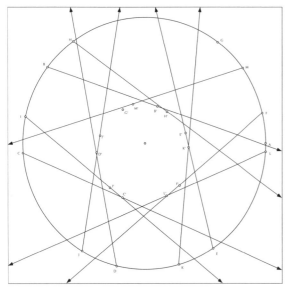

Fig. 3.3

With those values, we calculate the semimajor axis (average distance from the Sun) of Mercury to be

$$\frac{0.47 \text{ AU} + 0.31 \text{ AU}}{2} = 0.39 \text{ AU}.$$

Given that aphelion distance = $(a + c) = (a + a \cdot e) = a(1 + e)$, and that $a = 0.39$, we calculate

$$0.47 \text{ AU} = (0.39 \text{ AU})(1 + e),$$
$$1.205 = 1 + e,$$
$$0.205 = e.$$

These values are very close to the accepted values reported elsewhere in this unit.

## Investigation 5—Orbital Motion: How Far? How Fast?

1. Given that $G$ and $m_e$ are constants, first simplifying the velocity equation, as shown below, may be helpful.

$$v = \sqrt{\frac{Gm_e}{r}} = \sqrt{\frac{6.67(10^{-11})\frac{N-m^2}{kg^2} \cdot 6(10^{24})kg}{r \ m}}$$

$$= \sqrt{\frac{(6.67)(10^{-11})(6)(10^{24})}{r} \ \frac{kg \cdot m \cdot m^2 \cdot kg}{sec^2 \cdot kg^2 \cdot m}}$$

$$= \sqrt{\frac{6.67(10^{-11}) \cdot 6(10^{24})}{r} \ \frac{kg \cdot m}{sec^2} \cdot \frac{m^2}{kg^2} \cdot kg}{m}}$$

$$= \sqrt{\frac{4(10^{14})}{r} \ \frac{m^2}{sec^2}}$$

$$= \sqrt{\frac{4(10^{14})}{r}} \ \frac{m}{sec}$$

At an altitude of 300 km, $r = (6400 + 300)$ km, or $6.7(10^6)$ meters. Solving the equation above for this value of $r$ gives

$$v = 0.77(10^4)\frac{m}{sec} = 7.7\frac{km}{sec} = 27{,}720\frac{km}{hr} \ .$$

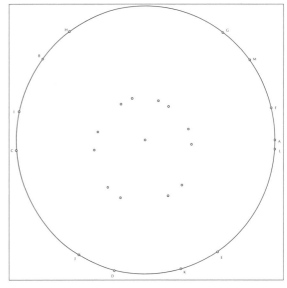

Fig. 3.4

2. The length of one orbit is $d = 2\pi r = 2\pi(6,700)\text{km} = 42,100\,\text{km}$. To complete one orbit requires

$$t = \frac{42,100\,\text{km}}{27,720\,\dfrac{\text{km}}{\text{hr}}} = 1.52\,\text{hr},$$

or about 91 minutes.

3. The velocity equation tells us that

$$v = \sqrt{\frac{4\,(10^{14})}{r}}\ \frac{\text{m}}{\text{sec}}$$

From the distance equation,

$$v = \frac{d}{t} = \frac{2\pi r}{24}\frac{\text{m}}{\text{hr}} = \frac{2\pi r}{86,400}\frac{\text{m}}{\text{sec}}.$$

Because the two values of $v$ must be equal, the two expressions are $r = 4.23(10^7)\,\text{m} = 42,300\,\text{km}$. Subtracting the radius of Earth gives the altitude of 35,900 km (about 22,300 miles). Substituting the value $r = 42,300$ km into the distance equation gives a velocity of about 11,100 km/hr.

4. Solving the equation

$$v = \sqrt{\frac{0.012 \cdot 4(10^{14})}{1.85(10^6)}}\ \frac{\text{m}}{\text{sec}}$$

yields a velocity of approximately 1,600 m/sec, or 5,760 km/hr. Solving the distance equation for $t$ gives an orbital period of just over 2 hours.

## Investigation 6—Cartesian Coordinate Models for Elliptical Orbits

1. Using the information provided and applying a conversion factor of 1.61 km for 1 mile, an equation for the ellipse that represents the orbital path of Transit is

$$\frac{(x-(-0.186))^2}{6.999^2} + \frac{y^2}{\left(\sqrt{6.999^2 + 0.186^2}\right)^2} = 1,$$

where 1 unit represents 1000 km. Two functions resulting from this equation can be used to plot the orbit on a graphing utility:

$$y_1(x) = \frac{\sqrt{6.999^2 - 0.186^2}}{6.999}\sqrt{6.999^2 - (x + 0.186)^2}$$

$$y_2(x) = -\frac{\sqrt{6.999^2 - 0.186^2}}{6.999}\sqrt{6.999^2 - (x + 0.186)^2}$$

At the right is a plot of these two functions superimposed on a plot representing Earth with a radius of 6,440 km.

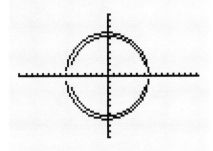

2. An equation for the ellipse that represents the orbital path of COMETS is

$$\frac{(x-(-8.6))^2}{15.54^2} + \frac{y^2}{\left(\sqrt{15.54^2 - 8.6^2}\right)^2} = 1,$$

where 1 unit represents 1000 km. Two functions resulting from this equation can be used to plot the orbit on a graphing utility:

$$y_1(x) = \frac{\sqrt{15.54^2 - 8.6^2}}{15.54} \sqrt{15.54^2 - (x+8.6)^2}$$

$$y_2(x) = -\frac{\sqrt{15.54^2 - 8.6^2}}{15.54} \sqrt{15.54^2 - (x+8.6)^2}$$

At the right is a plot of these two functions superimposed on a plot representing Earth with a radius of 6,440 km.

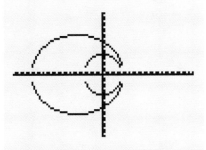

The plot shows an orbital path that is much more elliptical than circular. The differences in apogee and perigee are apparent in the plot. The display of the graphing calculator shows a gap in the plot near the x-axis because of the finite pixels available for graphing.

3. Here is a representative solution for the comet Crommelin. Note that the Sun has a radius of approximately 695,000 km, and its diameter is approximately 0.009 AU. The solution that follows does include this small contribution to the length of the major axis of the ellipse that represents the path of the comet. An equation for the ellipse that represents the orbital path of Crommelin around the Sun is

$$\frac{(x-(-4.2285))^2}{4.976^2} + \frac{y^2}{\left(\sqrt{4.976^2 - 4.2285^2}\right)^2} = 1,$$

where 1 unit represents 1 AU. Two functions resulting from this equation can be used to plot the orbit on a graphing utility:

$$y_1(x) = \frac{\sqrt{4.976^2 - 4.2285^2}}{4.976} \sqrt{4.976^2 - (x+4.2285)^2}$$

$$y_2(x) = -\frac{\sqrt{4.976^2 - 4.2285^2}}{4.976} \sqrt{4.976^2 - (x+4.2285)^2}$$

At the right is a plot of these two functions. The Sun is one of the foci, at (0, 0).

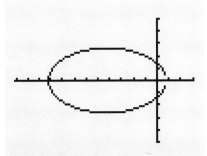

The plot shows an elliptical orbital path whose eccentricity is 0.8498. As in task 2, the differences in apogee and perigee are apparent when one considers the Sun as the point (0, 0).

## Investigation 7—Models for Elliptical Orbits: Parametric Equations

2.–4. For the parametric plot of the orbital path of the ISS, we use values calculated previously: $a = 4.25$, $c = 0.025$, and $b = \sqrt{a^2 - c^2}$, where 1 unit = 1000 miles. The resulting parametric equations are

$$x(t) = 4.25\cos(t) - 0.025,$$
$$y(t) = \sqrt{4.25^2 - 0.025^2}\,\sin(t).$$

When we plot the orbit on a graphing utility and carry out a trace, the ISS moves through the exact apogee and perigee given in the specifications. Students will likely comment on how complete the orbit is under a parametric model compared with the Cartesian plots. No gaps will appear near the x-axis, and students should also note how well the trace models the actual movement of the space station around Earth.

5. Here, $a = 6.999$ and $c = 0.186$, with 1 unit equal to 1000 km. The parametric equations for the path of the orbit of Transit are

$$x(t) = 6.999\cos(t) - 0.186,$$
$$y(t) = \sqrt{6.999^2 - 0.186^2}\,\sin(t).$$

## Investigation 8—Connecting the Model

Cartesian: the line $y = 5$    Polar: $\begin{cases} R(t) \cdot \sin(t) = 5 \\ R(t) = \dfrac{5}{\sin(t)} \\ R(t) = 5 \cdot \csc(t) \end{cases}$

Cartesian: $x = 2$    Polar: $\begin{cases} R(t) \cdot \cos(t) = 2 \\ \text{or} \\ R(t) = 2 \cdot \sec(t) \end{cases}$

Cartesian: $y^2 = 4x$    Polar: $R(t) = 4\cos(t)\csc^2(t)$

Cartesian: $\dfrac{x^2}{9} + \dfrac{y^2}{4} = 1$    Polar: $R(t) = \dfrac{6}{\sqrt{4\cos^2(t) + 9\sin^2(t)}}$

## Investigation 9—Modeling Low-Earth Orbits with Polar Models

1.–4. Note that the equation $R(t) = \dfrac{ed}{1 + e\cos(t)}$ has the advantage of being applicable to all conic sections. Use tasks 1 through 4 to encourage students to explore the meaning of this equation with the graphing utilities of their calculators, paying particular attention to what happens to the graph as they change the values of *e* and *d*.

5.–7. To illustrate the usefulness of the polar model, which may not be immediately apparent, ask students to use the polar form to graph the ISS orbit from the previous problems, as well as the orbit of a Space Shuttle mission, STS-73, which flew in October 1995. Note that the altitudes of apogee and perigee for the Shuttle orbit are given in nautical miles. Students will need the conversion factor 1 nautical mile = 1.151 statute miles. These tasks also present the opportunity to discuss the number of significant figures that students can reasonably use and their effect on the precision of the plots.

8.–9. These questions reinforce one of the most important elements in our study of orbits: how to change an orbit while in space. Changing orbits is accomplished by firing small rocket engines called *thrusters* to effect a change in speed or direction, or both. As described previously in this chapter, when a thruster is fired, the change in the spacecraft's velocity occurs in the opposite direction. Thus, to increase the forward motion of the spacecraft, the rocket is fired in the reverse direction, which is known as a *posigrade burn*. A *retrograde burn* fires the thruster in the forward direction, causing the spacecraft to decrease its forward velocity. For simplicity, we assume that the thruster burn occurs instantaneously, although in reality, the burn takes seconds or even minutes. This assumption of instantaneous burn leads to an important principle of orbital flight: The point at which the burn occurs is a point on both the original and the new orbits. In other words, the burn changes every point on the new orbit except the burn point. These questions involve a rendezvous with the Hubble Space Telescope. In the initial orbit, $H_p = 200$ miles and $H_a = 400$ miles; in the desired orbit, $H_a = 800$ miles and the burn occurs at perigee—hence, $H_p$ remains 200 miles. Orbital elements for the two orbits are as follows:

|  | Initial Orbit | Final Orbit |
|---|---|---|
| *a* | 4,300 miles | 4,500 miles |
| *c* | 100 miles | 300 miles |
| *e* | $\dfrac{100}{4,300} = 0.02326$ | $\dfrac{300}{4,500} = 0.06667$ |
| Perigee | (4,200, 0°) | (4,200, 0°) |
| Apogee | (4,400, 180°) | (4,800, 180°) |

Task 9 provides a reality check for the modeling activities. If carried out properly, the trace will move in the initial orbit for three revolutions, then simulate the burn and change to the final orbital path. One way to represent this orbit with a polar model is as follows:

$$R(t) = \left\{ \frac{4300\left(1-\left(\dfrac{100}{4300}\right)^2\right)}{1+\left(\dfrac{100}{4300}\right)\cos(t)}, \quad 0 \le t < 3 \cdot 360° \right.$$

$$R(t) = \left\{ \frac{4500\left(1-\left(\dfrac{300}{4500}\right)^2\right)}{1+\left(\dfrac{300}{4500}\right)\cos(t)}, \quad 3 \cdot 360° \le t \le 8 \cdot 360° \right.$$

Students will likely experience a true sense of accomplishment when their traces actually model the mission. The orbits plotted on a graphing utility will resemble the screen print in the following figure:

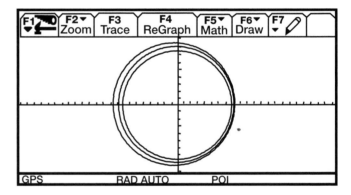

10. This problem represents a rich extension of the application of polar models to orbital paths. Values for the orbital elements of some comets can be found in astronomy books and on several Internet sites. Recall that the perihelion is the minimum distance of the comet from the Sun, analogous to the perigee in orbits around Earth. The perihelion is typically given in AUs, where 1 AU is the distance of Earth from the Sun, approximately 93,000,000 miles. The semimajor axis, $a$, can be calculated using the relationship

$$H_p = (a - c) = (a - a \cdot e) = a(1 - e).$$

Students can gain an appreciation for the profound effect that a small change in the eccentricity has on the orbit. They should also compare the orbits of comets, with their large eccentricities, with the planetary orbits whose eccentricities can be found in the scaling unit.

## Investigation 10—Applications of Polar Models for Orbital Paths

Encourage students to choose from among these projects or to design their own modeling investigations.

### Eccentric—or Not?

A polar plot of this orbit should look something like the graph in figure 3.5a or the screen print in figure 3.5b. From this plot, we can see that the television analyst was wrong about the eccentricity. Note that this orbit is the same one used in the earlier Hubble rendezvous problem, in which we calculated the eccentricity to be 0.06667. (This activity is adapted from an example in *To Rise from Earth* [Lee 1994, p. 32].)

### Modeling the Rendezvous with Mir

This activity is a variation on the Hubble rendezvous activity presented previously. Different graphing utilities will present different options for the small-window (zoom) investigation.

### Modeling the Orbit of the Moon

After studying many examples of LEOs, students may be surprised to observe the difference between the tight-fitting orbits of spacecraft and the lunar orbit, and they should arrive at a new appreciation of the Apollo missions. The scale of the window is essential for this model. In a representation of the orbit of the Moon in the graphing-utility window, Earth is likely to appear as a single pixel, hardly visible on the screen.

### Exploring the Solar System

This activity is a natural extension of the models of the solar system developed in the scaling unit, in which, for simplicity, we assumed circular orbits. Here, students can plot the elliptical orbits of the planets using the data on planetary distances and eccentricities of the orbits. After plotting these orbits, students should be asked to evaluate the appropriateness of our earlier assumption of circular orbits.

A window of [–2, 2] by [–2, 2] seems to be convenient for displaying the four inner planets, and the minimum number of windows to best display the solar system on a graphing utility is two. A second window [–50, 50] by [–50, 50] gives a nice display of the outer planets.

### A Final Challenge

Students who have mastered the technique of modeling orbits on their graphing utilities are challenged to extend their study by investigating how to plot orbits that are inclined to the equatorial plane of Earth. This question is left as an open-ended challenge for both students and teachers.

**Fig. 3.5a. Tight-fitting orbit**

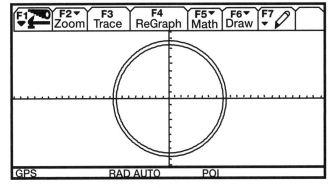

**Fig. 3.5b. Screen print from a graphing utility**

# Global Positioning System

## Finding Our Way

Travelers are always interested in knowing where they are at any point in a journey. Early explorers navigated the seas to find out about their world. The technology of the day helped them know their approximate locations and reach their destinations. For example, the magnetic compass gave sailors directional headings. The quadrant allowed sailors to measure the altitude of the Pole Star, thus helping them determine the latitude of their ships. The astrolabe and the Jacob's staff were other devices used to determine latitude. The sextant was invented as a means to help find the longitude of a ship at sea.

Cumulative information about sailing the seas was published as tables that all sea captains could use. An American mathematician and astronomer, Nathaniel Bowditch (1773–1838), played an important role in developing these navigational tables. Bowditch used his mathematical knowledge to correct the tables commonly used in the 1700s. His corrections were remarkably accurate. In fact, a prospective sea captain enrolled in a navigational course today will likely use a copy of Bowditch's tables.

Early aviators used visual landmarks to navigate in the air just as sailors used them at sea. Because airplanes were faster than ships, sextants and astrolabes were not appropriate tools for determining an aircraft's position. Pilots could not sight and compute fast enough to make accurate estimates of location. The need arose for faster calculations relative to position. Radio techniques filled this need and signaled the beginning of a new era in navigation. Navigation technologies originally developed for pilots were soon adopted by sailors.

Advanced aviation and space travel heightened the need for fast and accurate navigational aids, especially for the Department of Defense. The security of the nation depended on the ability to position its military assets accurately and to quickly determine the exact location of the military units of other countries. NASA's efforts in the development of satellites led to the creation of the U.S. Navigation System with Timing and Ranging (NAVSTAR). As a global positioning system (GPS), NAVSTAR is a constellation of twenty-four satellites launched and maintained by the Department of Defense. By " locking on" to the radio signals transmitted from at least three of these satellites and using a process known as triangulation, or more accurately, trilateration, a GPS receiver can provide navigation information to virtually anyone anywhere in the world in almost any weather conditions.

Today's handheld units use multichannel parallel-processing receivers together with integrated circuitry. These units can be purchased at sports-equipment outlets, from catalogs, and directly from manufacturers. Anglers use GPS units to record favorite fishing spots, enabling them to return another day; hunters use them to find locations where game has been sighted. Hikers use GPS to supplement topographical maps. Many golf courses now equip golf carts with GPS to allow players to determine the distance to the green with pinpoint accuracy.

GPS-based systems have been installed in emergency vehicles and are used in public and private transportation. Commercial aviation relies on the precise location and navigation capacities of GPS. North American farmers have embraced precision farming, a new science of agronomy that situates GPS and computer technology at its foundation. Hollywood studios use GPS for highly accurate measurement of time. For location, navigation, tracking, mapping, and timing, this immensely powerful technology has become available to everyone and will continue to be used in many creative ways in our changing world.

# Mathematics and Applications of a Global Positioning System

The union of GPS with state-of-the-art mapping techniques may help us to better locate, manage, and enjoy Earth's resources and to navigate more precisely on and above Earth. Smart-vehicle location and navigation systems will help travelers avoid busy freeways by identifying more efficient travel routes. Travel by air and sea will be safer in all weather conditions. Commercial and public enterprises with significant mobile resources, such as utilities, bus lines, and package delivery fleets, will be more efficient and effective in resource management.

Geometry offers a means of describing, analyzing, and understanding the world and seeing beauty in its structures. Geometric ideas can be useful both in other areas of mathematics and in applied settings.

*(NCTM 2000, p. 309)*

Aglobal positioning system (GPS) is a space-based, time-of-arrival radio-positioning system that provides twenty-four-hour, three-dimensional position, velocity, and time information to suitably equipped users anywhere on or near Earth's surface. On June 26, 1993, the U.S. Department of Defense set into Earth's orbit the last of twenty-four satellites that together make up the Navigation System with Timing and Ranging (NAVSTAR), a GPS that was conceived in the 1970s to provide its users with nothing short of a quantum leap as a utility for navigation and positioning. Seven years later, on May 1, 2000, the president of the United States authorized the removal of selective availability, that is, the intentional inclusion of noise in the GPS that had reduced the accuracy of civilian units. With appropriate technology—equipment that has decreased in price yet grown in features, sophistication, and availability—today's GPS users can accurately pinpoint their positions virtually anywhere on Earth.

## Purposes

This unit presents the mathematics that underlies a GPS. Students will develop a conceptualization of GPS through examples in one, two, and three dimensions; identify the mathematics inherent in the systems; and complete a series of activities involving GPS applications.

## Introduction

A GPS is defined by three components. The first is the *space segment.* NAVSTAR consists of twenty-four satellites, called the *operational constellation.* Twenty-one navigation satellites and three active spares circle Earth in twelve-hour orbits. The orbits repeat the same ground track once each day, and the orbit altitude is such that each satellite repeats the same track and configuration approximately each twenty-four hours. This operational constellation provides GPS users with five to eight satellites visible from any point on Earth.

The *control segment* is the second component of a GPS. It consists of a system of tracking stations throughout the world. The system monitors satellite signals, from which it creates orbital models for those satellites. The models compute precise orbital data, known as *ephemeris,* as well as clock corrections for each satellite. A master control station in Colorado sends ephemeris and clock data to the satellites, which then relay some of that information by radio signal to GPS receivers, part of the third segment of a GPS known as the *user segment.*

The user segment is made up of the GPS receivers and their users. GPS receivers convert satellite signals into position, velocity, and time

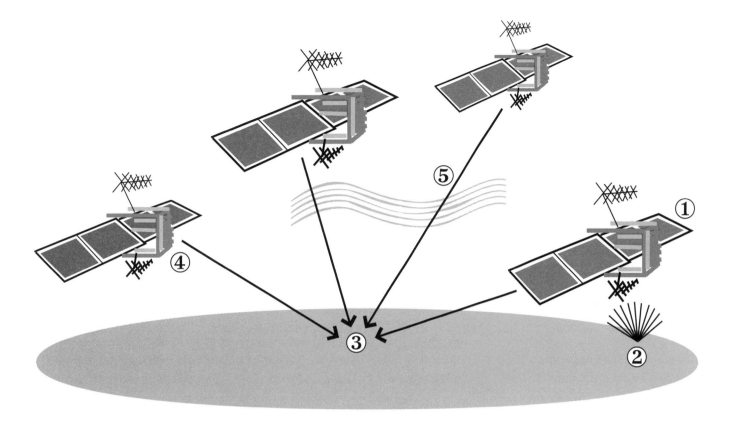

**Components of a Global Positioning System (GPS).**

① In the U.S. system called NAVSTAR (for **NAV**igation **S**atellite **T**iming **a**nd **R**anging), twenty-four satellites orbit Earth, providing GPS users with at least five satellites visible from any point on Earth.

② A worldwide monitoring system tracks the GPS satellites and generates an orbital model for each satellite. A master control station in Colorado sends each satellite orbital data and clock corrections that are relayed to GPS users.

③ GPS users on or near Earth use GPS receivers to convert satellite signals to position, velocity, and time estimates.

④ Each satellite has four atomic clocks, accurate to within a billionth of a second per year.

⑤ The speed of GPS satellite signals may be altered as the signals travel through the atmosphere. At the speed of light, even slight changes in transmission speed introduce significant errors into the system.

estimates. Data from four satellites are required to compute the earthly dimensions of position (latitude, longitude, altitude) and time.

The representation above shows the essential elements of a GPS. The mathematics of *trilateration* is the focus of this chapter. Trilateration refers to the determination of an unknown position using distances from one or more known positions. The process is generally referred to as *triangulation,* although technically, that term describes the determination of position using angle measures rather than distances. In the text that follows, the more conventional term, triangulation, is used.

In a three-dimensional GPS, we know the positions of the satellites that send radio signals to be picked up by a GPS receiver. Because radio signals travel at a constant speed, we can determine how far away we are from each satellite by knowing the travel time for each signal; however, errors creep into the system from several sources. For example, the calculations of a radio signal's travel time may be inaccurate, depending

The blackline master on page 137 can be used to make a transparency of the information shown above.

*Trilateration* refers to the determination of an unknown position using distances from one or more known positions; *triangulation* describes the determination of position using angle measures.

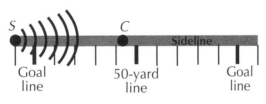

Note: The yard marks on the field are 10 yards apart.

on the synchronization of a satellite's clock with the one in the receiver. Because the radio signal is traveling in Earth's atmosphere, not in a vacuum, the speed of the radio wave may not be constant. At a signal speed of about 186,000 miles per second, even a slight change in speed can drastically alter the determination of the GPS receiver position.

In the investigations that follow, the intent is to help students conceptualize two essential components of the triangulation process: (1) the use of signal-travel time to determine distance and (2) methods for dealing with errors inherent in a positioning system. The investigations begin with examples of sound waves traveling in one and two dimensions and are drawn from familiar settings. The examples are intended to help students explore the mathematics of time-of-arrival positioning in systems that are less complex than the three dimensions of a true GPS.

## Investigation 1—Determining Position in One Dimension

Investigation 1 on pages 138–39 describes a one-dimensional setting for determining position. Students are asked to locate a coach somewhere along the sideline of a football field. The description and questions help emphasize and describe three calculations required in a time-of-arrival positioning system such as a GPS. These calculations are as follows:

1. Determine the travel time of a signal from a transmitter in a known position to a receiver in an unknown position: In the one-dimensional scenario, a coach is moving along the sideline of a football field. Positioned at one or both ends of the field are sound-wave transmitters, and the coach wears a special receiver designed to record the time of arrival of a sound wave. Two elements of the system are required to determine the travel time of the signal from the transmitter to the receiver:

   — The signal transmitter must maintain a clock that is highly accurate. Each satellite of the NAVSTAR GPS has four atomic clocks, each accurate to within a billionth of a second a year.

   — We must have some way of knowing when each broadcast is made from the transmitter. In our one-dimensional scenario, we assume that a sound is broadcast every minute on the minute. By comparing the time of arrival with a known transmission time, we can determine the travel time of the signal. In the NAVSTAR GPS, each satellite transmits a radio signal that contains a code unique to that satellite. A GPS receiver has a copy of each satellite's code. The receiver compares its copy of the code with the code it receives and, through the offset in the two copies of the identical code, calculates the transmission time of the satellite's signal.

2. Determine the distance traveled by a signal: In the one-dimensional activities, the speed of sound is assumed to be 1,100 feet per second. Knowing the travel time and travel rate, students can calculate

distance using the familiar relationship distance = rate · time. In subsequent activities, students will consider radio waves sent from orbiting satellites traveling at 186,000 miles per second.

3. Determine the position of the receiver: In one dimension, if we know the position of the signal transmitter and the distance traveled by the signal, we can add or subtract along a straight line to identify the receiver's position. Inherent in the position determination is the use of a coordinate system within which that calculation can be performed. The culminating activity in the investigation of a one-dimensional time-of-arrival positioning system is to describe the system using a conventional number line rather than a football-field sideline (task 8 in Investigation 1).

*Clock Error*

Under ideal conditions, only one transmitter would be required in a one-dimensional system. A user would determine the transmission time for a signal, use that time to calculate the distance traveled by the signal, then move that distance from the known position of the transmitter to identify the position of the receiver. Under such ideal conditions, assumptions must also be made about the general position of the receiver, because a signal broadcast from a single point on a line could identify a receiver on either side of the transmitter. In the football-field scenario, the coach is along the playing-field sideline, not along the part of the line that extends beyond the end zone of the field.

Conditions are seldom ideal in applications of a time-of-arrival positioning system such as a GPS. Just one of several errors that typically occur in a GPS is *clock error:* What happens if a receiver clock is not precisely synchronized with a transmitter clock? Given an asynchronous relationship between the two clocks, how can the time-of-arrival system be modified to ensure that precise locations are determined? For example, suppose that the clock in the coach's receiver is, unknowingly, running a constant 0.01 second faster than true time. If a signal is broadcast from the transmitter at 1:00:00.0000 and the receiver registers its reception at 1:00:00.1247, the signal actually took 0.1147 second to go from the transmitter to the receiver.

Using only the receiver clock, without knowing that it is running a constant 0.01 second fast, we would have erroneously determined that the coach was at $C_e$, near the 36-yard line:

Because discussions of navigation and positioning systems can cut across grade levels and mathematics courses, this unit begins with an example in one dimension. Teachers must determine both the entry point at which they and their students should begin the investigations and the level of mathematics they intend to draw on in working through and extending the ideas. The activities can be done using informal, visual techniques or a more advanced analytical approach.

See the unit "Advanced Communication Systems" for a consideration of the mathematics involved in transmitting signals through space.

Times are given as hours:minutes:seconds. The time 1:00:00.1247 represents 0.1247 second past 1:00.

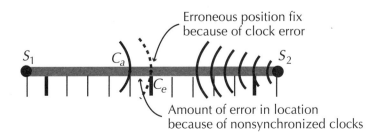

Erroneous position fix because of clock error

Amount of error in location because of nonsynchronized clocks

$$0.1247 \text{ sec} \cdot 1{,}100 \text{ ft/sec} \div 3 \text{ ft/yd} = 45.7233 \text{ yd from } S_1$$

The signal, however, traveled only 0.1147 second, positioning the coach at $C_a$, near the 32-yard line:

$$0.1147 \text{ sec} \cdot 1{,}100 \text{ ft/sec} \div 3 \text{ ft/yd} = 42.0567 \text{ yd from } S_2$$

In this situation involving clock error, a second transmitter at the opposite end of the sideline, sending to the same receiver that has a constant error in its time stamp, is required to accurately fix the position of the receiver, as follows:

(a) The distance between $S_1$ and $S_2$ is 360 feet. Regardless of the location of the coach at any point between the two transmitters, the sum of the transmission times for the signals must be

$$t = 360 \text{ ft} \div 1{,}100 \text{ ft/sec} = 0.3273 \text{ sec.}$$

(b) Because the clock error is in the receiver, it is constant regardless of the source of the signal. Let $e$ represent this constant error.

In this example, the coach's receiver runs a constant 0.01 second fast; thus, the calculated transmission times from the two transmitters are incorrect. Call these erroneous times $t_1$ and $t_2$. They are related to the actual transmission times, $T_1$ and $T_2$, respectively, as follows:

$$T_1 = t_1 - e$$

and

$$T_2 = t_2 - e.$$

We can use these equations and the information in (a) to determine the following relationships:

$$T_1 + T_2 = (t_1 - e) + (t_2 - e) = 0.3273$$
$$t_1 + t_2 - 2e = 0.3273$$
$$e = \tfrac{1}{2}(t_1 + t_2 - 0.3273)$$

These relationships furnish sufficient information to determine $d_1$, the distance from $S_1$ to the receiver at $C$:

$$d_1 = (t_1 - e) \cdot 1100$$
$$= [t_1 - \frac{1}{2}(t_1 + t_2 - 0.3273)] \cdot 1100$$
$$= \frac{1}{2}(1100)(t_1 - t_2 + 0.3273)$$
$$= 550(t_1 - t_2 + 0.3273)$$

In a similar manner, $d_2 = 550(t_2 - t_1 + 0.3273)$. Tasks 6 through 8 in Investigation 1 offer an opportunity to carry out additional calculations in time-of-arrival positioning where clock error is a factor.

## Investigation 2—Determining Position in Two Dimensions

Investigation 2 on pages 139–40 extends students' conceptualization of time-of-arrival positioning to a two-dimensional system using the context of a ship traveling on Lake Superior in the north-central United States. The ship has left the harbor at Duluth, Minnesota, and uses time-of-arrival positioning to track its progress across Lake Superior. Sound waves are again used as the signal, broadcast from foghorns on the lake and received by the ship's navigator.

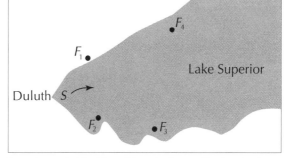

Locations of ship ($S$) and four foghorns ($F_1$, $F_2$, $F_3$, $F_4$)

The two-dimensional positioning problem is first explored under ideal circumstances with no clock error inherent in the system. By using travel times for sound waves broadcast from foghorns at fixed locations, the ship's navigator can determine broadcast ranges from one or more foghorns. At the two-dimensional level, each broadcast range defines a circle whose center is a foghorn, and the navigator must consider intersections of two or more circles to pinpoint the ship's location.

Again, some assumptions about the general position of the receiver are necessary. Transmissions broadcast from two points (here, the foghorns) on a plane often result in two potential locations for a ship: the two points of intersection of the two circles emanating from the foghorns. Some knowledge of the ship's point of departure, or at least its general path across the lake, must be assumed to allow a correct choice to be made from the two possible ship locations. Without knowledge to make such an assumption, time-of-arrival data from three foghorns would be needed to rule out an erroneous position fix.

Investigation 2 continues to explore two-dimensional positioning through consideration of clock error and concludes with a summary of two-dimensional time-of-arrival positioning. When the receiver clock is not synchronized with the transmission clocks, the ship's navigator must deal with a constant but unknown clock error. In two dimensions, this error translates into foghorn signal ranges that are a constant distance beyond or inside the true signal ranges. One approach to determining position and clock error is presented in the following paragraphs, and others are encouraged.

### Conceptualizing the System

Investigation 2 is based on the following scenario:

A sailing vessel, $S$, travels on Lake Superior from the harbor at Duluth. The diagram in the margin shows the lake, the ship, and the location of four foghorns. Onboard the ship is a receiver that records sound waves from foghorns. The receiver picks up sound waves that are broadcast on the minute at one-minute intervals from foghorn transmitters located at fixed points $F_1$, $F_2$, $F_3$, and $F_4$. How can such a transmitter-receiver system be used to determine the ship's position?

Compare the components of the two-dimensional positioning system with those of the one-dimensional system:

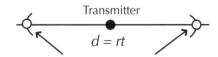

Two possible position fixes in a one-dimensional system

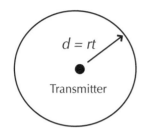

An infinite number of possible position fixes in a two-dimensional system

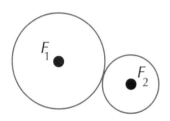

Transmission broadcast circles are tangent: one possible position fix

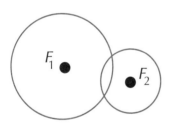

Transmission broadcast circles intersect: two possible position fixes

1. Both use transmitters and receivers to determine sound-wave travel time.

2. Both use the relationship distance = rate · time to determine how far a sound wave has traveled.

3. Instead of identifying two possible position fixes, as in the one-dimensional system, a two-dimensional system has an infinite number of possible position fixes from one signal, represented by a circle.

4. Accurate information from two transmitters can be used to fix, at most, two possible positions. Additional information—for example, a ship's existing course or information from additional signals—is needed to fix one true position.

5. Because of the possibility of receiver-clock error, information from no fewer than three transmitters is required for an accurate position fix.

*A Closer Look*

Investigation 2 also allows students to explore calculations of two-dimensional position determination. In task 1, for instance, they verify that the first recorded signal from $F_1$ is four miles from the ship. Using the distance equation and the reception time indicated for record 1, students perform the following calculation:

$$19.2000 \text{ sec} \cdot 1{,}100 \text{ ft/sec} = 21{,}120 \text{ ft} = 4 \text{ mi from } F_1$$

One way to verify the ship's location is to determine the equations for the transmission-broadcast circles from two foghorns, then solve those equations simultaneously. Using distance information and the coordinates of $F_1$ and $F_2$ yields these equations for the broadcast circles:

$$F_1: \quad x^2 + (y - 6)^2 = 4^2$$
$$\text{or}$$
$$x^2 + y^2 - 12y = -20$$

$$F_2: \quad (x - 1)^2 + y^2 = 5^2$$
$$\text{or}$$
$$x^2 - 2x + y^2 = 24$$

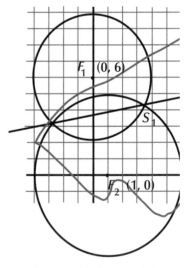

Broadcast circles for $F_1$ and $F_2$

The simultaneous solution of these two equations is the line

$$y = \frac{1}{6}x + \frac{11}{3}.$$

This expression for $y$ can be substituted into either circular equation to determine the two $x$-coordinates where the circles intersect. Substituting into the expanded equation for $F_2$, we find $x^2 - 2x + \left(\frac{1}{6}x + \frac{11}{3}\right)^2 = 24$, which simplifies to $37x^2 - 28x - 380 = 0$; the solutions for this equation are $x = 3.605$ or $x = -2.849$. When these values are returned to the linear equation, the ordered pairs that represent the intersection points of the two circles are (3.605, 4.268) and (–2.849, 3.192).

How did the navigator know to choose the first of these ordered pairs as the ship's correct position on the basis of record 1? Perhaps the navigator knew that the ship was farther from Duluth than was indicated by the ordered pair (–2.849, 3.192), or the navigator may have realized that the ship was not as close to shore as indicated by the rejected ordered pair.

Other methods exist to determine the ship's position on the basis of the information in the first transmission record. A scale drawing and a compass can be used to draw the two transmission circles. A compass construction may furnish an adequate position fix, depending on the desired degree of accuracy.

Task 2 in Investigation 2 shows the navigator's work in beginning to fix the ship's position from transmission 4. Students can determine locations $S_4$ and $S_5$ using a variety of methods. Assuming that the ship does not travel in an erratic path, the analytic method described earlier yields $S_4 = (7.993, 5.666)$ and $S_5 = (9, 6)$.

Task 3 reinforces the two-dimensional time-of-arrival positioning methods explored thus far. Although signal-reception times are provided from four foghorns, no more than three are necessary to ensure an accurate position fix. In fact, if we assume that the ship is on the lake and not on shore, a correct position fix can be made using information from only two foghorns. The correct location of the ship is at (5, 8), which may be closer to the shore than the ship's captain had intended!

## Investigation 3—Determining Position in Two Dimensions: Clock Error

What if a receiver clock is not precisely synchronized with a transmitter clock? Given an asynchronous relationship between the two clocks, how can we modify a two-dimensional time-of-arrival system to ensure precise location determination?

A constant one-second error in a receiver clock translates into an error of 1,100 feet in position fixing when sound waves are broadcast. When radio signals are used, a one-second error represents 186,000 miles! At the right is a sketch to represent an attempted position fix with a receiver clock that is constantly running slightly fast. In the Lake Superior shipping context, clock error raises the following questions, among others:

✦ How will a ship's navigator know whether the receiver clock is in error?

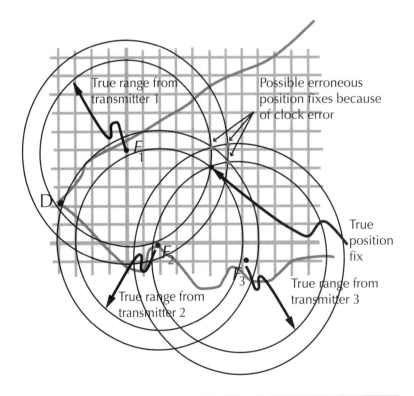

True range from transmitter 1

Possible erroneous position fixes because of clock error

$F_1$

D

$F_2$

$F_3$

True position fix

True range from transmitter 2

True range from transmitter 3

◆ How will a ship's navigator know whether the receiver clock is registering a time earlier or later than actual time?

◆ What must the navigator do to account for the receiver-clock error to make an accurate position fix?

◆ How can the amount of receiver-clock error be determined?

Investigation 3 on page 141 addresses problems such as these. Task 1 asks students to determine a position fix in the Lake Superior setting when clock error is a factor. The discussion in the following paragraphs illustrates one approach to solving that problem; students should be encouraged to generate others.

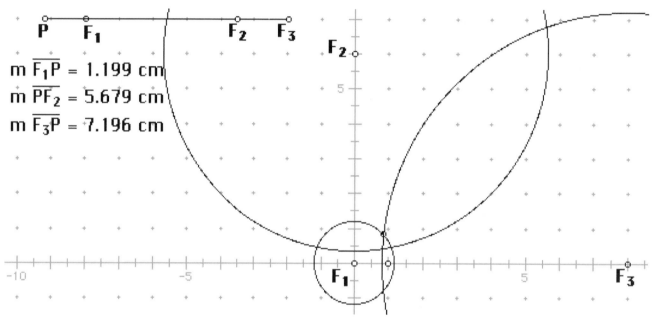

Scale drawing created by the Geometer's Sketchpad. The common point appears to be within the region enclosed by the three circles near the point (1, 1). The receiver clock is running fast.

Electronic technologies provide access to problems and methods that until recently were difficult to explore meaningfully in high school.

*(NCTM 2000, p. 362)*

The Geometer's Sketchpad was used to create a scale drawing, with 1 centimeter equal to 1 mile. Using the signal transmission times given in task 1 of Investigation 3 and 186,000 miles per second as the speed of light (the speed at which radio waves also travel), Sketchpad measurements show the radius of each broadcast transmission circle ($d_1 = 1.1904$ mi, $d_2 = 5.6637$ mi, $d_3 = 7.1908$ mi). The segment in the upper-left corner of figure 4.1 was constructed with points $F_1$, $F_2$, and $F_3$ on the segment, and the points were dragged until the segment lengths, whose measures are shown, corresponded as closely as possible to the calculated radii of the broadcast transmission circles.

The transmitter locations $F_1$, $F_2$, and $F_3$ were positioned on the grid, and circles were constructed with those points as centers and the segments $PF_1$, $PF_2$, and $PF_3$ as radii. Although accuracy was limited by the precision of measurements in the software, the construction shows that the three circles do not intersect in a common point, indicating the presence of receiver-clock error.

To approximate the location of the ship, point $P$ in the upper-left corner was moved uniformly closer to each of the points $F_1$, $F_2$, and $F_3$ on the segment until the three circles appeared to share one common point, near (1, 1) on the grid. Sketchpad was then used to identify this common point, whose coordinates were given as (0.940, 0.560), the approximate location of the ship. The new values for the three radii, as given by the software, were $PF_1 = 1.094$ cm, $PF_2 = 5.573$ cm, and $PF_3 = 7.091$ cm. Again, accuracy was limited by the precision of the software.

An estimate of the clock error can be generated by subtracting the estimates of distance taken from the construction (where 1 cm = 1 mi) from the distances that were calculated from the reported transmission times. Each pair of values yields a difference of approximately 0.09 mile, the amount by which the distance from the transmitters was overestimated. Traveling at the speed of 186,000 miles per second, the signals required approximately 0.0000004 second (4 ten-millionths of a second) to traverse 0.09 mile. Even the smallest of clock errors has a profound effect when radio signals are involved.

Given that the receiver clock is running fast, the segments $PF_1$, $PF_2$, and $PF_3$ overestimate the distances from the respective transmitters. Decreasing the lengths of the segments allows us to estimate the true distances.

*Further Exploration*

The Geometer's Sketchpad can be used to carry out an additional exploration of the scale drawing. Select the intersection points of each pair of circles, and turn on the Sketchpad command "trace points." Point $P$ on the segment in the upper-left corner of the screen can then be moved back and forth along the segment, allowing the intersection points to be traced. The locus of those points is shown in figure 4.1, with the three circles hidden from view to allow a clearer look at the locus of the traced points. Each pair of transmitter points appears to have a hyperbola associated with it. How can we account for that phenomenon?

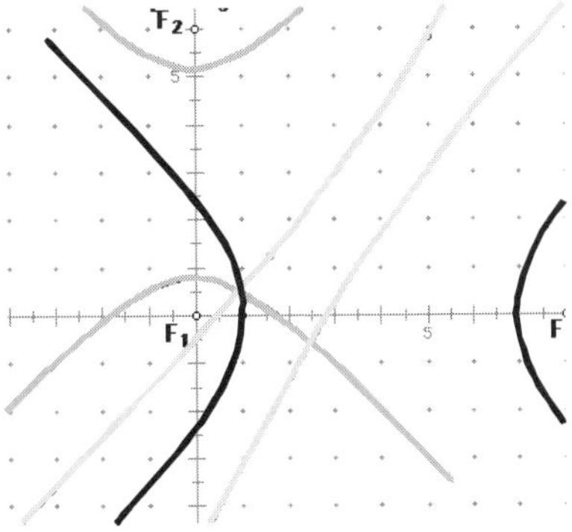

What qualities of a hyperbola may relate to the context that students are exploring? Recall the definition of a hyperbola: the set of all points in the plane that have a constant absolute difference in distance from two fixed points.

To verify the conjecture that the locus of intersection points is a hyperbola, concentrate on the apparent hyperbola with foci at $F_1$ and $F_3$. Segments $F_1A$ and $F_3A$ have been added to figure 4.2. The lengths of these segments correspond to the radii of circles $F_1$ and $F_3$, respectively, and represent the distances from the signal transmitters to the ship when calculated with some unknown receiver-clock error. If $r_1$ and $r_3$

More advanced students can explore the effect of changing the amount of receiver-clock error. The interpretation involves the analysis of the equation of a hyperbola.

**Fig. 4.1. Locus of intersection points**

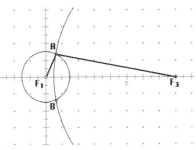

**Fig. 4.2. Signal transmission circles**

represent the true distance from each transmitter to the ship and $e$ represents the error distance common to each distance calculation, then

$$F_1 A = r_1 + e$$

and

$$F_3 A = r_3 + e.$$

Look at the absolute difference of these values:

$$|r_1 - r_3| = |r_1 + e - (r_3 + e)| = |F_1 A - F_3 A|$$

Regardless of the error distance introduced through receiver-clock error, a constant difference remains in the calculated distances from each pair of transmitters to the ship. The set of points that satisfies this condition generates a hyperbola, as we informally observed through the Sketchpad trace points.

As suggested by the trace points of the three hyperbolas, if we can determine the intersection point of the hyperbolas, we will have determined the possible location of the ship. With accurate scale drawings, we can find a precise position fix. To determine the hyperbolas' intersection points analytically, we first need equations for the hyperbolas. We again use the hyperbola associated with $F_1$ and $F_3$, this time to generate its equation.

Recall that in the hyperbola with center at $P = (h, k)$ and equation

$$\frac{(x-h)^2}{a^2} - \frac{(y-k)^2}{b^2} = 1,$$

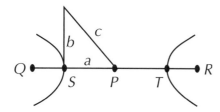

Fig. 4.3. Basic hyperbola relationships

each focus is $c$ units from $(h, k)$, each vertex is $a$ units from $(h, k)$, and $a^2 + b^2 = c^2$ (see fig. 4.3, basic hyperbola relationships, in the margin). For the situation on the navigator's map (fig. 4.4), we have foci at $(0, 0)$ and $(8, 0)$. The center is at $(4, 0)$, and $c = 4$ represents half the distance from $F_1$ to $F_3$. We determine $a$ by calculating half the constant difference $|F_1 A - F_3 A|$, using the signal-transmission times given in the problem:

$$F_1 A = 0.00000640 \text{ sec} \cdot 186{,}000 \text{ mi/sec} = 1.19040000 \text{ mi}$$

$$F_3 A = 0.00003866 \text{ sec} \cdot 186{,}000 \text{ mi/sec} = 7.19076000 \text{ mi}$$

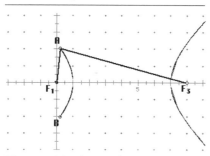

Fig. 4.4. Navigator's map

This result shows that $|F_1 A - F_3 A|$ is very close to 6 miles, resulting in the value $a = 3$ miles. Given that $b^2 = c^2 - a^2$, where $c = 4$ and $a = 3$, we determine that $b = \sqrt{7}$ and that the equation of our hyperbola is

$$\frac{(x-4)^2}{9} - \frac{(y-0)^2}{7} = 1.$$

In a similar manner, we can show that the hyperbola involving transmitter points $F_1$ and $F_2$ has the equation

$$\frac{(y-3)^2}{5} - \frac{(x-0)^2}{4} = 1.$$

Plotting these two hyperbolas with a graphing utility reveals an intersection point with coordinates (0.9406, 0.5290). Note that this ordered pair is close to the one we previously approximated using a Sketchpad scale drawing.

Finally, we can determine the receiver-clock error by comparing the transmitter broadcast radius with the true distance from a transmitter to the ship. Focusing on $F_1$, we have already computed 1.19040000 miles as the transmitter broadcast radius that includes clock error. Using the foregoing ordered pairs, we can calculate the true distance from $F_1$ to the ship to be 1.07916298 miles. The difference is 0.11123702 mile. Dividing this result by 186,000 mi/sec yields a clock error of 0.0000006 second. The receiver clock runs a constant 0.0000006 second fast, a discrepancy that agrees well with the error estimated from the Sketchpad solution method.

*Looking Back*

Students can summarize and generalize their work with two-dimensional time-of-arrival positioning by addressing the following question:

> *Describe how to use a two-dimensional time-of-arrival positioning system to determine the location of point P on a coordinate plane when broadcast transmitters are located at known coordinates $F_1$, $F_2$, and $F_3$ on the plane. Consider the situation both with and without clock error.*

If no clock error is present, signal broadcast-transmission times can be used to determine broadcast-transmission circles. With no error, the three circles will have one common point. The common point can be identified through analysis by determining the intersection points and the lines from the equations of the broadcast-transmission circles. Scale drawings, from pencil-and-paper or computer-generated models, can also be used to generate position estimates.

If receiver-clock error is present, scale-drawing estimates that employ a dynamic constant change in the radii of the broadcast-transmission circles can be used. As shown in the Sketchpad figures associated with the previous discussion, this technique provides reasonable position estimates. Analytic techniques that require determining intersection points of hyperbolas can also be used, especially when coordinate systems are established that place two or more transmitters on the same horizontal or vertical line.

## Investigation 4—Determining Position in Three Dimensions

In this investigation, students complete the mathematical conceptualization of time-of-arrival positioning by extending and applying the triangulation concepts and procedures developed for one and two dimensions. The setting is a three-dimensional system on Earth, as described below:

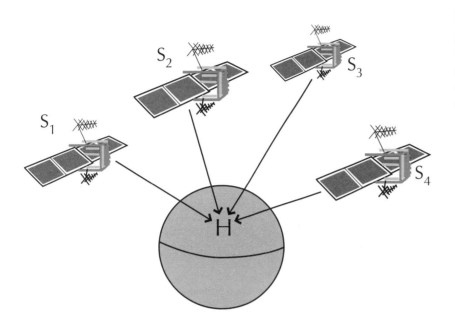

*A mountain climber is hiking in the Rocky Mountains. The figure shows Earth, the hiker at point H, and radio signals transmitted from four satellites, $S_1$, $S_2$, $S_3$, and $S_4$. Each satellite orbits approximately 11,000 miles above Earth, and the hiker has a handheld unit that receives the satellites' signals. A coded signal from each satellite helps determine the signal transmission time and provides information about the satellite's position. The hiker's receiver records the time of arrival of each radio signal. How can such a transmitter-receiver system be used to determine the hiker's position?*

*Use the three-dimensional coordinate system shown here to write a system of equations that can be solved to determine the position of the hiker at point H(x, y, z) in the mock-up, where the center of Earth is at the coordinate (0, 0, 0).*

> Geometric modeling and spatial reasoning offer ways to interpret and describe physical environments and can be important tools in problem solving.
>
> *(NCTM 2000, p. 41)*

Here is a system of equations generated from this situation:

$$\begin{cases} D_1 = \sqrt{(x - x_1)^2 + (y - y_1)^2 + (z - z_1)^2} \\ D_2 = \sqrt{(x - x_2)^2 + (y - y_2)^2 + (z - z_2)^2} \\ D_3 = \sqrt{(x - x_3)^2 + (y - y_3)^2 + (z - z_3)^2} \end{cases}$$

Students may be motivated to solve this set of equations for the unknown point (x, y, z), or they may find other ways to use technology to approximate the values for x, y, and z. The tasks in Investigation 4 on page 142 illustrate the calculations of time and distance that are part of a three-dimensional time-of-arrival positioning system. The tasks may lead to further discussion of the impact of clock error in a GPS, where a difference of even a fraction of a second translates into hundreds of miles (or more) of error.

Unknown position of hiker
(x, y, z)

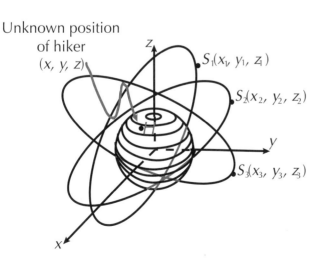

In considering a solution to the three-dimensional positioning problem, students should first identify the fundamental components of the system:

✦ Broadcast signals from known locations

✦ Signal receptions at the unknown location

✦ Determination of elapsed time for signal broadcasts

✦ Calculation of distances between known and unknown locations

✦ Position fixes based on calculated distances

✦ Allowance for clock error within a system

These components form the basis for a three-dimensional time-of-arrival positioning system. Any discussion of the triangulation process applied to a three-dimensional system should focus on concepts rather than calculations, as illustrated through the following questions and responses:

✦ How can we calculate the distance between two points in a three-dimensional coordinate system? (Extend the distance calculations from two dimensions to three by repeated application of the Pythagorean theorem.)

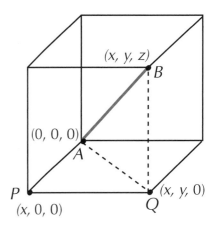

✦ What geometric shape represents the set of all possible locations that are a known distance r from a satellite? (The shape is a sphere of radius $r$.)

✦ How many different satellites' signals are required to pinpoint one unique point of signal reception? (Two unique spheres can have zero, one, or an infinite number of points in common. In the last instance, the set of points represents a circle. If the time-of-arrival positioning system has no errors, three spheres will have exactly two points in common, one of which is typically an impossible position fix if the general location of the GPS receiver is known.)

✦ How many satellites' signals are required to correct for clock error? (A fourth satellite is required to fix a unique position.)

## GPS Applications

The third task in Investigation 4 offers a transition into GPS applications. The reality of GPS is that a coordinate system different from a typical Cartesian system builds the framework for the location and navigation information available on GPS readouts.

Several coordinate systems may be used to report location through a GPS receiver, but the system most familiar to many GPS users is the system of longitude and latitude typically expressed in degrees, minutes, and seconds. The latitude and longitude readouts are coupled with a measure of altitude expressed in feet or meters above or below sea level. These three measures form the basis for many maps and other location and navigation aids in use today.

The prime meridian through Greenwich, England, supplies a reference circle for east and west longitude measurement; the equator is a reference circle for north and south latitude measurement.

The need to understand and be able to use mathematics in everyday life and in the workplace has never been greater and will continue to increase.

*(NCTM 2000, p. 4)*

The applications explored in Investigations 5 through 10 are intended to help students become familiar with ways to use the information available from a GPS receiver. Although the applications focus on aspects of location and navigation, GPS can be used in many more ways in personal, recreational, commercial, agricultural, and governmental settings. The reference list on page 135 shows additional resources that students can use to learn more.

## Investigation 5—GPS Application: Lake Superior Navigation

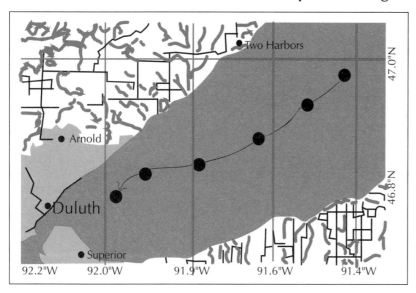

Investigation 5 on page 143 returns to the Lake Superior setting, this time with a more detailed map and instructions to plot a ship's course on Lake Superior on the basis of six GPS readouts. The figure at left shows approximate locations of the ship determined by the GPS readout.

Students are asked to determine the direction of the ship, in part to focus on the date information shown on the GPS readouts. Because the two readouts dated July 6, 2002 are the two closest to Duluth, students can safely assume that the ship is moving toward the harbor. A specific path, however, such as the one shown on the map, is only a suggestion. No information indicating the ship's location is available other than the six GPS readouts. In particular, the elapsed time between GPS readings is unknown. In subsequent applications, students will need to interpret both time and date information contained in the GPS readouts.

Note that the longitude and latitude on the maps are expressed in degrees to the nearest tenth of a degree, whereas the sample readouts from the GPS units express longitude and latitude in degrees and minutes or in degrees, minutes, and seconds. Teachers should bring this distinction to the attention of students and help them make conversions when necessary.

## Investigation 6—GPS Application: San Antonio–Phoenix Air Travel

In Investigation 6 on page 144, the GPS readouts include more information. In addition to the date, the first line of the position readout shows the time in hours, minutes, and seconds. The displayed time is Greenwich Mean Time (GMT). Line 3 shows the altitude of the GPS unit.

The map on the following page shows a flight path based on estimates of position using the GPS data. Readings 1 and 2 show identical values except for a time difference of 25 minutes, which probably means that the aircraft did not move from the San Antonio airport during that time. Assuming that the first two readings show time on the ground in San Antonio and that reading 8 occurred on touchdown at the Phoenix airport, we can determine that the flight lasted no longer than 1 hour, 32 minutes, 35 seconds. On the basis of the altitudes shown in the readouts, we can conclude that the plane must have reached an altitude of at least 29,976 feet. It may have flown higher.

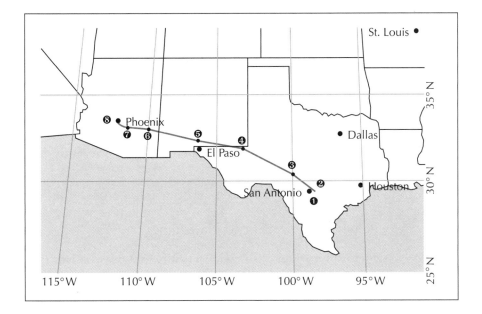

St. Louis

Phoenix

El Paso

Dallas

San Antonio  Houston

35° N

30° N

25° N

115° W    110° W    105° W    100° W    95° W

For greater precision in solving these problems, secure a larger map of the region, either a road map or a map from an atlas. Maps can also be downloaded from the Internet or from CD-ROM software.

## Investigation 7—GPS Application: Anaheim Deliveries

Investigation 7 on pages 145–46 extends the task of estimating location using longitude and latitude to an analysis of a situation for which GPS data may provide additional information. The package-delivery setting highlights the popular use of GPS and other types of location and navigation technology in transportation settings. The situation described here is a much simplified version of what may occur in reality, yet it offers a rich context for analysis and discussion.

Note that the longitude and latitude of location *D* are given, although this information is not necessary to complete the problem; it is provided as a reference point for those who need one. With no longitude or latitude lines shown on the map, students will need to compare the longitudes and latitudes for the GPS readouts. Because the six points of delivery are shown on the map, students can match the GPS readouts with the map locations by independently ordering the set of six longitudes and the set of six latitudes. Location 6, for instance, has the northernmost latitude and the easternmost longitude. Similar relative positioning analyses result in the matches shown in the GPS readouts at the right.

With this information, students can trace a path that connects the locations in the order determined. Starting at the distribution center (*D*), the driver traveled to locations 6, 5, 3, 2, 1, and 4, in that order, and finished the deliveries by returning to *D*. The map shows one of many paths that reasonably represent this sequence of deliveries.

| 28APR97 08:45:12<br>LAT N 33° 51.48' ⑥<br>LON W 117° 51.54' | 28APR97 08:52:21<br>LAT N 33° 51.30' ⑤<br>LON W 117° 51.90' | 28APR97 09:03:15<br>LAT N 33° 51.06' ③<br>LON W 117° 52.86' |
|---|---|---|
| 28APR97 09:11:52<br>LAT N 33° 50.52' ②<br>LON W 117° 53.28' | 28APR97 09:17:20<br>LAT N 33° 50.70' ①<br>LON W 117° 53.76' | 28APR97 09:31:01<br>LAT N 33° 50.58' ④<br>LON W 117° 52.08' |

GPS readouts

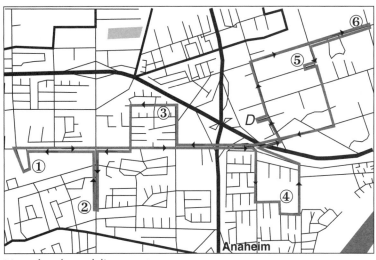

Map of package-delivery route

With the increasing popularity of GPS among drivers, boaters, hunters, and others, some students may have firsthand experience with GPS and may even own GPS units that they can demonstrate to the class.

An evaluation of the routes the driver could have taken may raise the following issues:

✦ The total distance traveled may vary from one route to another.

✦ The map does not clearly show underpass or overpass options near what seem to be two freeways transversing Anaheim, nor does the map indicate areas of known or potential traffic congestion.

✦ The character of the area shown on the map, whether primarily commercial or residential, is unknown.

✦ A careful look at distances traveled may bring into question the elapsed times between deliveries. Again, many unknowns may account for longer-than-anticipated travel times.

If students suggest other routes, ask them to justify their alternatives on the basis of one or more of the concerns discussed above. Some students may be interested in pursuing these questions in more detail. They might search reference materials for information about this part of Anaheim or talk to a local delivery service about the factors that affect times and routes for deliveries.

## Navigation Applications Using a GPS Receiver

The NAVSTAR GPS is comprised of a constellation of high-orbit satellites. In an unobstructed area, five to eight satellites are typically "visible" to a GPS receiver. Data are sent by radio waves—at about 186,000 miles per second—from a satellite to a GPS receiver similar to the one drawn here. The receiver stores information about each satellite—its location and status, for instance—using data sent from the satellites. The screen here represents a receiver's viewable satellites, working from the horizon (the outer circle) to directly overhead (the center point). Each satellite's position is identified by a number on the screen. Numbers surrounded by a black box (numbers 1, 6, 11, and 19 in the illustration) indicate that the GPS receiver is tracking those satellites. If a number is not surrounded by a black box, as shown for satellite 8, the receiver is not receiving position data from that satellite.

A GPS receiver's position screen reveals such information as the user's location, direction of travel, and speed of travel. The screen here shows that the receiver is—

✦ heading 211 degrees clockwise from true north;

✦ moving at 3.7 miles per hour;

✦ 11.1 miles from its initial position;

✦ at the position 36° 24' 32" north latitude, 82° 51' 07" west longitude;

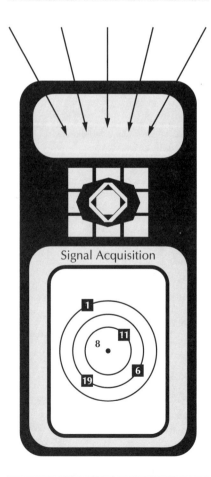

Signal Acquisition

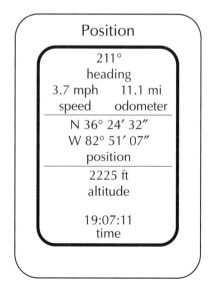

Position

211°
heading

3.7 mph      11.1 mi
speed        odometer

N 36° 24' 32"
W 82° 51' 07"
position

2225 ft
altitude

19:07:11
time

✦ at an altitude of 2225 feet; and

✦ operating at a local time of just after 7:00 P.M.

Position information can be stored in a GPS receiver for later use. Each stored position is called a *waypoint,* and a series of related waypoints is called a *route.*

The navigation features of a GPS receiver monitor the receiver's movement to or from a waypoint. The receiver screen here shows the waypoint "Fishing" as the desired target or destination. Other information on the screen includes the following:

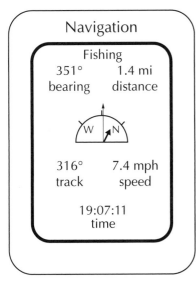

✦ The compass guide shows the current ground track of the receiver, indicated by the faint arrow pointing straight up on the screen and the reading of 316 degrees over the track label.

✦ The guide also shows the direction to the destination, indicated by the solid arrow on the screen and the reading of 351 degrees over the bearing label.

✦ This navigation screen shows that the receiver is 1.4 miles from the "Fishing" waypoint.

The previous three investigations focus on reading a GPS receiver and using its information for recreational navigation. Investigation 8 on pages 146–47 discusses location and navigation information provided by GPS, followed by application tasks in Investigations 9 and 10 (pages 148–49) that focus on the use of GPS in fishing and hiking.

## Investigation 8 — Information at Your Fingertips: Exploring Position and Navigation

In Investigation 8 on page 146–47, two people are hiking in the vicinity of Tupper Lake in upstate New York. They set out from point *A,* intending to hike directly to point *B.*

The hikers use a GPS receiver to record their location at point *A;* earlier, they had stored information about point *B* in the receiver. At point *A,* the hikers set the GPS receiver for navigation and select point *B* as their destination. After turning off the receiver and hiking for a while, they take another reading and find that they have gone off track to point *P.* Investigation 8 shows students how the GPS information enables the hikers to determine their position and correct their course to reach their desired destination.

The blackline master on page 145 duplicates this information about GPS displays. It can be copied for students to use as a reference in interpreting GPS readouts.

Spatial reasoning is helpful in using maps, planning routes, designing floor plans, and creating art.

*(NCTM 2000, p. 41)*

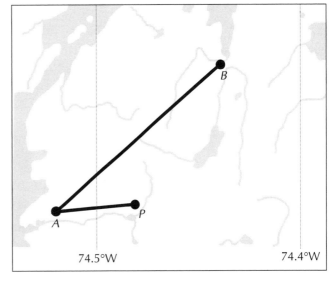

## Investigation 9—Information at Your Fingertips: GPS Navigation

Investigation 9 on page 148 involves an angler who sets out from shore (A) to return to a favorite fishing spot (B) on Little Mantrap Lake. Students are asked to interpret GPS readouts and determine what the angler must do to get back on course after drifting.

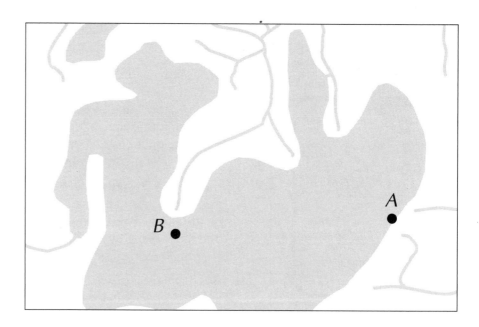

## Investigation 10—Information at Your Fingertips: GPS Navigation Routes

In Investigation 10 on pages 148–49, students determine the location, P, of hikers in Bryce Canyon National Park who attempt to follow a ten-waypoint route from Ruby's Inn to the Pump House. Stopping to make a GPS position reading en route, they find that they must adjust their route to get back on track.

### Looking Back and Looking Ahead

Students who are interested in investigating GPS further may select one or more of the following explorations:

1. Review the concepts and procedures for using time-of-arrival positioning systems. Identify the essential components of any such system, and show how mathematics is used to make accurate position fixes.

2. Use interactive geometry software, such as the The Geometer's Sketchpad or Cabri Geometry II, to create an interactive application to make position fixes in one, two, or three dimensions.

3. Write a program for a graphing calculator to make position fixes in one, two, or three dimensions.

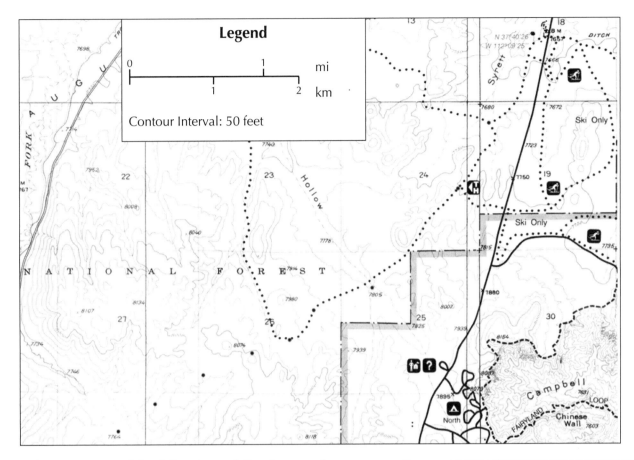

4.  Read one or more of the following publications, and present a written or oral summary to the class:

—Ferguson, Michael, Randy Kalisek, and Leah Tuck. *GPS Land Navigation: A Complete Guidebook for Backcountry Users of the NAVSTAR Satellite System.* Boise, Idaho: Glassford Publishing, 1997. ISBN 0965220257.

—Herring, Thomas A. "The Global Positioning System." *Scientific American* (February 1996): 44–50.

—Hotchkiss, Noel J. *A Comprehensive Guide to Land Navigation with GPS.* 3rd ed. Leesburg, Va.: Alexis Publishing, 1999. ISBN 189268800X.

—Huang, Jerry. *All about GPS: Sherlock Holmes' Guide to the Global Positioning System.* n.p.: Acme Services, 1999. ISBN 9579738971.

—Larijani, L. Casey. *GPS for Everyone: How the Global Positioning System Can Work for You.* New York: American Interface Corporation, Publishing Division, 1998. ISBN 0965966755.

—Letham, Lawrence. *GPS Made Easy: Using Global Positioning Systems in the Outdoors.* 3rd ed. Seattle, Wash.: Mountaineers Books, 2001. ISBN 0898868025.

—Vest, Floyd, William Diedrich, and Kenneth Vos. "Mathematics and the Global Positioning System." *Consortium* (spring 1994). Includes HiMap pullout section.

5. Look through recent issues of *GPS World* (ISSN 10485104), and pick out a GPS application that is of interest to you. Use that application as a basis for a research report. Try to include an interview with someone who actually uses GPS in his or her professional or recreational activities.

6. Create a three-dimensional, scale-model representation of the spheres of intersection that result when three or four satellite signals are used to fix a position on or near Earth. Identify the geometric shapes that result when two or more spheres intersect.

## Components of a Global Positioning System (GPS)

At the heart of a GPS is triangulation, the determination of an unknown position using distances from known positions. A GPS receiver uses signal-transmission times from orbiting satellites to calculate distances from those satellites, which in turn are used to determine receiver position.

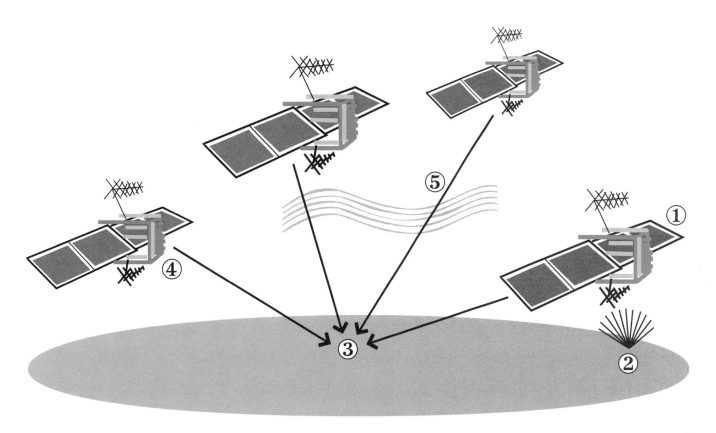

**Components of a Global Positioning System (GPS).**

① In the U.S. system called NAVSTAR (for **NAV**igation **S**atellite **T**iming **a**nd **R**anging), twenty-four satellites orbit Earth, providing GPS users with at least five satellites visible from any point on Earth.

② A worldwide monitoring system tracks the GPS satellites and generates an orbital model for each satellite. A master control station in Colorado sends each satellite orbital data and clock corrections that are relayed to GPS users.

③ GPS users on or near Earth use GPS receivers to convert satellite signals to position, velocity, and time estimates.

④ Each satellite has four atomic clocks, accurate to within a billionth of a second per year.

⑤ The speed of GPS satellite signals may be altered as the signals travel through the atmosphere. At the speed of light, even slight changes in transmission speed introduce significant errors into the system.

## Investigation 1—Determining Position in One Dimension

The diagram at the left shows a bird's-eye view of a football-field sideline. A coach is at point C on the sideline. The coach is wearing a headset with a special receiver. The receiver picks up sound waves that are broadcast at one-minute intervals from a transmitter located at point S at one end of the sideline. If the coach moves only along the sideline, how can a transmitter-receiver system like this one be used to determine the coach's position?

Answer the following questions; use the assumption that sound travels at 1100 feet per second.

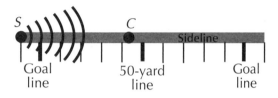

Note: The yard marks on the field are 10 yards apart.

1. The coach is at a point C on the 50-yard line; how much time is needed for a sound wave to travel from S to C?

2. A sound wave requires 0.14 second to travel from S to C. What is the coach's position?

3. The coach is at one of the 30-yard lines. What two travel times are possible for a sound wave to move from the transmitter to the coach?

4. Determine the time difference in a sound wave traveling from S to each goal line.

5. Sound waves are broadcast from S at one-minute intervals starting on the hour. The coach's receiver includes a clock synchronized with the one in the transmitter. Determine the missing information in the table below.

| Time Sent (Transmitter) (hr:min:sec) | Time Received (Receiver) (hr:min:sec) | Coach's Position |
| --- | --- | --- |
| 0:02:00.0000 | 0:02:00.0762 | (a) |
| 0:25:00.0000 | 0:25:00.1238 | (b) |
| 0:57:00.0000 | (c) | 12-yard line farthest from S |

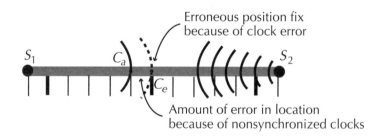

6. The coach is positioned at the 40-yard line that is closer to the transmitter at $S_1$. Because the coach's receiver is not synchronized with the transmitters, using only the $S_1$ transmission will

erroneously locate the coach at the 50-yard line. Use this information to complete the following tasks:

(a) Determine how fast or how slow the receiver clock is registering times.

(b) If a broadcast is sent from $S_2$ at 1:27:00.0000, calculate what the receiver clock will read when it receives this transmission.

7. Sound waves are broadcast from $S_1$ and $S_2$ at 0:23:00.0000. The coach's receiver records the $S_1$ transmission at 0:23:00.0892 and the $S_2$ transmission at 0:23:00.2981. Determine the coach's position, and verify that the coach's receiver is not synchronized with the clocks in the transmitters. Determine how fast or slow the receiver clock registers reception times.

8. Generalize a method for using a one-dimensional time-of-arrival positioning system to determine accurately the location of point $P$ on a number line and the amount of receiver-clock error when transmitters are located at known coordinates $X_1$ and $X_2$ on the number line.

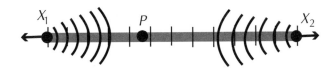

## Investigation 2—Determining Position in Two Dimensions

A ship is traveling on Lake Superior in the north-central United States. The ship has left the harbor at Duluth, Minnesota, and is tracking its progress across the lake using sound waves broadcast from foghorns on the lake and received by the ship's navigator.

Here is a simplified version of a map that the navigator might use to record and track the ship's position. Note the use of rectangular coordinates with grid marks each 1 mile apart.

1. Study the table on the following page. It shows data recorded after the ship left the Duluth harbor. The ship sailed at 15:12:30.0000. What calculations and assumptions has the navigator made to fix the ship's position?

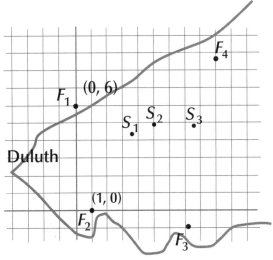

| Record # | Signal Reception Times | | Foghorn Distance (miles) | | Ship's Position | |
|---|---|---|---|---|---|---|
| | $F_1$ | $F_2$ | $F_1$ | $F_2$ | X | Y |
| 1 | 15:40:19.2000 | 15:40:24.0000 | 4.00 | 5.00 | 3.605 | 4.268 |
| 2 | 15:50:24.0000 | 15:50:28.8000 | 5.00 | 6.00 | 4.810 | 4.635 |
| 3 | 16:10:36.0000 | 16:10:38.4000 | 7.50 | 8.00 | 7.403 | 4.796 |
| 4 | 16:20:38.4000 | 16:20:43.2000 | | | | |
| 5 | 16:30:43.2000 | 16:30:48.0000 | | | | |

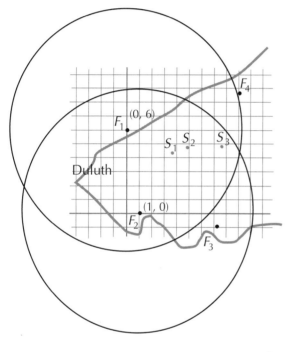

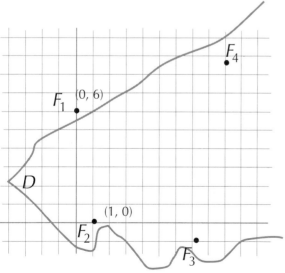

2. The three lightly shaded dots on the map at the left ($S_1$, $S_2$, and $S_3$) indicate the first three position fixes made by the navigator, using the data from the foregoing navigator's table. The navigator has begun to fix a fourth position. Complete the data entry for records 4 and 5 in the navigator's table. Locate the fourth and fifth position points.

3. A ship has lost its bearing on Lake Superior. The only information to aid navigation is the transmission data, shown below, from the four foghorns. Each foghorn broadcasts a signal every minute on the minute. Determine the ship's location, and show the point on the grid below. Is the ship in trouble?

| Signal Reception Times | |
|---|---|
| $F_1$ | 23:09:25.8488 |
| $F_2$ | 23:09:42.9325 |
| $F_3$ | 23:09:44.2538 |
| $F_4$ | 23:09:19.7909 |

## Investigation 3—Determining Position in Two Dimensions: Clock Error

1. At the right are a navigator's map and data table from a voyage on a lake. Use the information to determine the ship's position and the amount of receiver-clock error. Grid lines on the map are 1 mile apart, and each transmitter broadcasts radio signals traveling at 186,000 miles per second.

For tasks 2–4 below, you are shown transmitter locations and signal-reception times. Use the information to determine the receiver's position and the amount of receiver-clock error in each situation. Assume that each transmitter broadcasts a radio signal every minute on the minute, that radio signals travel at 186,000 miles per second, and that the broadcast-transmitter clocks in each set are synchronized.

| | Signal Reception Times (seconds) |
|---|---|
| $F_1$ | 0.00000640 |
| $F_2$ | 0.00003045 |
| $F_3$ | 0.00003866 |

2.

| | Transmitter Location | Signal Reception Times |
|---|---|---|
| $T_1$ | (–8, 0) | 8:36:00.000 077 77 |
| $T_2$ | (–2, 0) | 8:36:00.000 067 02 |
| $T_3$ | (10, 0) | 8:36:00.000 088 52 |

3.

| | Transmitter Location | Signal Reception Times |
|---|---|---|
| $T_1$ | (–5, 0) | 1:41:00.000 034 98 |
| $T_2$ | (5, 0) | 1:41:00.000 013 48 |
| $T_3$ | (0, –3) | 1:41:00.000 024 10 |
| $T_4$ | (0, 3) | 1:41:00.000 007 97 |

4.

| | Transmitter Location | Signal Reception Times |
|---|---|---|
| $T_1$ | (–8, 0) | 16:21:00.000 053 94 |
| $T_2$ | (2, 0) | 16:21:00.000 027 38 |
| $T_3$ | (0, 6) | 16:21:00.000 024 13 |

## Investigation 4—Determining Position in Three Dimensions

A mountain climber is hiking in the Rocky Mountains. The figure shows Earth, the hiker at point $H$, and radio signals transmitted from four satellites, $S_1$, $S_2$, $S_3$, and $S_4$. Each satellite orbits approximately 11,000 miles above Earth, and the hiker has a handheld unit that receives the satellites' signals. A coded signal from each satellite helps determine the signal transmission time and provides information about the satellite's position. The hiker's receiver records the time of arrival of each radio signal. How can such a transmitter-receiver system be used to determine the hiker's position?

Radio signals from an Earth-orbiting satellite travel at 186,000 miles per second. The $(x, y, z)$ coordinates used in the diagram below are expressed in miles and refer to an Earth-centered three-dimensional system. The atomic clocks in the NAVSTAR GPS satellites are accurate to within a billionth of a second a year, whereas the clocks in GPS receivers are typically much less accurate.

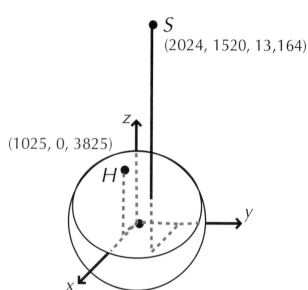

$S$
(2024, 1520, 13,164)

(1025, 0, 3825)

1. A handheld GPS receiver is 18,456 miles from a specific satellite.

   (a) How long will a signal take to travel from that satellite to the receiver?

   (b) If the clock in the handheld unit registers times that are 0.0001 second faster than actual time, what is the error in the distance calculated from the satellite to the receiver?

   (c) The GPS receiver calculated the receiver-to-satellite distance to be 18,078 miles. If receiver-clock error is the only factor affecting accuracy, what is the receiver-clock error?

2. A hiker, $H$, is positioned on Earth at the point (1025, 0, 3825), and a satellite, $S$, is orbiting Earth at the point (2024, 1520, 13,164) (see figure above).

   (a) Use a coordinate system like the one shown above to estimate the location of points $H$ and $S$.

   (b) How far is $S$ from $H$?

   (c) How long will a satellite signal take to travel from $S$ to $H$?

3. A location readout from a GPS receiver, simulated at left, is typically expressed in longitude, latitude, and altitude. The time shown represents the local time at the receiver location. Suggest reasons for the use of longitude, latitude, and altitude in GPS location readouts rather than $(x, y, z)$ coordinates.

| 6 MAY 2000 | 3:18 PM |
|---|---|
| LAT | 44° 08′ 02.4″ N |
| LON | 74° 31′ 15.6″ N |
| ALT | +1513 FT |

## Investigation 5—GPS Application:
## Lake Superior Navigation

Below is a map of a portion of Lake Superior, together with simulations from six screens of a handheld GPS unit that show longitude and latitude for a ship near the harbor. Use the GPS readings to mark on the map the path and direction of the ship.

Explain how you used the GPS information to arrive at your conclusions about the ship's path.

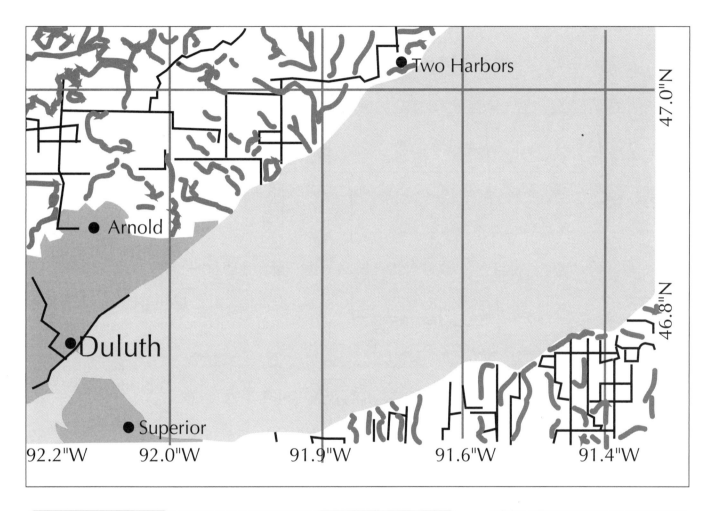

| LAT  N 46° 55.482' | LAT  N 46° 52.094' | LAT  N 46° 49.714' |
| --- | --- | --- |
| LON  W 91° 31.572' | LON  W 91° 39.657' | LON  W 91° 53.920' |
| date      22 NOV 02 | date      22 NOV 02 | date      23 NOV 02 |
| LAT  N 46° 50.681' | LAT  N 46° 58.613' | LAT  N 46° 43.810' |
| LON  W 91° 46.510' | LON  W 91° 26.217' | LON  W 91° 58.873' |
| date      22 NOV 02 | date      22 NOV 02 | date      23 NOV 02 |

### Investigation 6—GPS Application: San Antonio–Phoenix Air Travel

Here is a map of the southern United States, together with simulated readings from a handheld GPS unit onboard an aircraft flying from San Antonio to Phoenix.

1. Use the GPS readings to draw the path of the flight on the map.

2. Determine the length of the flight in hours, minutes, and seconds.

3. What do you suppose occurred during the time that readings 1 and 2 were taken?

4. What is the lowest possible maximum altitude the aircraft could have reached?

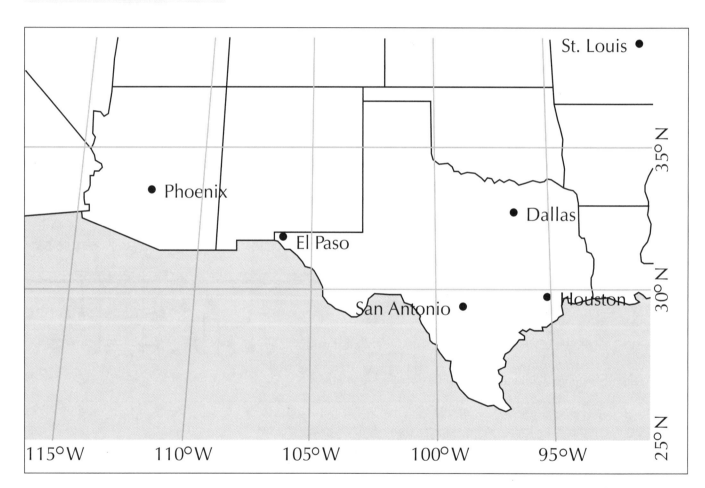

| 15MAR04 02:12:10 Z<br>LAT  N 29° 23.043'<br>LON W 98° 29.047'<br>MSL +701 ft        ❶ | 15MAR04 02:37:29 Z<br>LAT  N 29° 23.043'<br>LON W 98° 29.047'<br>MSL +701 ft        ❷ | 15MAR04 02:55:23 Z<br>LAT  N 30° 13.679'<br>LON W 100° 09.962'<br>MSL +12842 ft        ❸ | 15MAR04 03:17:01 Z<br>LAT  N 31° 43.620'<br>LON W 103° 35.104'<br>MSL +28976 ft        ❹ |
| --- | --- | --- | --- |
| 15MAR04 03:28:42 Z<br>LAT  N 32° 20.221'<br>LON W 106° 21.602'<br>MSL +25212 ft        ❺ | 15MAR04 03:52:38 Z<br>LAT  N 32° 54.011'<br>LON W 109° 56.038'<br>MSL +14922 ft        ❻ | 15MAR04 04:02:11 Z<br>LAT  N 32° 54.361'<br>LON W 111° 19.800'<br>MSL +5480 ft        ❼ | 15MAR04 04:10:04 Z<br>LAT  N 33° 32.585'<br>LON W 112° 05.259'<br>MSL +1090 ft        ❽ |

## Investigation 7—GPS Application: Anaheim Deliveries

Here is a map of Anaheim, California, showing GPS readings taken at the points marked 1 through 6. A local distribution center for American Package Systems (APS) is at point *D* (33.851°N, 117.871°W). Points 1 through 6 represent the locations of six deliveries made by an APS driver on a weekday morning.

1. Match the GPS readings with the delivery locations.

2. On the map, trace a possible route the APS truck may have followed in making the six deliveries, beginning and ending the route at *D*.

3. After you have completed the route, evaluate it by considering the following issues:

   —Do you think the driver took an efficient route?

   —What additional information would you like to have to evaluate the route more accurately?

   —Suggest one or more alternative routes the driver could have followed that may have been more efficient.

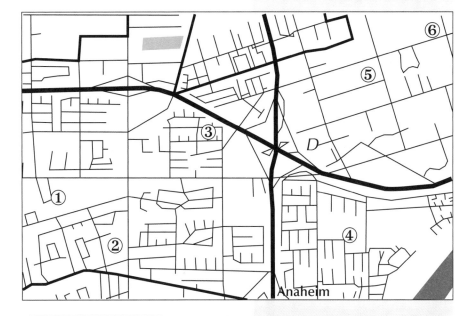

| 02AUG04   08:45:12<br>LAT N 33 ° 51.48'<br>LON W 117° 51.54' | 02AUG04   08:52:21<br>LAT N 33 ° 51.30'<br>LON W 117° 51.90' | 02AUG04   09:03:15<br>LAT N 33 ° 51.06'<br>LON W 117° 52.86' |
|---|---|---|
| 02AUG04   09:11:52<br>LAT N 33 ° 50.52'<br>LON W 117° 53.28' | 02AUG04   09:17:20<br>LAT N 33 ° 50.70'<br>LON W 117° 53.76' | 02AUG04   09:31:01<br>LAT N 33 ° 50.58'<br>LON W 117° 52.08' |

## Navigation Applications Using a GPS Receiver

The NAVSTAR GPS is comprised of a constellation of high-orbit satellites. In an unobstructed area, five to eight satellites are typically "visible" to a GPS receiver. Data are sent by radio waves—at about 186,000 miles per second—from a satellite to a GPS receiver similar to the one drawn on the following page. The receiver stores information about each satellite—its location and status, for instance—using data sent from the satellites. The screen here represents a receiver's viewable satellites, working from the horizon (the outer circle) to directly overhead (the center point). Each satellite's position is identified by a number on the screen. Numbers surrounded by a black box (numbers 1, 6, 11, and 19 in the illustration) indicate that the GPS receiver is tracking those satellites. If a number is not surrounded by a black box, as shown for satellite 8, the receiver is not receiving position data from that satellite.

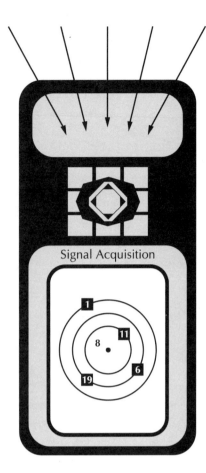

Signal Acquisition

A GPS receiver's position screen reveals such information as the user's location, direction of travel, and speed of travel. The screen at the right shows that the receiver is—

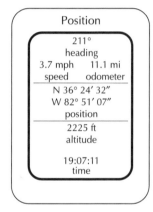

Navigation

Fishing

351°      1.4 mi
bearing    distance

316°      7.4 mph
track       speed

19:07:11
time

- heading 211 degrees clockwise from true north;

- moving at 3.7 miles per hour;

- 11.1 miles from its initial position;

- at the position 36° 24′ 32″ north latitude, 82° 51′ 07″ west longitude;

- at an altitude of 2225 feet; and

- operating at a local time of just after 7:00 P.M.

Position information can be stored in a GPS receiver for later use. Each stored position is called a *waypoint,* and a series of related waypoints is called a *route.*

The navigation features of a GPS receiver monitor the receiver's movement to or from a waypoint. The receiver screen at the right shows the waypoint "Fishing" as the desired target or destination. Other information on the screen includes the following:

Position

211°
heading
3.7 mph    11.1 mi
speed     odometer
N 36° 24′ 32″
W 82° 51′ 07″
position
2225 ft
altitude

19:07:11
time

- The compass guide shows the current ground track of the receiver, indicated by the faint arrow pointing straight up on the screen and the reading of 316 degrees over the track label.

- The guide also shows the direction to the destination, indicated by the solid arrow on the screen and the reading of 351 degrees over the bearing label.

- This navigation screen shows that the receiver is 1.4 miles from the "Fishing" waypoint.

## Investigation 8—Information at Your Fingertips: Exploring Position and Navigation

The map on the next page shows a portion of Tupper Lake in upstate New York. Two hikers set out from point *A*, intending to hike directly to point *B*. The hikers have reached point *P*. The following discussion focuses on how GPS is used for navigation.

At point *A*, the hikers use a GPS receiver to record their location as waypoint "Lake TS" (Lake Tupper South). Screen (a) on the next page shows the waypoint information for point *A*. Screen (b) on the next page shows information about point *B* that the hikers had previously stored in their GPS receiver as waypoint "Lake TE" (Lake Tupper East).

At point *A*, the hikers set the GPS receiver for navigation, choosing Lake TE as their destination. Screen (c) below is the navigation screen that the hikers see as they leave point *A*. The screen may be interpreted as follows:

✦ The waypoint Lake TE is named at the top of the screen.

✦ The bearing and track are the same, 62 degrees, shown numerically and graphically. This reading indicates that the hikers are actually moving (or tracking) directly toward their destination (or their bearing).

✦ The navigation screen shows that the hikers are 6.20 miles from Lake TE and that they are hiking at 1.4 mi/h.

✦ The current time is also shown.

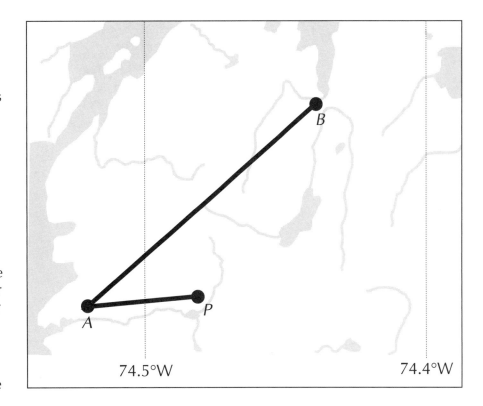

74.5°W       74.4°W

The hikers turn off the GPS receiver and hike on. When they make another navigation reading, at point *P*, they see screen (d) below. This screen indicates that the hikers have not stayed on course. Their current ground track, or heading, is 87 degrees, and their bearing is 47 degrees. The compass guide shows that the hikers should bear to the left—the direction from the faint (tracking) arrow to the solid (bearing) arrow—until their track and bearing are again equal.

The sketch at the right shows the situation. The cross-track error (XTE) shown in the drawing indicates that the hikers are just over 1 mile off course.

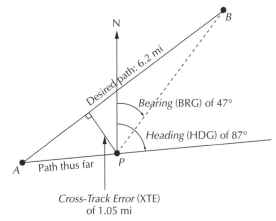

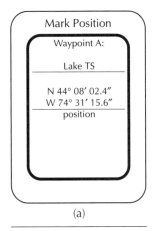

(a)

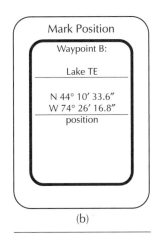

(b)

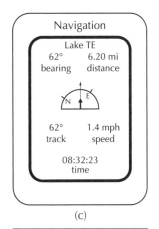

(c)

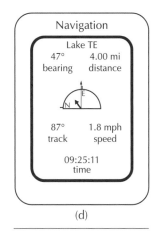

(d)

## Investigation 9—Information at Your Fingertips: GPS Navigation

Someone in a fishing boat sets out from shore (A) to return to a favorite fishing spot (B) on Little Mantrap Lake. Equipped with a GPS receiver, the boater sees the GPS navigation readouts shown below. Reading 1 was taken from shore (A), and reading 2 was taken on the lake, en route to B.

Interpret the readings and locate the boat's position when the second reading was made. Suggest what the boater should do to get back on course.

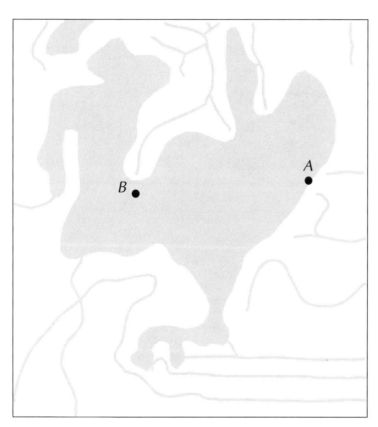

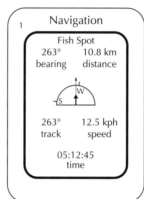

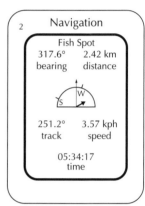

## Investigation 10—Information at Your Fingertips: GPS Navigation Routes

Jan and Chris planned a hike from Ruby's Inn to the Pump House near Utah's Bryce Canyon National Park. They entered a ten-waypoint route into their GPS receiver. The first waypoint is Ruby's Inn, and the last waypoint is the Pump House. The latitude and longitude for Ruby's Inn were on a topographical map, and Jan and Chris interpolated latitude and longitude readings from the map to estimate the positions of the other nine waypoints. The table on the next page shows the ten waypoints, and the map shows the hikers' planned route.

Jan and Chris stopped once to make a GPS position reading and saw the position screen shown on the next page. Without moving, they

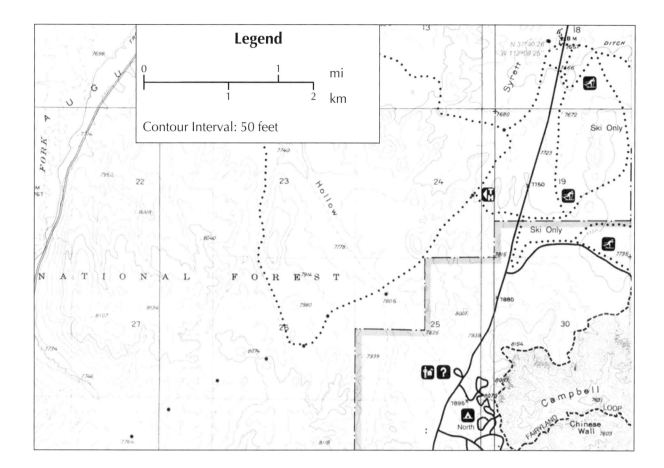

changed to GPS navigate mode and chose the Pump House as their desired target. Determine the following information about the hikers:

✦ On the map, locate the point where they made the position reading.

✦ Calculate (a) the bearing and (b) the distance that would appear on their navigation screen.

✦ Describe what they should do to get back on track.

| Position |
| --- |
| 207° heading |
| 1.9 mph     4.19 mi |
| speed     odometer |
| N 37° 38′ 25.7″ |
| W 112° 12′ 21.3″ |
| position |
| 7946 ft |
| altitude |
| 14:19:29 |
| time |

| Waypoint | Latitude | Longitude |
| --- | --- | --- |
| RI | 37° 40′ 26.0″ | 112° 09′ 25.0″ |
| 01 | 37° 39′ 52.8″ | 112° 09′ 46.6″ |
| 02 | 37° 39′ 29.5″ | 112° 09′ 58.6″ |
| 03 | 37° 38′ 55.2″ | 112° 10′ 42.1″ |
| 04 | 37° 38′ 47.5″ | 112° 11′ 07.2″ |
| 05 | 37° 38′ 35.8″ | 112° 11′ 20.7″ |
| 06 | 37° 38′ 30.3″ | 112° 11′ 40.0″ |
| 07 | 37° 38′ 24.5″ | 112° 12′ 03.9″ |
| 08 | 37° 38′ 14.7″ | 112° 12′ 25.9″ |
| PH | 37° 38′ 02.1″ | 112° 12′ 43.0″ |

# Solutions and Teacher Commentary

## Introduction

The master "Components of a Global Positioning System (GPS)" introduces the components of a three-dimensional GPS. Discuss with students the meaning of *triangulation,* and ask them for examples of triangulation that they might know about in their lives. Talk about the speed of light and the speed of sound, which are numerical constants that students will need for calculations in many of the GPS activities. Give students an overview of the activities that you intend to carry out in class, including the development of one-, two-, and three-dimensional cases.

## Investigation 1—Determining Position in One Dimension

Investigation 1 illustrates the calculations associated with time-of-arrival positioning.

1.  A sound wave will travel from $S$ to $C$ in 0.1636 second. The distance from $S$ to $C$ is 60 yards, or 180 feet; using $d = r \cdot t$, we find that

    $$t = 180 \text{ ft} \div 1100 \text{ ft/sec} = 0.1636 \text{ sec.}$$

2.  $C$ is just outside the 40-yard line closer to $S$:

    $$d = 1100 \text{ ft/sec} \cdot 0.14 \text{ sec} = 154 \text{ ft} = 51.3 \text{ yd}$$

3.  If $C$ is on the 30-yard line nearer to $S$, $C$ is 40 yards, or 120 feet, from $S$. Using the technique shown in task 1 yields

    $$t = 0.1091 \text{ sec.}$$

    If $C$ is on the 30-yard line farther from $S$, $C$ is 80 yards, or 240 feet, from $S$; thus, $t$ equals 0.2182 second.

4.  If $C$ is at the goal line closer to $S$, $d$ is 10 yards and $t$ is 0.0273 second. If $C$ is at the other goal line, $d$ is 110 yards and $t$ is 0.3000 second. The difference is 0.2727 second. Another way to approach this problem is to realize that the goal lines are 100 yards, or 300 feet, apart and that the time required for a sound wave to travel that distance is

    $$t = 300 \text{ ft} \div 1100 \text{ ft/sec, or } 0.2727 \text{ sec.}$$

5.  (a) The elapsed time is 0.0762 second, and

    $$d = 83.8200 \text{ ft} = 27.9400 \text{ yd.}$$

    $C$ is just inside the 18-yard line closer to $S$. (b) The elapsed time is 0.1238 second, and

    $$d = 136.1800 \text{ ft} = 45.3933 \text{ yd.}$$

C is between the 35- and 36-yard lines closer to S. (c) If C is at the 12-yard line farther from S,

$$d = 98 \text{ yd}$$

and

$$t = 0.2673 \text{ sec.}$$

The receiver clock reads 0:57:00.2673.

*Clock Error*

6.  (a) The receiver clock generates a positioning error of 10 yards, or 30 feet, which is equivalent to a clock error of

$$30 \text{ ft} \div 1100 \text{ ft/sec} = 0.0273 \text{ sec.}$$

The receiver clock is running 0.0273 second fast. (b) The transmitter at $S_2$ is 70 yards, or 210 feet, from C. Sound requires

$$210 \text{ ft} \div 1100 \text{ ft/sec} = 0.1909 \text{ sec}$$

to travel that distance. Using the clock error determined in (a), we find that the receiver clock will read 1:27:00.2182.

7.  Use the relationship $d_1 = 550(t_1 - t_2 + 0.3273)$ to determine the distance in feet from $S_1$ to C. The relationship

$$d_2 = 550(t_2 - t_1 + 0.3273)$$

can also be used to determine the distance from $S_2$ to C. Transmission times are

$$t_1 = 0.0892 \text{ sec}$$

and

$$t_2 = 0.2981 \text{ sec};$$

therefore,

$$\begin{aligned} d_1 &= 550(0.0892 - 0.2981 + 0.3273) \\ &= 65.12 \text{ ft} \\ &= 21.7067 \text{ yd} \end{aligned}$$

and

$$\begin{aligned} d_2 &= 550(0.2981 - 0.0892 + 0.3273) \\ &= 294.91 \text{ ft} \\ &= 98.3033 \text{ yd.} \end{aligned}$$

These calculations show that C is between the 11- and 12-yard lines closer to $S_1$. Note that $d_1$ and $d_2$ sum to 120 yards.

Students can use several methods to verify that the clocks are not synchronized. One method is to compare the sum of the two transmission times, $t_1$ and $t_2$, with the time required for a sound wave to travel from $S_1$ to $S_2$. Here,

$$t_1 + t_2 = 0.3873 \text{ sec,}$$

yet previously, we determined that sound travels from $T_1$ to $T_2$ in 0.3273 second. Because these values differ, we can conclude that the clocks are not synchronized. Another way to confirm that the clocks are not synchronized is to compare the position of $C$ determined from each transmission. Using $t_1$ in the $d = r \cdot t$ equation, we know that $C$ is 32.7 yards from $S_1$, between the 22- and 23-yard lines closer to $S_1$; using $t_2$, we know that C is 109.3 yards from $S_2$, between the goal line and the 1-yard line closer to $S_1$. These position fixes are not the same.

To determine the clock error, we can use the relationship

$$e = \frac{1}{2}\left(t_1 + t_2 - 0.3273\right)$$

$$= \frac{1}{2}\left(0.0892 + 0.2981 - 0.3273\right)$$

$$= 0.0300.$$

The receiver clock runs 0.03 second fast. (How do we know whether the clock is running slow or fast?)

8. The generalization is similar to the foregoing situations, except that the distance between $X_1$ and $X_2$ is fixed but unknown. When fixed on a number line, that distance is $|x_1 - x_2|$, and the time required for a sound wave to travel that distance is

$$t = \left(|x_1 - x_2| \text{ ft} \div 1100 \text{ ft/sec}\right)$$

seconds. The receiver-clock error is

$$e = \frac{1}{2}\left(t_1 + t_2 - |x_1 - x_2|\text{ft} \div 1100\text{ft/sec}\right)$$

$$= \frac{1}{2}\left(t_1 + t_2\right) - \frac{1}{2200}|x_1 - x_2|\text{sec.}$$

The distance from $x_1$ to $P$ is

$$d_1 = 550\left(t_1 - t_2 + |x_1 - x_2|\text{ft} \div 1100\text{ft/sec}\right)$$

$$= 550\left(t_1 - t_2\right) + \frac{1}{2}|x_1 - x_2|\text{ft.}$$

In a similar manner, we have

$$d_2 = 550(t_2 - t_1) + \frac{1}{2}|x_1 - x_2|\text{ft}.$$

## Investigation 2—Determining Position in Two Dimensions

1. The situation is discussed at length in the section "A Closer Look" beginning on page 122.

2. Record 4 (ship's position): $x = 7.993$, $y = 5.666$; record 5 (ship's position): $x = 9$, $y = 6$

3. The ship is at $(5, 8)$.

## Investigation 3—Determining Position in Two Dimensions: Clock Error

1. Ship's position: (0.9406, 0.5290)

   Clock error: receiver clock is 0.0000006 second faster than the transmitter clocks

2. Receiver position: (–2/3, 11.9257)

   Clock error: receiver clock is 0.0000025 second faster than the transmitter clocks

3. Receiver position: (2.17458, 1.95609)

   Clock error: receiver clock is 0.000005 second slower than the transmitter clocks

4. Receiver position: (0, 3)

   Clock error: receiver clock is 0.000008 second faster than the transmitter clocks

## Investigation 4—Determining Position in Three Dimensions

1. (a)   18,456 mi ÷ 186,000 mi/sec = 0.099226 sec

   (b) The receiver clock will determine a travel time of 0.099326 second. Then,

   $$0.099326 \text{ sec} \cdot 186,000 \frac{\text{mi}}{\text{sec}} = 18,474.6 \text{ mi.}$$

   The error is slightly less than 19 miles.

   Be sure to discuss the issue of significant digits in this context. This problem highlights the dilemma of using extremely precise readings from the GPS (for example, time given in thousandths or ten-thousandths of a second) in calculations with estimates having, perhaps, two- or three-digit precision (for example, the speed of sound or light). Clearly, the resulting calculations will not be as precise as those above indicate. The digits are retained here simply to illustrate the steps in the computations.

   (c) A difference of 378 miles exists between the actual and computed distances, and

   $$378 \text{ mi} \div 186,000 \text{ mi/sec} = 0.002032 \text{ sec.}$$

   The receiver clock is 0.002032 second slow.

2. A satellite signal will take 0.051153 second to travel the distance from *S* to *H*.

3. Longitude, latitude, and altitude are more useful and familiar in GPS applications involving location, navigation, mapping, and tracking.

### Investigations 5–7

These investigations are discussed in the body of this unit.

### Investigation 8—Information at Your Fingertips: Exploring Position and Navigation

This investigation illustrates for students how GPS information is used in navigation.

### Investigation 9—Information at Your Fingertips: GPS Navigation

For the approach to the Little Mantrap Lake fishing application, refer to the sketch at the left. We know that *AB* is 10.8 kilometers and that *BP* is 2.42 kilometers. We can determine that the measure of ∠*BAP* is 11.8 degrees, the difference between the bearing from point *A* and the current track at point *P*. From the diagram, we can see that *PC*, representing the cross-track error, is 7 degrees west of north. We can then determine that ∠*BPC* measures 35.4 degrees because the bearing at *P* is 317.6 degrees. Therefore, ∠*B* measures 54.6 degrees.

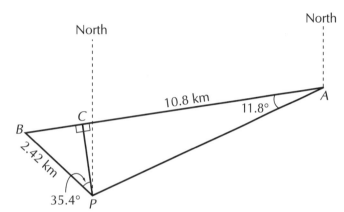

Using trigonometry, we determine that the cross-track error is approximately 1.97 kilometers and that *BC* is approximately 1.40 kilometers; thus, *CA* measures 9.40 kilometers. We can then determine that *P* is approximately 9.6 kilometers from *A*.

The boat should be steered to the right (starboard) 66.4 degrees or until the GPS readings for bearing and track are the same (317.6° – 251.2° = 66.4°). The boater should monitor the bearing and track and maintain the starboard course until GPS distance shows 0 km on the navigation screen.

### Investigation 10—Information at Your Fingertips: GPS Navigation Routes

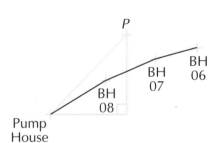

To determine the hikers' location, *P,* in Bryce Canyon National Park, compare the latitude and longitude shown on the GPS position screen with the waypoints given in the table. The latitude of 37° 38′ 25.7″ is approximately one-fifth the vertical distance from waypoint 07 to waypoint 06. Likewise, the longitude of 112° 12′ 21.3″ is just over one-seventh the horizontal distance from waypoint 08 to waypoint 07. Using a ruler, we can carefully position point *P,* as shown.

To determine the missing distance and bearing, draw a right triangle that includes a hypotenuse from *P* to the Pump House. With a ruler, approximate the distance in the drawing from *P* to the Pump House, then use the scale provided with the map to determine an actual distance of approximately 0.54 mile. Use trigonometry to determine that in the right triangle, the acute angle at *P* is approximately 35.4 degrees. Add this measurement to 180 degrees to get the bearing 215.4 degrees. Because the hikers' current heading is 207 degrees, they should turn approximately 8 degrees to the right.

# Communicating through Space

## Advanced Communication Systems

Our improved ability to receive television signals in our homes is one visible example of how NASA's research in advanced communication systems affects us daily. Only a short time ago, television signals originated from a limited number of local and network television stations. Those stations used omnidirectional broadcast systems, which were limited in radiating their broadcast signals to the geographic horizon. The signals decayed in strength in relation to the square of the distance from the station to the receiver. Hills, valleys, and buildings also interfered with those straight-line signals.

Home television reception of many channels and an improved signal are products of communication technology developed and tested in orbit by NASA in the 1960s and 1970s. This effort led to the development, manufacture, and operation of commercial communication satellites. Satellite communication of television signals paved the way for cable television and satellite transmission. Cable companies invested in powerful satellite-dish receivers and miles of cable to individual homes. Those technological advances allowed the reception of many channels and improved the quality of the transmission. Now, many people have home satellite dishes and receive satellite transmission directly into their homes. More recently, the concept of direct television has become popular even in areas where cable and broadcast television are available. Direct television gives access to 100 or more television channels, including special "packages" of programming, such as sports.

The success of the television industry is one example of how NASA technology has affected the communication industry. Today, the United States leads the world in advanced communication systems, a position that has had a positive impact on our economy. To remain competitive, NASA and its industry partners continue to explore new communication technologies. The purpose of this effort is to allow our communication industries to meet worldwide needs.

Another example of the joint effort of NASA and industry in the field of communication systems is the Advanced Communications Technology Satellite. This large and highly innovative satellite was launched in September 1993. During its time in orbit, it has been used by more than eighty organizations in field trials of advanced communication applications designed to increase communication performance while reducing operational costs. The results of these trials indicate that the potential exists to make practicable such services as remote medical-imaging diagnostics, global personal communications, real-time television for airliners, the direct transmission of image data to battlefield commanders, the interconnection of distantly located super-computers, and high-speed off-ramps for the National Information Infrastructure. NASA continues to provide the technology that fuels the communication industry, an important segment of our economy.

# Communicating through Space

On July 4, 1997, observers on Earth watched their television screens in amazement as NASA's Mars Pathfinder landed on the Red Planet and began to transmit images from the surface of our planetary neighbor. During the days and weeks that followed, terrestrial viewers saw Pathfinder deploy the small robot Sojourner and watched as Sojourner explored the Martian landscape, sending never-before-seen pictures of another world to viewers on Earth, images that were received almost "live" (see figs. 5.1 and 5.2).

In this age of satellites and modern telecommunications, we have become accustomed to seeing images of galaxies millions of light-years away or current events broadcast directly to our television screens as they happen on the other side of Earth; for this reason, we may have given little thought to those stunning views from the surface of Mars. But how did we get those pictures from a planet tens of millions of miles away? The Mars landing craft did not return to Earth. Neither did it beam back tiny canisters of film to be hurried to the local one-hour photo booth. The answer, which may sound like science fiction, is in fact, an indispensable form of mathematical communication that now permeates our lives.

To appreciate the complexities of this type of communication requires an understanding of the basics of telemetry, the technique by which the images are converted into data that can be transmitted via radio signals to receivers at distant locations, where the data are interpreted and translated back into visual images. This unit introduces three crucial problems associated with this process:

1. Information is gathered by a sensor that detects radiation from an object. An ordinary camera, for example, detects light reflected from the subject of interest and focuses that light through a lens system onto a photosensitive film or plate, causing the film to be exposed in a manner that replicates the appearance of the original object. Other kinds of sensors are used by NASA to study such things as the temperature of the oceans, the amount of ozone in the atmosphere, and the extent of the polar ice caps. Whatever the nature of the data, they must be represented in a manner that permits their communication to remote receivers; finding a way to represent the data mathematically, then, is the first problem.

2. The amount of data that must be communicated, even to transmit a single black-and-white image, is enormous and, thus, costly in

Given that the distance between Earth and Mars ranges from about 50 million to about 235 million miles, images captured on Mars take 5 to 20 minutes to reach Earth, even though the images travel at the speed of light.

Fig. 5.1. The Mars Sojourner rover visits the rock named Yogi.

Fig. 5.2. The Martian landscape as seen by the Mars Pathfinder

We live in a time of extraordinary and accelerating change. New knowledge, tools, and ways of doing and communicating mathematics continue to emerge and evolve.

*(NCTM 2000, p. 4)*

[A] major goal of high school mathematics is to equip students with knowledge and tools that enable them to formulate, approach, and solve problems beyond those that they have studied.

(NCTM 2000, p. 335)

terms of both time and technology. Consequently, to achieve greater efficiency, scientists turn to mathematics to solve the second problem: finding ways to minimize, or compress, the data that must be sent.

3. The data must be transmitted across exceedingly long distances through the "noisy" environment of space, where such factors as atmospheric conditions, sunspots, solar flares, electromagnetic radiation, and other influences can interfere in unpredictable ways to distort the signal and introduce errors into the data stream. As a result, mathematical strategies are sought for detecting and correcting data errors whenever possible.

This unit provides a basis for understanding the mathematical aspects of these three telecommunication problems.

# Problem 1: Representing Image Data

Suppose we want to send a picture from the surface of Mars. The first thing we must do is represent the image as a set of data that can be transmitted as a radio signal to receivers on Earth. Because those receivers involve computers and because all communication with computers is ultimately binary, the information must be digitized—that is, presented as binary data, which are represented as 0's and 1's. Communication in a binary system offers only two possibilities for any message. For example, a location on a computer disk is magnetized either positively or negatively; a location on a punch-card either has a hole or it does not; a statement is either true or false; a switch is either on or off, open or closed, up or down, in or out. The digitized data are transmitted to a receiver on Earth or are stored on magnetic tape for transmission at a later time. Delayed transmission may be necessary if, for example, the spacecraft is about to pass behind a planet, where signals would be blocked. Radio signals to Earth are received by a system of large dish antennas called the Deep Space Network (DSN), which is made up of three stations around the globe at locations approximately 120 degrees apart. One is at Goldstone, California; a second is near Madrid, Spain; and the third is near Canberra, Australia. From these locations, the DSN is capable of providing twenty-four-hour coverage; as antennas at one location lose contact because of Earth's rotation, another station is in position to take up the reception. Data received by DSN antennas are relayed to the Jet Propulsion Laboratory in Pasadena, California, which manages the DSN. There, computers re-create the images by reading the data and converting their values to recompose the original image.

## Investigation 1—Pixels in the News

To understand what happens when a picture is digitized, have students examine some photographs in newspapers or magazines using a hand-held magnifier. Under magnification, what appears to the unaided eye as a continuous black-and-white photograph can be seen, in fact, as a collection of tiny dots in various shades of gray from white to black.

This phenomenon offers a clue about what must be done to transmit the picture of the Martian landscape: it must be encoded as a pattern of cells, or *pixels* ("picture elements"), that can be filled with appropriate shades of gray.

Figures 5.3 and 5.4 show "pictures" of Mars's smaller moon, Deimos, and of the Sun as they appeared to Mars Pathfinder; these images nicely illustrate the pixellated nature of digitized transmissions.

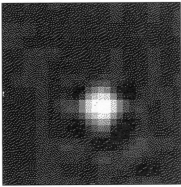

**Fig. 5.3. Image of Mars' smaller moon, Deimos, as it appeared to Mars Pathfinder**

**Fig. 5.4. This image shows Mars Pathfinder images of the Sun taken with different colors and with the Sun at different elevations in the sky. When the Sun is lower in the sky, the light passes through more dust and becomes fainter.**

A somewhat more down-to-earth analogy may help to clarify this concept. Crafters who create pictures in needlepoint or counted cross stitch work from charted designs that represent the desired image in a manner analogous to digitizing. For example, figure 5.5 is a charted design in which the picture has been divided into 575 pixels—23 columns by 25 rows—and each pixel has been filled with a symbol corresponding to the color of the stitch that is to be made in that location. In this example, a blank pixel indicates that no stitch is to be placed in that spot. When the picture is stitched using the proper colors, the rose in figure 5.6 emerges. Notice that the closer one is to the image when viewing it, the more apparent the individual pixels are; at greater distances, the colors seem to blend into a more continuous depiction. If the pixels are made smaller, the result is a smoother, more detailed rendering of the rose, as shown in figure 5.7, but the number of pixels is greatly increased, in this instance, from 575 to 2300. If more shades of pink and green are used, the resolution becomes even greater.

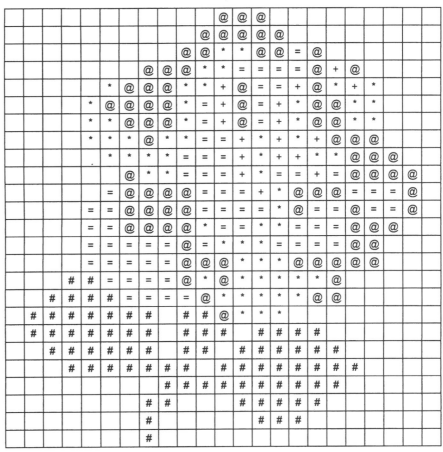

Figure 5.5. Charted design for counted cross stich. Legend:
@—medium pink; *—dark pink; =—light pink;
+—pale pink; #—medium green.

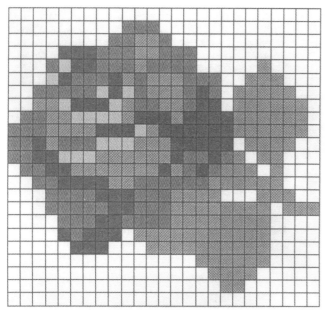

Fig. 5.6. Counted-cross-stich rose design

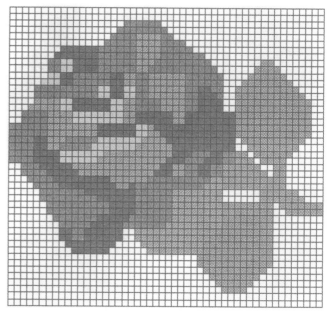

Fig. 5.7. Rose design resulting from use of smaller pixels

In grades 9–12, students' knowledge and use of representations should expand in scope and complexity.

*(NCTM 2000, p. 361)*

| Chart Symbol | Binary Code |
|:---:|:---:|
| / | 0 |
| * | 1 |
| @ | 00 |
| = | 01 |
| + | 10 |
| # | 11 |

## Investigation 2—Crafty Coding

Charts similar to the one in figure 5.5 are readily available in craft stores and craft magazines. Obtain a charted design, or copy the one in figure 5.5, and have students color the represented picture on graph paper to see how the image is developed from the symbols. Then guide students through the discussion outlined in the following paragraphs.

If we wanted to tell someone at a distant location how to reproduce the picture of the rose, we could do so by sending the symbols that occur in the cells, starting in the upper-left corner and reading from left to right across the top row, then repeating the same procedure for the second row, and so on. If we use / to represent a blank pixel, the chart would resemble the one shown in figure 5.8, and the data in row 6 would be sent as ////*@@@@*=+@=+*@@**///. Although the image of the rose is now encoded, it is not yet digitized, because we used six symbols in the code. To digitize the image, we will need a binary code.

In attempting to redefine the six symbols using the fewest number of 0's and 1's, we might come up with a code like the one shown in the margin.

Using those binary digits instead of the six symbols in the chart, row 6 would be encoded as follows:

0000100000000010110000110100000110000

```
/ / / / / / / / / / @ @ @ / / / / / / / / /
/ / / / / / / / / @ @ @ @ @ / / / / / / / /
/ / / / / / / / @ @ * * @ @ = @ / / / / / /
/ / / / / / / @ @ @ * * = = = = @ + @ / / /
/ / / / / * @ @ @ * * + @ = = + @ * + * / /
/ / / * @ @ @ @ * = + @ = + * @ @ * * / / /
/ / / * * @ @ @ * = + @ = + * @ @ * * / / /
/ / / / * * * @ * * = = + * + * + @ @ @ / /
/ / / / * * * * = = = + * + + * * @ @ @ / /
/ / / / / @ * * = = * + * = = + = @ @ @ @ /
/ / / / / = @ @ @ @ = = = + * @ @ @ = = = @
/ / / / = = @ @ @ @ = = = = * @ = = @ = = @
/ / / = = @ @ @ @ * = = * * = = = @ @ @ / /
/ / / = = = = @ = * * * = = = = @ @ / / / /
/ / / = = = = = @ @ @ * * * @ @ @ @ @ / / /
/ / # # = = = = @ * @ * * * * * @ / / / / /
/ / # # # # = = = = @ * * * * * @ @ / / / /
/ # # # # # # # / # # @ * * * / / / / / / /
/ # # # # # # # / # # # / # # # # / / / / /
/ / # # # # # # / # # / # # # # # # / / / /
/ / / # # # # # # # / # # # # # # # # / / /
/ / / / / / / / # # # # # # # # # # # / / /
/ / / / / / / / # # / / / # # # # / / / / /
/ / / / / / / / # / / / / # # # / / / / / /
/ / / / / / / / # / / / / / / / / / / / / /
```

**Fig. 5.8. Symbolic representation of rose design**

## Investigation 3—Ambiguity in the Code

Have students try decoding the line of binary symbols on page 160 using only the table given in the margin. What problems do they discover?

The binary representation given in the table introduces a new problem. We had no trouble translating the chart symbols into binary code, but the person who receives the binary message on page 160 will not be able to decode it because it is ambiguous. For example, consider the sequence of digits …00101100… that appears near the center of the row. Reading from left to right, this sequence could be translated as //*/**// or @+#@, or perhaps, /=/*+/, or any of a number of other possibilities. Translating the sequence with certainty is impossible.

To be sure that the digitized message is interpreted correctly, we need a binary code that is unambiguous. The problem in the example above arose when we began to read "001…" and could not be sure whether the first 0 represented /, whether it was the leading digit in the symbol 00 indicating @, and so on throughout the string. To put it another way, 0 is used not only as a symbol in its own right but also as the "prefix" of the symbols 00 and 01. To avoid confusion, our representation must be chosen so that no symbol is the prefix of any other.

Mathematics is one of humankind's greatest cultural achievements. It is the "language of science," providing a means by which the world around us can be represented and understood. The mathematical representations that high school students learn afford them the opportunity to understand the power and beauty of mathematics and equip them to use representations in their personal lives, in the workplace, and in further study.

(NCTM 2000, p. 364)

A set of code words has the prefix property if no code word is a prefix of any other code word.

The new code in the margin, using three binary digits for each symbol, has the desired property. To illustrate, we express row 6 of the chart using the three-digit code, as follows:

001001001010101001001001000100111011000111010101001000100100010010001001001

## Investigation 4—Does a New Code Do the Trick?

Have students complete the following tasks:

1. Try decoding the line of binary symbols above using only the table given in the margin. Does the ambiguity problem persist?

2. Identify the sets of code words that have the prefix property from the following list.

   {0, 10, 11}

   {0, 100, 101, 11, 1011}

   {000, 001, 10, 111, 1101}

   {00, 11, 010, 100, 011}

   {00, 10, 11, 1101, 0011}

3. Create a binary code for the symbols +, −, ×, ÷, $\pi$, and $\infty$ that has the prefix property.

The three-digit code shown in the chart in the margin presents no ambiguity, but clarity has been achieved at a great cost because now we must send 69 binary digits, or bits of information, to communicate the 23 symbols in row 6. To digitize the entire chart with this encoding scheme, we will need $(575 \times 3)$, or 1,725 bits. This outcome leads us to the second problem: dealing with the enormous amount of data required to send pictures from Mars.

# Problem 2: Compressing the Data

The *Voyager* spacecraft that were launched in the late 1970s explored the outer planets Jupiter, Saturn, Uranus, and Neptune using a camera system that divided images into 640,000 pixels (800 rows by 800 columns). As the camera scanned its target, a computer assigned to each of the pixels a value between 0 and 255, corresponding to the brightness of the light reflected from the particular location, where 0 signified black, 255 signified white, and the intervening numbers represented gradations in shades of gray. Each of these numbers, of course, had to be expressed in binary form (see fig. 5.9), which can be done with eight-digit binary numerals between **00000000** (black) and **11111111** (white). With this system, eight bits of information were required for each of the 640,000 pixels; to send a single black-and-white image required the transmission of 5,120,000 bits $(640,000 \times 8)$, each containing either a **0** or a **1**. When colored images are produced, the camera takes three images, or frames, in succession, each through a different colored filter (*Voyager* used blue, green, and orange filters);

| Chart Symbol | Binary Code |
|:---:|:---:|
| / | 001 |
| * | 010 |
| @ | 100 |
| = | 011 |
| + | 101 |
| # | 110 |

As recently as December 2002, NASA engineers picked up radio signals from *Pioneer 10*, which was launched more than thirty years earlier in 1972. At the time, *Pioneer 10* was beyond Pluto, 7.5 billion miles from Earth. From that distance, a radio signal traveling at the speed of light takes more than eleven hours to reach Earth.

when the data are received on Earth, the three frames are combined and blended together to produce the color image. To produce that image, however, three times as much data must be sent—15,360,000 bits for one color image. Furthermore, as we shall see later, the amount of data sent must be increased to build in additional information for error detection and correction. Finding methods to reduce the amount of data without losing information is one problem that mathematical thinking has helped to solve.

As the *Voyager* spacecraft flew by Jupiter, the nearest to Earth of the four planets it surveyed, it transmitted data to Earth at a rate of more than 100,000 bits per second. At that pace, transmission of the 5,120,000 bits that defined a single black-and-white image required nearly a minute. But as the spacecraft ventured farther out in the solar system, the quality of the radio transmission decreased; to compensate, NASA slowed the rate of data transmission so that space noise produced less interference. (Think about the difficulty of trying to understand someone who is speaking rapidly over a telephone with static on the line. "Slow down!" you tell the caller, "I can't understand you when you talk so fast.") By the time *Voyager* passed Uranus, it was transmitting at about one-sixth to one-eighth of its earlier rate, meaning that transmission of a single image would take six minutes or more. Such a situation prompts us to find a way to achieve greater efficiency.

Obviously, the distance from Earth to the planet we are trying to study cannot be changed. Nor can we increase the speed at which radio signals travel, because they are traveling at the speed of light. However, to reduce the time required to send and receive a set of data between the distant planet and Earth, we can decrease the amount of data to be sent—in other words, compress the data.

## Investigation 5—Data Transmission in the News: *Galileo*

In 1989, NASA launched the spacecraft *Galileo* on a mission to study the planet Jupiter. Plans called for the craft to descend into orbit around Jupiter in December 1995 and to transmit information about the Jovian atmosphere, as well as thousands of pictures of the giant planet. However, in 1991, the main data-transmitting antenna refused to unfurl, forcing NASA to depend on a backup antenna. Then, in October 1995, a data recorder onboard the spacecraft failed, further complicating and slowing the process of data transmission. Data-compression technology and NASA engineers came to the rescue, preventing the failure of *Galileo's* mission.

Have students read the account of the *Galileo* situation and answer the questions posed in Investigation 5 on pages 175–76. This investigation sets the stage for addressing the second problem mentioned previously, that is, finding ways to compress the data that must be transmitted.

The outer planets, Jupiter, Saturn, Uranus, Neptune, and Pluto, achieve a favorable alignment for a multiplanetary flyby only once every 176 years. Such a window occurred between 1976 and 1978, and NASA was able to take advantage of it to launch the *Voyager* probes.

Artist's Conception showing *Pioneer 11*

Photograph of Saturn from *Voyager 1*

## Computers, Codes, and Compression

Computers understand only binary numbers, that is, sequences of **0**'s and **I**'s. Each pixel in a drawing or each character in a word-processor document must be translated into a binary number for the computer to understand it. The American Standard Code for Information Interchange (ASCII) is the code that computers most frequently use for converting characters to binary numbers. In ASCII, each letter of the alphabet, each numerical digit, and each special character, such as $, &, and #, is represented by a string of seven binary digits. Even though ASCII uses only seven bits, it is always represented by eight bits with a leading bit of **0**.

ASCII is an example of a block code in which each symbol to be encoded is represented by the same number of binary digits. In Morse code, which was invented for the telegraph and was later used in radio communication by military and amateur radio operators, the length of the code word used to represent a symbol is variable. Morse code uses a system of dots and dashes to produce electrical pulses, in which the duration of the dash is three times as long as the dot and the letters and digits have different numbers of dots and dashes assigned to them. In Morse code, the letter *E*, the most-frequently used letter in the English language, is represented by a single •, whereas the less common *Q* is represented as − − • −. The assignment of shorter codes to commonly used letters, such as *E*, *T*, *A*, or *I*, and longer codes to such letters as *J*, *Q*, or *Z* means that the number of symbols required to send a paragraph of text is greatly reduced compared to what would be needed if all letters used the same number of symbols. The chart below shows the difference between the two codes for selected letters.

The method of using longer code words for less frequently used symbols and shorter code words for more frequently used symbols is one form of data compression. To explore how the frequency of letters of the alphabet affects codes, have students complete Investigation 6.

| Letter | Approx Freq. (%) | ASCII | Morse |
|--------|------------------|----------|-------|
| A | 7.9 | 01000001 | •− |
| E | 13.0 | 01000101 | • |
| L | 3.6 | 01001100 | •−•• |
| N | 7.3 | 01001110 | −• |
| P | 2.3 | 01010000 | •−−• |
| T | 9.8 | 01010100 | − |

## Investigation 6—Letters! We Get Lots and Lots of Letters!

Use Investigation 6 on pages 176–77 to have students construct a frequency table for the occurrence of letters of the alphabet in English text. The results of this activity will be used in future activities related to data compression. To introduce the "Letters" activity, discuss with students which letters appear with the greatest or least frequency in the English language.

You can obtain text samples from newspapers, magazines, and books. Try to obtain samples of different types of text, such as from different sections of the newspaper. You may want students to investigate whether their results differ for samples taken from the news or editorial pages, for example, compared with samples from the sports or entertainment sections. Make copies so that students can mark on them, and give each pair of students a different passage of text.

First, have students complete the Individual Letter-Frequency Chart on page 177. After they have finished counting the characters in their samples, combine the results from all pairs of students to complete the Class Letter-Frequency Chart on page 178. The results should be similar to the table below (taken from NCTM's *Student Math Notes* [1983]). Students should save the final letter-frequency table to use in future activities.

A number of approaches can be used to create a coding scheme that condenses data by varying the length of the symbols according to the frequency of their occurrence, but one of the oldest methods was developed by David Huffman while he was a graduate student in the 1950s. Huffman codes are developed with the aid of *binary trees,* a special kind of directed graph that is illustrated in the example that follows. The compression code that results always has the desired prefix property discussed previously.

To use Huffman's method, we first must know the relative frequencies of the symbols we want to encode. For the rose in figure 5.8, the frequencies of the six symbols are shown here.

| Letter | Frequency (Percent) |
|:------:|:-------------------:|
| A | 8.2 |
| B | 1.4 |
| C | 2.8 |
| D | 3.8 |
| E | 13.0 |
| F | 3.0 |
| G | 2.0 |
| H | 5.3 |
| I | 6.5 |
| J | 0.1 |
| K | 0.4 |
| L | 3.4 |
| M | 2.5 |
| N | 7.0 |
| O | 8.0 |
| P | 2.0 |
| Q | 0.1 |
| R | 6.8 |
| S | 6.0 |
| T | 10.5 |
| U | 2.5 |
| V | 0.9 |
| W | 1.5 |
| X | 0.2 |
| Y | 2.0 |
| Z | 0.07 |

(From "Codes and Counting" in NCTM *Student Math Notes,* January 1983)

| Symbol: | / | * | @ | = | + | # |
|---------|-----|------|------|------|-----|------|
| Frequency: | 259 | 62 | 88 | 69 | 17 | 80 |
| Percent: | 45.0 | 10.8 | 15.3 | 12.0 | 3.0 | 13.9 |

We will use the percents to construct a "Huffman tree" from the bottom up, as follows:

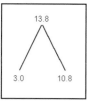

Step 1

*Step 1:* Select the two lowest frequencies, in this example, 3.0 and 10.8, and form a binary tree. For consistency, we will always place the lower frequency on the left. If this convention is not followed, a different but equivalent tree will result. Add the two frequencies, and write the sum at the vertex, as shown.

*Step 2:* Repeat step 1 using the remaining frequencies. In our example, the remaining values are 13.8, 45.0, 15.3, 12.0, and 13.9. The two lowest values in this set are 12.0 and 13.8. Use these values to form a new binary tree, as shown.

After step 2, the frequencies are reduced to four: 25.8, 45.0, 15.3, and 13.9. Of these, the least values are 13.9 and 15.3.

*Next steps:* Repeat the tree-formation process until just one binary tree results. For the example of the rose, three more steps are required, as shown below.

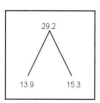

Step 2

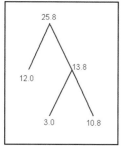

Step 3

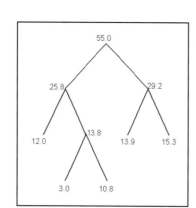

Step 4

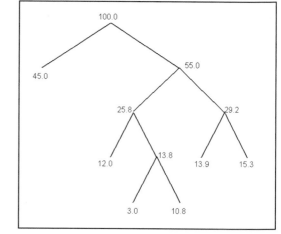

Step 5

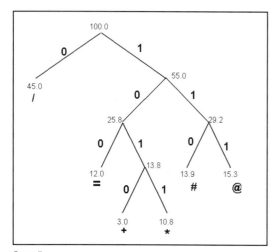

Step 5

To obtain the desired binary code, from each vertex, or node of the tree where two branches emanate, assign a value of **0** to the left branch and a value of **1** to the right branch. Next, write the original symbols next to their respective percentages at the lowest levels of the branches. Starting at the top, this final tree can now be used to read the Huffman codes for each of the symbols, as follows:

| Symbol: | / | * | @ | = | + | # |
|---|---|---|---|---|---|---|
| Huffman Code: | 0 | 1011 | 111 | 100 | 1010 | 110 |

## Investigation 7—Show Your Encoding Expertise

To test students' understanding of this method for developing a binary code, have them perform some or all of the following activities:

1. Try the foregoing procedure for developing a binary tree using the letters *A, E, L, N, P, T* and the frequencies shown in the previous table.

2. Use your Huffman code to represent such words as PLANET or PATENT or to decode the messages **010011011011101** and **110011010000110**. The Huffman code preserves the desired prefix property; therefore, it can be interpreted unambiguously.

3. Use the Class Letter-Frequency Chart from Investigation 6 to create your own Huffman tree. Begin by writing the letters in your last name; below each letter, write the frequency of occurrence according to your letter-frequency chart. (Each letter in your name should occur only once in the tree even if it is repeated in your name.) Construct a Huffman tree using the weights from the table. Assign **0** to each left branch and **1** to each right branch in your tree, and encode your last name using the Huffman code you created. Try to make some other words from the letters in your name. Encode them using your Huffman tree. Give the tree and the coded words to a classmate to decode.

To see how the Huffman code that we created previously compresses data, consider once more the picture of the rose that we want to digitize, and compare the requirements of the three-digit binary code suggested previously (on page 162) with the Huffman code. The Huffman code requires 1,286 bits, or 74.6 percent of the 1,725 bits that would be needed if each symbol was represented with a uniform 3 bits. In this example, we have compressed the data by more than 25 percent. For NASA, data compression on a large scale is essential. In the case of *Voyager*, NASA reprogrammed the spacecraft as it traveled to the more distant planets and achieved a data compression of about 60 percent to compensate for slowing the rate of transmission. As a consequence, we were able to gaze at images of worlds never before seen on Earth.

| Symbol | Frequency | Huffman Code | # Bits Compressed |
|--------|-----------|--------------|-------------------|
| / | 259 | 0 | 259 |
| * | 62 | 1011 | 248 |
| @ | 88 | 111 | 264 |
| = | 69 | 100 | 207 |
| + | 17 | 1010 | 68 |
| # | 80 | 110 | 240 |
| Total | 575 | | 1,286 |

# Problem 3: Detecting and Correcting Errors

So far, we have seen how images can be represented as binary data, and we have looked at ways to compress the data to economize on time and costs. One more consideration remains: How can we be sure that the messages we receive are accurate? In other words, if errors are introduced into the data, will we be able to detect and correct those errors? The answer is "sometimes."

The transmission of information between Earth and a spacecraft is subject to various errors caused by electromagnetic interference or equipment malfunction. The situation is similar to the old game "gossip," in which a message is whispered to a participant, who in turn whispers it to the next participant, and so on until the last participant has received the message. Frequently, the last message has little resemblance to the starting message. At the end of the game, the original message is compared with the final one, and everyone has a good laugh. In transmissions from space, scientists and engineers have found that ensuring that the message received is identical to the message sent is virtually impossible; however, they have developed techniques that can detect and correct errors in the transmission of information.

## Investigation 8—Gossip

Divide the class into teams of approximately eight members each, and have the team members form a line. The first member of the team writes down a sequence of seven digits and whispers the sequence to the second person, who in turn whispers the message to the third person, and so on. No repeats of the message are allowed. The last person in the line writes down the sequence he or she has received. Compare the original message with the message received by the last person. Did errors occur in transmission?

Have students repeat this process several times with seven-digit sequences, then experiment with sequences of fewer digits and sequences of more digits. Lead a discussion about what students discovered. Did they find that a particular sequence length transmitted accurately most of the time? Did a particular sequence length always seem to have errors in transmission? What do students propose as the causes of the transmission errors? Can they pinpoint more than one source of error?

The problems encountered with transmissions of data in the "Gossip" activity are similar to the problems encountered by NASA in the transmission of data across space. In this section, students learn some of the ways that mathematics helps NASA detect and correct errors in the transmission of data.

### Redundancy in Human Communication

In written and oral communication, errors are detected and corrected because of built-in redundancies in language. Letters or even entire words can be omitted or be written or spoken incorrectly, yet the reader or listener can still understand the message. This built-in redundancy has made the television game show *Wheel of Fortune* successful. The home viewer may be amazed that she or he can so often determine the hidden message when only a few letters have been revealed. This feat is not really that amazing; it is simply an example of redundancy in the English language.

Music, another mode of communication, also has built-in redundancies that enable trained musicians, and sometimes even untrained listeners, to detect errors. A sour note is obvious to all listeners even though they may not immediately know how to fix it. Someone once said that the professional musician is not one who never makes mistakes but one who knows how to cover up mistakes so that they are not noticed. The musician does his or her own error correction.

Mathematicians and engineers have used various methods to build redundancy into communication. A simplified diagram of the process of error correction is shown in the margin.

## Investigation 9—Wheel of Fortune

Have students complete the phrases given in Investigation 9 on pages 178–79. Most are familiar proverbs or idiomatic expressions, such as "A stitch in time saves nine."

*Experimenting with Error Detection and Correction: The Switch*

Ask students to imagine the following scenario:

*You are the controller for an unmanned Earth-orbiting satellite, and you need to know the position of a certain switch on the spacecraft. The spacecraft transmits all information in the form of strings of binary digits, that is, sequences of 0's and 1's, where 0 means "switch off" and 1 means "switch on."*

*Suppose that you receive a 0 from the spacecraft, indicating that the switch is off. Is the 0 correct? How would you know? What could you do to increase the likelihood of receiving a correct message? Can you think of a way to add redundancy to the message to enable you to detect and correct an error?*

*One form of redundancy is to repeat the message. That is, off = 0 would be sent as 00; on = 1 would be sent as 11. If the received message is 10 or 01, you would know that an error had occurred, but you would not know which bit, or digit, was in error. In other words, the error could be detected but not corrected. Of course, if two errors had occurred and you received the message as 00 or 11, you would never know about the problem. This form of redundancy assumes that only one error will occur and employs a code that will detect just one error.*

*Repeating each digit twice increases our level of confidence; in this code, off = 0 would be sent as 000 and on = 1 would be sent as 111. This time, if you received the messages 100, 010, or 001, you would know that an error had occurred. Assuming that only one error*

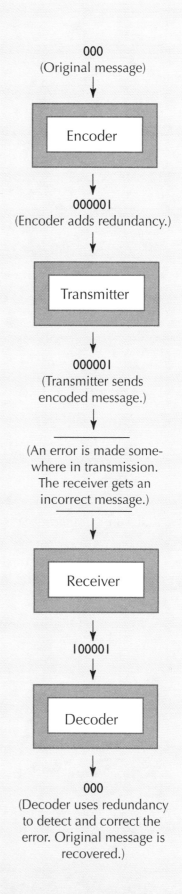

000
(Original message)

↓

Encoder

↓

000000
(Encoder adds redundancy.)

↓

Transmitter

↓

000000
(Transmitter sends encoded message.)

――――

(An error is made somewhere in transmission. The receiver gets an incorrect message.)

――――

↓

Receiver

↓

100001

↓

Decoder

↓

000
(Decoder uses redundancy to detect and correct the error. Original message is recovered.)

*occurred, you would translate any of those three messages as **000** because each of them differs from **000** in only one digit. Similarly, any of the messages **011**, **101**, or **110** would be translated as **111**. Again, however, this coding scheme can detect and correct only one error. Of course, the possibility exists that two errors might occur; for example, you might receive the message **110**, which should actually be read as **000**. This system would not detect two errors but would, instead, assume that only one error occurred and change the **110** to **111**.*

Obviously, redundancy runs counter to our efforts to economize on the amount of data transmitted. The example above requires us to triple the amount of data sent. As the lengths of the code words increase, the situation becomes more complex. In the previous example, only two message words were involved, **0** and **1**, which were tripled to produce the code words **000** and **111**. For a three-digit binary number, only eight possibilities exist, our two desired codes and six others. As we have seen, three of those others differ from **000** in one digit (that is, they have distance 1 from **000**) and are corrected to read **000**; the other three are distance 1 from **111** and are corrected to read **111**. If we had four message words (**00**, **01**, **10**, and **11**) in our system, however, tripling the message would produce four 6-bit code words: **000000**, **010101**, **101010**, and **111111**. The number of possible 6-bit combinations of 0's and 1's is $2^6$, or 64; 24 of these combinations are distance 1 from one of the four code words, meaning that single errors can be both detected and corrected, as follows:

| If any of the following messages is received … | Translate it as … | Original message was … |
| --- | --- | --- |
| 100000, 010000, 001000, 000100, 000010, 000001 | 000000 | 00 |
| 110101, 000101, 011101, 010001, 010111, 010100 | 010101 | 01 |
| 001010, 111010, 100010, 101110, 101000, 101011 | 101010 | 10 |
| 011111, 101111, 110111, 111011, 111101, 111110 | 111111 | 11 |

The other thirty-six combinations represent two or more errors that can be detected but not corrected.

### Error-Detecting and Error-Correcting Codes

Any scheme for error correction will involve adding information to the original message before it is sent. When the message is received, the additional information is used to interpret the message, evaluate it for errors, correct the errors if possible, and reproduce the original data. Using redundancy is one way to add information, but perhaps we can find a scheme that will not require so much extra input.

One approach to this problem is to add what are called check digits to the original message. An everyday application that uses a check digit for error detection is the ZIP code used by the U. S. Postal Service and the bar-coded "ZIP strip" that appears beneath the address on the cards and letters we receive. The following paragraphs use ZIP codes to illustrate error detection and correction.

Originally, ZIP codes consisted of five digits. The left-most digit corresponds to one of ten large regions of the United States, with 0 in New England (Agawa, Massachusetts, has the lowest ZIP code in the fifty states: 01001) and increasing in a generally westward direction to 9 on the West Coast (Wrangell, AK 99929). The second and third digits correspond to smaller regions in a state. For example, Michigan ZIP codes range from 480XX through 499XX; the digits 80 through 99 denote subregions in the state. The final two digits direct the letter to the local post office in the subarea. In rural areas and smaller towns, these last two digits are usually assigned to local post offices in alphabetical order (in the 499XX area, for example, Ahmeek has ZIP code 49901, whereas White Pine has 49971); in urban areas with multiple ZIP codes, the last two digits denote a local delivery zone. Later, the Postal Service adopted nine-digit "ZIP + 4" codes and, more recently, eleven-digit codes, in which the additional digits further direct the letter to the particular street, block, and address of its destination.

The underpinnings of everyday life are increasingly mathematical and technological.

*(NCTM 2000, p. 4)*

To the five or nine or eleven digits that we write when we address an envelope, the post office appends one additional check digit that is seen only in the bar code; the check digit is the number that must be added to the sum of the ZIP-code digits to make the total a multiple of ten. For example, the ZIP code of NASA's Glenn Research Center (GRC) in Cleveland,

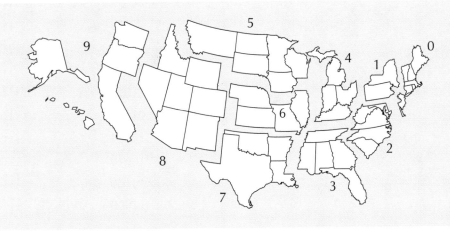

Ohio, is 44135. Adding the digits of the ZIP code yields 17, so the check digit is 3 because 17 + 3 = 20. Ask students, "What would the check digit be for GRC's ZIP + 4 code of 44135–3191?"

To automate the sorting of mail, the ZIP codes are transformed into a bar code that can be read by a scanner. Each digit in a ZIP code is encoded with five binary digits, or bars; the short bars in the code represent 0's, and the long bars represent 1s. A five-digit ZIP code consists of thirty-two bars that encode the five digits of the ZIP code plus one check digit; the ZIP + 4 bar code has fifty-two bars to encode the nine-digit ZIP code and one check digit. The bar codes always begin and end with a long bar, or 1; these bars, called *guard bars,* signal that a code is enclosed between them.

## Investigation 10—Speeding the Mail with ZIP + 4

Investigation 10 illustrates one example of the use of codes and check digits in everyday life. Bar codes are a rich area for further study of codes through student research and projects. Other examples of codes used in everyday life that could be topics for student research are the ISBN code used internationally for books; the UPC used by merchandisers to code products for sale; the codes used by banks, airlines, automobile manufacturers, and parcel delivery services; and the Soundex code used for genealogical research.

In Investigation 10, students should discover the codes for the digits 0 through 9. Notice that each 5-bit symbol for a digit is composed of three short bars (0's) and two long bars (I's). Conveniently, ten 5-bit combinations with exactly two I's are possible, and these combinations are assigned to the digits in increasing order (if 0 is considered as being greater than 9).

| Binary Code | Bar code | Digit |
|---|---|---|
| 00011 | ıııll | 1 |
| 00101 | ıılıl | 2 |
| 00110 | ııllı | 3 |
| 01001 | ılııl | 4 |
| 01010 | ılılı | 5 |
| 01100 | ıllıı | 6 |
| 10001 | lıııl | 7 |
| 10010 | lıılı | 8 |
| 10100 | lılıı | 9 |
| 11000 | llııı | 0 |

An envelope addressed to NASA's Glenn Research Center (GRC) in Cleveland, Ohio, ZIP code 44135–3191, would bear this ZIP strip:

lıluılılııluıllııllııllıılıuılluıılllılıuıulllılıul

To decode the GRC bar code, cross out the first and last long bars (the guard bars) and divide the remaining fifty bars into blocks of five. These bars are the nine digits of the ZIP code and the check digit, which can now be read using the codes in the table, as follows:

l   ılııl   ılııl   ıııll   ıllıı   ılılı   ıllıı   ıııll   lılıı   ıııll   lılıı   l
    4      4      1      3      5      3      1      9      1      9

How does the check digit serve as an error-detection, error-correction device? For convenience, consider only the five-digit GRC ZIP code, with check-digit 3, and its digitized ZIP strip. For ease of reading, the ZIP strip is separated into its component parts:

| ılııl ılııl ıııll ıllıı ılılı ıllıı |

The following are some possible error scenarios and their outcomes with the check digit as an error-detection, error-correction device:

1. A single error occurs in one of the blocks of five bars. For example, the message is transmitted as

   | ılııl ılııl ıılll ıllıı ılılı ıllıı |.

   The appearance of three long bars in the third block indicates that an error has occurred in that digit, but the rest of the digits can be interpreted, yielding 44E353. Because the sum of the six digits must be a multiple of 10, we can solve the resulting equation, $E + 19 = 10n$, and determine that $E$ must be 1. A single error in one block can be detected and corrected.

2. Two errors occur, one in each of two different blocks. For example, the message is received as

   | ılııl llııl ıııl ıllıı ılılı ıllıı |.

   By inspection, we can determine that errors occurred in the second and third blocks, because they have either one or three long bars. The message we receive is 4EF353, and we know that $E + F + 15 = 10n$, but we cannot determine $E$ and $F$. Either $E + F = 5$ or $E + F = 15$, but any of the pairs (0, 5), (1, 4), (2, 3), (3, 2), (4, 1), (5, 0), (6, 9), (7, 8), (8, 7), or (9, 6) is a possible solution. In this example, the two errors can be detected but not corrected.

3. Two errors occur in the same block, and the result is not another coded digit. For example, the message reads

   | ılııl ılııl llıll ıllıı ılılı ıllıı |.

   Again, we see by inspection that the third block contains two errors, but because llıll is not another digit, the situation is the same as the first example above. The error can be detected and corrected.

4. Two errors occur in the same block, but the result is another coded digit. For example, the message reads

   | ılııl ılııl ıllıı ıllıı ılılı ıllıı |

   where the third block has been sent as ıllıı instead of ıııll. Because ıllıı is a valid digit, the message is interpreted as 446353. Given that the sum of the digits is 25, we know that an error has occurred somewhere, but we are not able to determine where the error occurred, nor can we correct it.

5. Two digits are transposed. For example, the message

| ‖ .⅃‖ ⅃⅃ .⅃‖ ⅃⅃ .⅃ .⅃ |

is received and decoded as 414353. The error is neither detected nor corrected.

Task 5 in Investigation 10 asks students to examine several ZIP-code bar codes to detect, and when possible, correct, errors.

The ZIP strip is a relatively simple system that is able to detect and correct errors under certain conditions. More powerful systems for error detection and correction are possible, but they require more than just one check digit, and the mathematics becomes more complex. The extension titled "Other Coding Schemes" presents additional examples.

*Conclusion*

Numerous forms of telecommunication enter our lives daily. For every television show we watch, every fax we send, every CD or DVD we play, every bar code we have scanned in the checkout line, data are digitized, compressed, transmitted, analyzed, and interpreted. During the early decades of the twenty-first century, NASA will launch more robotic missions to Mars, to be followed in due time by manned missions; the ISS will become fully operational in Earth orbit; other voyages of exploration will enable humans to look deeper into space; and Earth-orbiting satellites will continue to study our home planet using remote sensing. As the images that come from these endeavors reach our computers, television sets, and newspapers, students should gain a heightened awareness of, and appreciation for, the unwritten caption that could accompany each of them: "This awesome image made possible by mathematics."

This "picture" of the planet Saturn was assembled from images obtained from the *Voyager 2* spacecraft in 1981. The image is not really a photograph in the sense that we think of photographs as images recorded on film. Instead, the image is composed of a pattern of dots assigned various shades of gray, from white to black, which measure the brightness of the light reflected from the planet.

## Investigation 5—Data Transmission in the News: *Galileo*

In 1989, NASA launched the spacecraft *Galileo* on a mission to study the planet Jupiter. Plans called for the craft to descend into orbit around Jupiter in December 1995 and to transmit information about the Jovian atmosphere, as well as thousands of pictures of the giant planet. However, in 1991, the main data-transmitting antenna refused to unfurl, forcing NASA to depend on a backup antenna. Then, in October 1995, a data recorder onboard the spacecraft failed, further complicating and slowing the process of data transmission. As the following excerpt from *Newsweek* magazine shows, data-compression technology and NASA engineers came to the rescue, preventing the failure of *Galileo*'s mission.

Read the excerpt from *Newsweek* below, then answer the questions that follow.

> *The first spacecraft to circle a giant planet for an extended time,* Galileo *will probe Jupiter's weather, photograph four of its 16 moons, investigate what makes its wind alternate direction and try to figure out what creates its colors....*
>
> *All this is possible only because NASA's space jocks performed the equivalent of a long-distance brain transplant. After losing the main antenna,* Galileo *had to rely on a backup that normally transmits no more than 16 bits per second, compared with the main antenna's 134,000. At that rate, scientists would have been receiving* Galileo's *data for years.... So, starting in March, the ground team reprogrammed* Galileo's *computers to compress the data they sent and eliminate the boring stuff (like black pictures of empty space). Such a maneuver had never been attempted before, says the JPL's Walt Hoffman, who likens it to "upgrading your word processor while you're using it." For 26 days the computer team radioed up digital code that rewrote on-board software. It was a feat akin to sending instructions over your modem in San Jose to reprogram a computer in Tokyo—except that this computer was speeding through space at 18,000 mph. The fix upped the data rate to 160 bits per second. That should allow* Galileo *to accomplish about 70% of its goals, though it will send no more than 4000 photos instead of the 50,000 once planned. (From "The Spacecraft That Could," Newsweek, 18 December 1995)*

1. What was the data-transmission rate of *Galileo*'s main antenna?

2. What was the transmission rate of the backup antenna?

3. What transmission rate was NASA able to achieve after reprogramming *Galileo*'s computers?

4. What fraction of the original rate was NASA able to achieve?

5. If each image is divided into a grid of 800 by 800 pixels and each pixel requires 8 bits to be transmitted, how many bits are required for the transmission of one image?

6. How much time would be required for *Galileo* to transmit one image using the original main-antenna rate?

7. At the original rate, how much time would have been required to transmit the 50,000 images of Jupiter that were originally planned?

8. How much time would be required to transmit one image using the backup antenna if the *Galileo* software had not been altered?

9. How much time would have been required to send the 50,000 images of Jupiter if the software had not been altered?

10. How much time was required to transmit one image after the *Galileo* software was changed?

11. How much time will be required to transmit the 4,000 images that were subsequently planned?

Note: The assumption here is that NASA scientists did not actually increase the transmission rate of the backup antenna, because doing so would have required a hardware change. Instead, they achieved a pseudo-rate of 160 bits per second (bps). That is, the data were compressed enough so that the transmission rate was the equivalent of 160 bps.

## Investigation 6—Letters! We Get Lots and Lots of Letters!

Suppose you picked up a newspaper or a book and counted the number of times each letter in the alphabet appears. Ask yourself the following questions:

✦ Which letter do you think would appear most frequently?

✦ Which letters would rank in the top five in frequency of occurrence?

✦ Which letter do you think would appear least frequently?

✦ Which letters would rank in the bottom five in frequency of occurrence?

Obtain a sample of text from your teacher, and, with your partner, complete the following activities:

1. Mark the text in groups of 10 letters. Continue until you have counted 300 letters. For example:

   A giant, gase / ous planet, S / aturn has an / intriguing / atmosphere /

2. Use tally marks to count the number of times each letter occurs in your text sample, and complete the Individual Letter-Frequency Chart. The easiest way to perform this task is for one partner to read the letter and the other partner to mark the tally in the chart.

3. Combine your results with those of other pairs of students in the class, and complete the Class Letter-Frequency Chart. Save this chart for future use.

4. How close are the class results to your predictions? How many of the top five letters did you predict? How many of the bottom five did you predict?

5. Write a paragraph summarizing the results shown in the Class Letter-Frequency Chart.

### Individual Letter Frequency Chart
*(Based on 300 Characters of English Text)*

| Letter | Tally | Total | Frequency (Percent) |
|--------|-------|-------|---------------------|
| A | | | |
| B | | | |
| C | | | |
| D | | | |
| E | | | |
| F | | | |
| G | | | |
| H | | | |
| I | | | |
| J | | | |
| K | | | |
| L | | | |
| M | | | |
| N | | | |
| O | | | |
| P | | | |
| Q | | | |
| R | | | |
| S | | | |
| T | | | |
| U | | | |
| V | | | |
| W | | | |
| X | | | |
| Y | | | |
| Z | | | |

## Class Letter Frequency Chart
*(Based on _____ Characters of English Text)*

| Letter | Tally | Total | Frequency (Percent) |
|--------|-------|-------|---------------------|
| A | | | |
| B | | | |
| C | | | |
| D | | | |
| E | | | |
| F | | | |
| G | | | |
| H | | | |
| I | | | |
| J | | | |
| K | | | |
| L | | | |
| M | | | |
| N | | | |
| O | | | |
| P | | | |
| Q | | | |
| R | | | |
| S | | | |
| T | | | |
| U | | | |
| V | | | |
| W | | | |
| X | | | |
| Y | | | |
| Z | | | |

## Investigation 9—Wheel of Fortune

In written and oral communication, errors are detected and corrected because of built-in redundancies in language. Letters or even entire words can be omitted or written or spoken incorrectly, yet the reader or listener can still understand the message. This built-in redundancy has made the television game show *Wheel of Fortune* successful. The home viewer may be amazed that she or he can so often determine the hidden message when only a few letters have been revealed. This feat is not really that amazing; it is simply an example of redundancy in the English language.

Complete as many of the following phrases as you can. Most are familiar proverbs or idiomatic expressions, such as "A stitch in time saves nine."

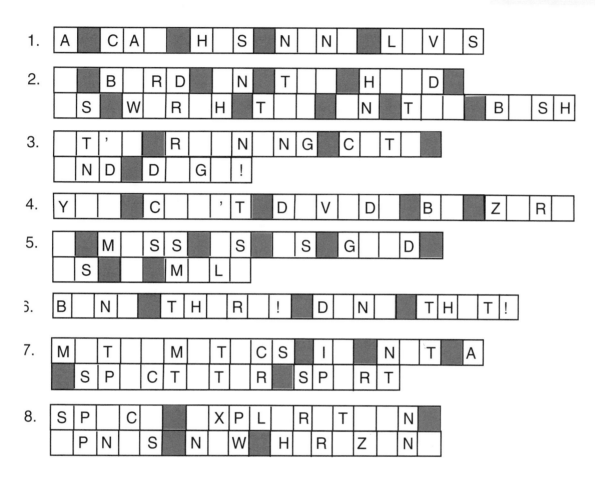

1. | A | | C | A | | | H | | S | | N | | N | | | L | | V | | S |

2. | | | B | | R | D | | | N | | T | | | | H | | | D | |
   | | S | | W | | R | | H | | T | | | | | N | | T | | | | | B | | S | H |

3. | | T | ' | | | R | | | N | | N | G | | C | | T | | |
   | | N | D | | | D | | | G | | ! |

4. | Y | | | | C | | | ' | T | | D | | V | | D | | | B | | | Z | | R | |

5. | | | M | | S | S | | | S | | | S | | G | | | D | |
   | | S | | | | | M | | L |

6. | B | | N | | | | T | H | | R | | ! | | D | | N | | | | T | H | | T | ! |

7. | M | | T | | | M | | T | | C | S | | I | | | | N | | T | | A |
   | | | S | P | | C | T | | T | | R | | S | P | | R | T |

8. | S | P | | | C | | | | | X | P | L | | R | | T | | | | N | |
   | | | P | N | | S | | | N | | W | | | H | | R | | Z | | N | |

## Investigation 10—Speeding the Mail with ZIP + 4

1. The nine patterns below each correspond to one of the ZIP codes listed. Break the code, and match the pattern with its corresponding ZIP code.

   (a) ‖ııı‖ıı‖ıı‖ıı‖ıı‖ıı‖ı‖ı‖ıı‖ı      ___ 90210

   (b) ‖ıı‖ıı‖ıı‖ı‖ı‖ıı‖ı‖ıı‖ı‖ı‖ı‖      ___ 53981

   (c) ‖ıı‖ı‖‖ı‖ıı‖ıı‖ıı‖ı‖ıı‖ı‖ı‖      ___ 69794

   (d) ‖‖ıııı‖ı‖ı‖ıı‖ı‖ı‖ı‖‖ı‖ı‖      ___ 12882

   (e) ‖ı‖ıı‖ıııı‖ı‖ıı‖‖‖ıı‖ıı‖ı      ___ 78964

   (f) ı‖ıı‖ı‖ı‖ı‖‖ıııı‖ıı‖ı‖‖ıııı‖‖      ___ 39048

   (g) ı‖ı‖‖ı‖ı‖ıı‖ıııı‖ıı‖‖ıı‖ı‖ı‖ı      ___ 29857

   (h) ı‖ı‖ı‖ı‖ı‖ıı‖‖ı‖ıı‖ı‖ı‖ı‖ı      ___ 45046

   (i) ı‖ı‖ıı‖‖ı‖ı‖ı‖ı‖ıı‖‖ı‖ıı‖‖      ___ 03823

2. Enter the bar code and the corresponding binary code for each digit.

| Decimal Digit | Bar Code | Binary Code |
|---|---|---|
| 1 | | |
| 2 | | |
| 3 | | |
| 4 | | |
| 5 | | |
| 6 | | |
| 7 | | |
| 8 | | |
| 9 | | |
| 0 | | |

3. Identify the following ZIP + 4 bar codes:

(a) ‖₁₁‖₁‖₁‖₁‖‖‖₁₁‖‖₁₁‖‖₁‖₁‖₁‖₁‖₁₁‖₁‖₁‖‖₁₁‖₁‖₁

(b) ‖₁‖₁‖‖₁‖₁‖₁‖₁‖₁‖₁‖₁‖₁‖₁₁‖‖₁‖₁‖₁‖₁‖‖₁‖₁

(c) ‖₁‖₁‖₁‖‖₁‖₁‖₁‖₁‖‖‖₁₁‖‖₁₁‖‖₁‖₁‖₁‖₁

(d) ‖₁‖‖₁‖₁‖₁₁₁‖‖₁‖‖‖₁₁₁‖₁₁‖‖₁₁‖₁‖₁‖₁‖‖‖

(e) ‖₁‖₁‖₁₁‖‖₁‖₁‖₁‖‖₁‖₁₁₁‖‖‖₁₁‖₁‖₁‖‖‖

(f) ‖‖₁‖₁₁‖₁‖‖‖₁₁‖‖₁₁‖₁‖₁₁‖‖‖‖₁₁‖‖₁₁‖₁‖₁

(g) ‖₁₁‖‖₁₁‖₁‖‖₁₁‖₁₁₁‖‖‖‖₁‖‖₁‖₁‖₁‖₁‖₁‖₁₁₁‖‖₁₁‖‖₁₁

(h) ‖₁‖₁‖₁‖‖‖₁₁‖₁‖₁‖‖‖‖₁₁‖‖‖₁‖₁‖₁‖₁‖₁₁‖‖‖₁‖₁‖₁

(i) ‖₁‖‖₁₁₁‖‖‖‖‖‖₁₁‖‖₁₁‖₁‖₁‖₁‖₁‖₁‖₁‖₁‖‖‖‖₁₁‖‖₁‖₁

4. The ZIP + 4 code for the NASA Marshall Space Flight Center, Huntsville, Alabama, is 35812–0001. Write a bar code for this ZIP code. Remember to include the check digit and the guard bars.

5. Examine the ZIP-code bar codes below for errors. Find the errors, and correct the ZIP codes when possible.

(a) ‖₁‖₁‖‖‖₁₁₁₁₁‖‖‖₁‖₁‖₁₁₁₁‖‖₁₁‖₁‖‖₁‖₁‖₁‖₁‖₁₁‖‖‖₁‖₁‖₁‖₁

(b) ‖‖‖₁₁₁₁‖₁₁‖₁‖₁‖₁₁‖‖₁₁‖‖₁‖₁‖₁‖₁‖₁‖₁₁‖‖‖‖₁‖₁‖₁₁

(c) ‖₁‖₁‖‖₁₁‖₁‖‖₁₁‖₁‖₁‖‖₁₁₁‖‖‖‖‖₁‖₁‖₁‖₁‖‖‖‖₁₁‖₁

(d) ‖₁‖₁₁‖‖₁‖₁‖₁‖‖₁₁‖‖‖₁₁‖₁‖₁‖₁‖₁‖₁‖‖₁‖₁₁‖₁‖‖‖₁₁₁₁‖‖₁

(e) ‖₁₁₁‖‖‖‖‖‖₁₁‖₁‖‖₁₁‖₁‖‖₁‖₁‖₁‖₁‖₁‖₁‖₁₁₁‖₁‖₁‖‖₁‖₁

(f) ‖₁‖₁‖₁₁₁₁₁‖‖₁₁‖₁‖‖‖‖₁‖₁‖₁‖₁‖₁‖₁‖₁‖₁‖₁‖‖‖₁₁‖₁‖‖₁‖₁

# Extension 1: Binary Trees

A binary tree is a special kind of graph; the points in this graph are called *vertices,* or *nodes,* and the line segments are called *edges.* Shown at the right are examples of graphs used in this activity to introduce vocabulary associated with graphs and to observe some of the properties of graphs.

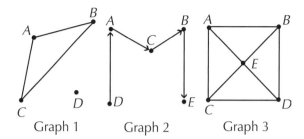

Graph 1     Graph 2     Graph 3

In graph 1, the vertices are *A, B, C,* and *D* and the edges are *AB, AC,* and *BC.* The *degree of a vertex* is the number of edges at that vertex. In graph 1, vertices *A, B,* and *C* each have degree 2, and *D* has degree 0. Graphs 2 and 3 are called *connected graphs* because every vertex has degree greater than or equal to 1. Graph 1 is not connected because vertex *D* is isolated.

Mathematicians speak of *traversing a graph* by moving from one vertex to another along the edges of the graph. Such a traversal is called a *path.* In graph 3, a path from vertex *A* to vertex *D* is *ABECD.* Another path is *AED.* Paths that traverse a graph and return to the starting vertex are called *circuits.* In graph 1, the path *ACBA* is a circuit, and in graph 3, *AECA* is a circuit. Graph 2 has no circuits.

Graph 2 is called a *directed graph,* or *digraph.* The arrows along the edges indicate the direction in which one must move in traversing the graph. In a directed graph, the number of edges leading into a vertex is called its *in-degree* and the number of edges leading away from the vertex is called its *out-degree.* In graph 2, vertex *D* has in-degree equal to 0 and out-degree equal to 1; vertices *A, B,* and *C* have in-degree equal to 1 and out-degree equal to 1; vertex *E* has in-degree equal to 1 and out-degree equal to 0.

Check your understanding of these terms by solving the following problems:

1.  What is the degree of each vertex in graph 3?

2.  Draw an example of a connected graph with six vertices in which each vertex has a degree of at least 2.

3.  In graph 3, find a circuit that passes only once through each vertex.

4.  Draw an example of a directed graph with five vertices and the following properties:

    —The graph is connected with no circuits.

    —Vertex *A* has in-degree equal to 0 and out-degree equal to 1 or 2.

    —Vertices *B, C, D,* and *E* have in-degree equal to 1 and out-degree equal to 0, 1, or 2.

The graph that satisfies the foregoing requirements is an example of a binary tree.

Binary trees are similar to real trees in that they have a root, branches, and leaves. They are also similar to the familiar family tree used in genealogy. The languages of biology and genealogy are both used in describing binary trees.

A binary tree is a directed graph that satisfies the following conditions:

✦ The graph is connected.

✦ The graph has no circuits.

✦ The number of edges is one less than the number of vertices.

✦ The graph has a single vertex, called the *root,* that has in-degree equal to 0 and out-degree equal to 1 or 2.

✦ All other vertices have in-degree equal to 1 and out-degree equal to 0, 1, or 2.

In the binary trees at the left, *R* is the root node. Note the absence of arrows showing the direction of travel in these diagrams. As in most binary trees, the direction of travel is understood to be downward from the root to the other vertices.

In tree 1, *A* is known as the *left-child* of *R,* and *B* is the *right-child* of *R.* Node *G* is the left-child of *C,* but *C* has no right-child. Node *D* is known as the *parent* of *H* and *I.* Node *B* is the *ancestor* of the nodes *E, J, F, K, L,* and *M;* these same nodes are known as *descendants* of *B.* The nodes *G, H, I, J, K,* and *M,* which have no children, are called *leaves.*

Check your understanding of these vocabulary terms by completing the following tasks:

5. Name the descendants of *B* in tree 2.

6. Name the children of *D* in tree 2.

7. Name the leaves of tree 2.

8. Draw a binary tree with seven nodes such that four nodes are leaves.

## Binary Trees Grow inside Computers

Binary trees, such as the Huffman trees used for data compression, are used frequently by computer programmers to generate efficient methods for manipulating data. One such tree, known as a binary search tree, offers a fast method for searching a list. In fact, you have probably used a binary search tree yourself if you have ever played the game "guess my number," in which one person picks a number between, say, 1 and 1000, and another person tries to guess the number by asking whether the chosen number is greater than or less than the guess. Do you remember the best strategy for playing this game? Here is a simple example:

*Player 1.* I am thinking of a secret number between 1 and 10.

*Player 2.* Is your number greater than or less than 5?

*Player 1.* Greater than 5.

*Player 2.* Is your number greater than or less than 7?

*Player 1.* Greater than 7.

*Player 2.* Is your number greater than or less than 9?

### Examples of Binary Trees

Tree 1

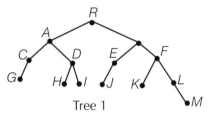

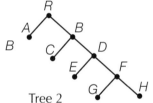

Tree 2

*Player 1.* Less than 9.

*Player 2.* Is your number 8?

*Player 1.* You got it!

When the secret number is between 1 and 10, player 2 can always win the game in four guesses or fewer by following an optimum strategy. The following paragraphs explain why this statement is true.

Imagine that the numbers from 1 through 10 are arranged in a binary tree, such as the one shown.

The game described above is equivalent to traversing the binary tree from the root 5 to node 7 to node 9 and, finally, to node 8. We can see that any node from 1 through 10

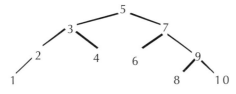

can be reached in four or fewer guesses because the binary tree has only three levels. The number of levels is defined as the number of edges that must be traversed to reach the bottom of the tree. Three levels are required because $2^3 < 10 < 2^4$. If "guess my number" is played with numbers from 1 through 100, at most seven guesses are required because $2^6 < 100 < 2^7$.

The binary tree shown has the special property that for each node, any left-child is less than the parent and any right-child is greater than the parent. Binary trees with this property are called *binary search trees*. This tree is also *evenly balanced* because each internal node has two children.

The same principle used in "guess my number" can be used in a computer program to search a long list of data. Suppose, for example, that a list of 10,000 names is stored in a computer. If the names are ordered alphabetically and stored sequentially, up to 10,000 guesses might be required to find a particular name in the list. However, if the names are stored in an evenly balanced binary search tree, the maximum number of guesses is reduced to 14 because $2^{13} < 10,000 < 2^{14}$. To find a given name in the list, a user would merely traverse the binary search tree until the name is found.

## Working with Binary Trees

1. Find a partner, and play "guess my number" for the numbers from 1 through 1000 several times, recording the number of guesses required to win each game. Find the average number of guesses required for all teams in the class. What is the maximum number of guesses required for numbers from 1 through 1000?

2. Have one person secretly choose a word from a dictionary. The second person then takes the dictionary and tries to guess the secret word by asking, "Does the word come before or after...?" Record the number of guesses required to guess the word. Play this version

of the game several times. The results may give some idea of the power of the binary search tree in locating data. For a shorter game, choose a word that begins with a certain letter of the alphabet.

3. Suppose a dictionary contains 60,000 words. Assuming that the remaining words can be divided exactly in half at each step, what is the maximum number of guesses needed to find a secret word? What if the dictionary has 100,000 words?

4. Make a binary search tree for the letters of the alphabet as follows:

Start with the letter *M* at the root of the tree. Add new letters to the tree, preserving the condition that each new left-child must be alphabetically less than the parent and each new right-child must be alphabetically greater than the parent. Use a randomizing device to select the letters to be added to the tree from the remaining letters.

Compare your tree with those created by your classmates. Do the trees all have the same shape? What is the average number of levels produced in the trees?

5. Make a binary search tree for the alphabet by starting with the letter *A* as the root and inserting the other letters in order into the tree. What kind of tree results? If you were creating a binary search tree for a large list of names, what recommendations would you make about how the tree should be created?

6. Make binary search trees for the words in the following phrases. Modify the binary search tree requirement so that each left-child is less than or equal to the parent and each right-child is greater than the parent.

   a. ONE SMALL STEP FOR MAN; ONE GIANT LEAP FOR MANKIND.

   b. TWINKLE, TWINKLE, LITTLE STAR. HOW I WONDER WHAT YOU ARE.

7. Traverse the trees above by using the following recursive algorithm:

Begin at the leftmost node. At each node, apply the rule "go left, visit the node, go right." What happens if you traverse the trees in this way? Hint: Traversing the binary tree given previously for the numbers 1–10 results in the sequence 1, 2, 3, 4, 5, 6, 7, 8, 9, 10.

# Extension 2: Other Coding Schemes

Imagine that you are the controller for an unmanned spacecraft and that you must know the status of a control that has four possible positions, called A, B, C, and D. To transmit the position of the control, you use the following binary code:

00 = position A
01 = position B
10 = position C
11 = position D

Suppose that you receive the message 01 from the spacecraft, indicating that the control is in position B. How do you know that the message is correct? What could you do to build in redundancy to ensure that one-bit errors can be detected and corrected?

A logical step is to try duplicating the message. That is, 00 would be sent as 0000, 01 would be sent as 0101, 10 would be sent as 1010, and 11 would be sent as 1111. If you analyze this code, however, you should be able to determine that it will not result in a one-bit error correction. For example, suppose that 10 is sent as 1010, but an error occurs in the first digit so that the received message is 0010. The receiver would not know whether the sent message was 0000 or 1010, because both differ from the received message in only one position.

The next step might be to triplicate the message. In this scheme, 00 would be sent as 000000; 01, as 010101; 10, as 101010; and 11, as 111111. This code will work, but the analysis of the message is more difficult. If the received message is 001000, then obviously, it should be decoded as 000000. But what if the received message is 010011? How should that message be decoded? The concept of Hamming distance is helpful in this analysis. Hamming distance is important because it completely defines the error-correcting capability of binary linear codes.

## Hamming Distance

The Hamming distance between two binary code words is the number of positions in which the digits are different. This number is named in honor of Richard Hamming, who first developed the concept in the late 1940s.

The first table below represents the code words 000100 and 111010, which have a Hamming distance of 5 because they differ in the first five positions. In the second table, the code words 000100 and 100100 have a Hamming distance of 1 because they differ only in the first position. The idea of Hamming distance can be used to help analyze the code obtained by triplicating the message bits 00, 01, 10, and 11 to produce the code words 000000, 010101, 101010, and 111111.

| 0 | 0 | 0 | 1 | 0 | 0 |
|---|---|---|---|---|---|
| 1 | 1 | 1 | 0 | 1 | 0 |
| ✔ | ✔ | ✔ | ✔ | ✔ |  |

| 0 | 0 | 0 | 1 | 0 | 0 |
|---|---|---|---|---|---|
| 1 | 0 | 0 | 1 | 0 | 0 |
| ✔ |  |  |  |  |  |

Complete the table in the worksheet "Hamming Distances from Code Words" (on page 187) to show the set of all sixty possible six-digit binary strings other than the four code words, as well as the Hamming distance of each string from each of the four code words 000000, 010101, 101010, and 111111. You may want to share the work on this task with one or two classmates.

Your completed table will show that each code word has six possible message words that are a distance of 1 from the code word and fifteen possible message words that are a distance of 2 from the code word. Thus, this code can detect and correct all one-bit errors. It can also detect and correct some but not all two-bit errors. For example, suppose that 111101 is the received message. We can assume that a one-bit error occurred and decode the message as 111111, but the possibility also exists that two errors occurred and that the actual message sent was 010101.

Because the goal was one-bit error correction and triplicating the code is expensive in terms of the number of digits that must be transmitted, the question arises of whether some code with fewer digits can offer one-bit error correction. The answer is yes. A more efficient error-correcting code exists for the two-bit messages 00, 01, 10, and 11. Because four bits were insufficient to detect one-bit errors and six bits were more than needed, one might logically assume that an optimal code for one-bit error correction would have five bits. To understand how to find such a code, one must know some of the mathematics and vocabulary of error-correcting codes.

## Addition of Binary Code Words

The addition of binary code words is a special form of addition with no "carrying," or regrouping. In Boolean logic, this operation is called "exclusive or." The rule is

$$0 + 0 = 1 + 1 = 0 \text{ and } 1 + 0 = 0 + 1 = 1.$$

A *binary linear code* is a set of binary code words with the property that the sum of any code words is another code word. The two codes shown in the tables below are examples of binary codes. The first example represents a switch with two positions: on (1) and off (0). To add redundancy, the symbols are tripled so that "on" is sent as 111 and "off," as 000. The second example represents the four-position switch described at the beginning of extension 2. The completed addition tables for those two codes are shown.

The following is an example of adding binary code words:

```
  00101
+ 11011
-------
  11110
```

A *binary linear code* is a set of binary code words with the property that the sum of any code words is another code word.

| + | 000 | 111 |
|-----|-----|-----|
| 000 | 000 | 111 |
| 111 | 111 | 000 |

Addition table for code {000, 111}

| + | 000000 | 010101 | 101010 | 111111 |
|--------|--------|--------|--------|--------|
| 000000 | 000000 | 010101 | 101010 | 111111 |
| 010101 | 010101 | 000000 | 111111 | 101010 |
| 101010 | 101010 | 111111 | 000000 | 010101 |
| 111111 | 111111 | 101010 | 010101 | 000000 |

Addition table for code {000000, 010101, 101010, 111111}

## Hamming Distance from Code Words

| Message Received | Distance from 000000 | Distance from 010101 | Distance from 101010 | Distance from 111111 | Message Received | Distance from 000000 | Distance from 010101 | Distance from 101010 | Distance from 111111 |
|---|---|---|---|---|---|---|---|---|---|
| 000001 | 1 | 2 | 4 | 5 | 111110 | | | | |
| 000010 | 1 | 4 | 2 | 5 | 111101 | | | | |
| 000100 | | | | | 111011 | | | | |
| 001000 | | | | | 110111 | 5 | 2 | 4 | 1 |
| 010000 | | | | | 101111 | 5 | 4 | 2 | 1 |
| 100000 | | | | | 011111 | 5 | 2 | 4 | 1 |
| 000011 | | | | | 111100 | 4 | 3 | 3 | 2 |
| 000101 | | | | | 111010 | | | | |
| 001001 | | | | | 110110 | 4 | 3 | 3 | 2 |
| 010001 | | | | | 101110 | | | | |
| 100001 | 2 | 3 | 3 | 4 | 011110 | | | | |
| 000110 | | | | | 111001 | 4 | 3 | 3 | 2 |
| 001010 | 2 | 5 | 1 | 4 | 110101 | | | | |
| 010010 | | | | | 101101 | 4 | 3 | 3 | 2 |
| 100010 | | | | | 011101 | | | | |
| 001100 | | | | | 110011 | 4 | 3 | 3 | 2 |
| 010100 | | | | | 101011 | | | | |
| 100100 | | | | | 011011 | | | | |
| 011000 | 2 | 3 | 3 | 4 | 100111 | | | | |
| 101000 | | | | | 010111 | | | | |
| 110000 | | | | | 001111 | | | | |
| 000111 | | | | | 111000 | 3 | 4 | 2 | 3 |
| 001011 | | | | | 110100 | 3 | 2 | 4 | 3 |
| 010011 | | | | | 101100 | | | | |
| 100011 | | | | | 011100 | | | | |
| 001101 | | | | | 110010 | 3 | 4 | 2 | 3 |
| 100101 | 3 | 2 | 4 | 3 | 011010 | | | | |
| 011001 | | | | | 100110 | | | | |
| 101001 | | | | | 010110 | | | | |
| 110001 | 3 | 2 | 4 | 3 | 001110 | | | | |

## Summary of Hamming Distance from Code Words

| Number of messages at distance | from code word 000000 | from code word 010101 | from code word 101010 | from code word 111111 |
|---|---|---|---|---|
| 1 | 6 | | | |
| 2 | | | | |
| 3 | | | | |
| 4 | | | | |
| 5 | | | | |

*Algebra Connection*

Recall the fundamental properties of the operation of addition for real numbers:

✦ Closure: The sum of any two real numbers is a real number.

✦ Commutative property: $a + b = b + a$.

✦ Associative property: $a + (b + c) = (a + b) + c$.

✦ Identity property: A number 0 exists such that $0 + a = a + 0 = a$ for all numbers $a$.

✦ Inverses property: For every number $a$, a number $-a$ exists such that $a + (-a) = -a + a = 0$.

For the addition of the code words in the examples on page 186, we check these properties by asking the following questions:

✦ Is every sum a code word?

✦ Is the addition commutative?

✦ Is the addition associative?

✦ Is an identity present?

✦ Does every code word have an inverse?

*Check Your Understanding*

1. Which of the algebraic properties do the foregoing two codes satisfy under the operation of addition?

2. Complete the addition tables for the following codes. Which of these codes are binary linear codes?

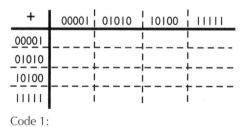

Code 1: _____

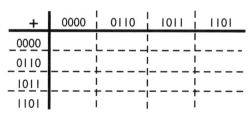

Code 2: _____

| + | 0000 | 0010 | 0111 | 0001 | 1000 | 1010 | 1101 | 1111 |
|---|------|------|------|------|------|------|------|------|
| 0000 | | | | | | | | |
| 0010 | | | | | | | | |
| 0111 | | | | | | | | |
| 0001 | | | | | | | | |
| 1000 | | | | | | | | |
| 1010 | | | | | | | | |
| 1101 | | | | | | | | |
| 1111 | | | | | | | | |

Code 3:

Binary linear codes have some properties that make designing error-correcting codes easier. Looking again at the code {000000, 010101, 101010, 111111}, we can see that the distance between any pair of code words is at least 3. For example, 010101 is at a distance of 3 from 000000 and 111111, and it is at a distance of 6 from 101010. We also note that except for the code word 000000, the minimum number of 1's in any code word is three. This occurrence is no coincidence.

For a binary linear code, the minimum distance between code words equals the minimum number of 1's in any code word except for the word containing all 0's. This minimum number of 1's is called the weight of the code. The weight of a binary linear code offers a simple way to determine the error-detecting and error-correcting capability of the code, as shown in the following rule:

*To detect k errors, a binary linear code must have a weight of at least k + 1. To correct k errors, the weight of the code must be at least 2k + 1.*

To detect one error, the code must have a weight of at least 2. To detect two errors, the code must have a weight of at least 3. To correct one error, the code must have a weight of at least 3, and to correct two errors, the code must have a weight of at least 5.

Returning to the problem of devising a code for the two-bit messages {00, 01, 10, 11}, we must construct a binary linear code with a weight of 3. One method is to use what are called *parity-check sums.*

A binary string is said to be of *even parity* if the sum of its bits is even and of *odd parity* if the sum of its bits is odd. For example, 0010110 has odd parity, whereas 1010110 has even parity.

Using the idea of parity, suppose that we add three additional digits, called *parity-check bits,* to our message bits so that the code word will be of the form $m_1m_2p_1p_2p_3$, where $m_1$ and $m_2$ are the message bits and $p_1$, $p_2$, and $p_3$ are the parity-check bits. For this first example, we choose $p_1$ as a parity check on $m_1$, $p_2$ as a parity check on $m_2$, and $p_3$ as a parity check on the sum of $m_1$ and $m_2$. That is, we choose $p_1$, $p_2$, and $p_3$ so that

The weight of a binary linear code is the minimum number of 1's in any code word except for the word containing all 0's.

| To detect | The weight must be |
|-----------|--------------------|
| One error | 2 |
| Two errors | 3 |
| ... | ... |
| $k$ errors | $k + 1$ |

| To correct | The weight must be |
|------------|--------------------|
| One error | 3 |
| Two errors | 5 |
| ... | ... |
| $k$ errors | $2k + 1$ |

To form code words from message words, some combinations of the message digits are used to form parity-check digits.

Example

*The message to be sent is* m$_1$m$_2$.

*The message with parity-check bits added is* m$_1$m$_2$p$_1$p$_2$p$_3$.

*To send the message*
m$_1$m$_2$ = 10,

$1 + p_1 = 0 \quad \Rightarrow \quad p_1 = 1$,

$0 + p_2 = 0 \quad \Rightarrow \quad p_2 = 0$,

$1 + 0 + p_3 = 0 \quad \Rightarrow \quad p_3 = 1$.

*The code word for* 10 *becomes* m$_1$m$_2$p$_1$p$_2$p$_3$ = 10101.

$$m_1 + p_1 = 0,$$

$$m_2 + p_2 = 0,$$

and

$$m_1 + m_2 + p_3 = 0.$$

Using this scheme, we encode the four message words as follows:

$$00 \rightarrow 00000 \qquad 01 \rightarrow 01011 \qquad 10 \rightarrow 10101 \qquad 11 \rightarrow 11110$$

The list below shows each code word and the five possible messages that are a distance of 1 from that word.

| | |
|---|---|
| 00000: | 10000, 01000, 00100, 00010, 00001 |
| 01011: | 11011, 00011, 01111, 01001, 01010 |
| 10101: | 00101, 11101, 10001, 10111, 10100 |
| 11110: | 01110, 10110, 11010, 11100, 11111 |

If any of these messages is received, it will be decoded as the corresponding code word. However, the number of possible five-bit messages is $2^5$, or 32, and we have accounted for only twenty-four, which leaves eight other messages that are a distance of at least 2 from any of the code words. If one of those eight messages is received, we assume that some error has occurred, but the error is not correctable.

*Check Your Understanding*

3. Find the other eight possible five-bit messages. Show that the distance between each of these and the four code words is at least 2.

4. The picture at the left is composed of eight different shadings. The eight shadings are each assigned a binary code according to the chart below the picture. Use parity-check bits to design a code for these eight shadings that will correct all one-bit errors. You will need three parity-check bits. Remember to check the following:

   —Your code should have weight 3.

   —Your code words should form a binary linear code; that is, the sum of any two code words must be another code word.

Write your results in the chart.

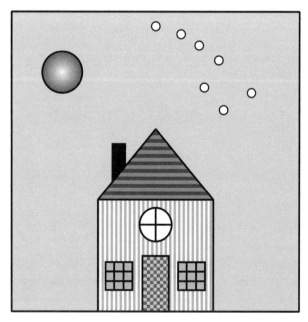

| | | | | | | | |
|---|---|---|---|---|---|---|---|
| 000 | 001 | 010 | 011 | 100 | 101 | 110 | 111 |

| Message | Code Word | Weight |
|---|---|---|
| 000 | | |
| 001 | | |
| 010 | | |
| 011 | | |
| 100 | | |
| 101 | | |
| 110 | | |
| 111 | | |

# Hamming Codes

Richard Hamming, a mathematician at Bell Laboratories, developed an infinite set of single-error-correcting, double-error-detecting codes in the late 1940s. His work laid a foundation for error-correction techniques that have become increasingly useful with the growth of digital technology. Satellite communication, home computers, fax machines, compact discs, cellular telephones, digital audiotape, and digital television are just a few examples of technologies that use error-correcting codes. The Hamming codes can be derived elegantly using matrices, thereby leading to an easy method for finding and correcting errors in received messages.

Hamming developed codes that work in certain situations. These codes can be described in terms of $m$ parity-check digits and $n = (2^m - 1 - m)$ message digits. We first examine codes for special values of $m$ and $n$ and subsequently look at codes for any value of $n$.

If $m = 2$, then $n = 2^2 - 1 - 2 = 1$ message digit.

If $m = 3$, then $n = 2^3 - 1 - 3 = 4$ message digits.

If $m = 4$, then $n = 2^4 - 1 - 4 = 11$ message digits.

You can develop a Hamming code by following these procedures:

(a) Form a matrix, $H$, with $m$ rows and $2^m - 1$ columns. The columns of the matrix are the binary representations of the integers $1, 2, 3, \ldots, 2^m - 1$. The matrices for $m = 2, 3,$ and $4$ are shown below, with the decimal integers written above the columns.

| Parity-Check Digits ($m$) | Message Digits ($n$) |
|:---:|:---:|
| 2 | 1 |
| 3 | 4 |
| 4 | 11 |
| ... | ... |
| $m$ | $2^m - 1 - m$ |

$$H_2 = \begin{array}{ccc} 1 & 2 & 3 \\ \left[\begin{array}{ccc} 0 & 1 & 1 \\ 1 & 0 & 1 \end{array}\right] \end{array}$$

$$H_3 = \begin{array}{ccccccc} 1 & 2 & 3 & 4 & 5 & 6 & 7 \\ \left[\begin{array}{ccccccc} 0 & 0 & 0 & 1 & 1 & 1 & 1 \\ 0 & 1 & 1 & 0 & 0 & 1 & 1 \\ 1 & 0 & 1 & 0 & 1 & 0 & 1 \end{array}\right] \end{array}$$

$$H_4 = \begin{array}{ccccccccccccccc} 1 & 2 & 3 & 4 & 5 & 6 & 7 & 8 & 9 & 10 & 11 & 12 & 13 & 14 & 15 \\ \left[\begin{array}{ccccccccccccccc} 0 & 0 & 0 & 0 & 0 & 0 & 0 & 1 & 1 & 1 & 1 & 1 & 1 & 1 & 1 \\ 0 & 0 & 0 & 1 & 1 & 1 & 1 & 0 & 0 & 0 & 0 & 1 & 1 & 1 & 1 \\ 0 & 1 & 1 & 0 & 0 & 1 & 1 & 0 & 0 & 1 & 1 & 0 & 0 & 1 & 1 \\ 1 & 0 & 1 & 0 & 1 & 0 & 1 & 0 & 1 & 0 & 1 & 0 & 1 & 0 & 1 \end{array}\right] \end{array}$$

(b) Write an $(m + n) \times 1$ matrix, $U$, in which the elements are the $n$ message digits and the $m$ parity-check digits. The message digits are represented by $w_1, w_2, \ldots, w_n$, and the parity-check digits are $p_1, p_2, \ldots, p_m$. Locate the columns of $H$ that contain only one 1, and write the parity-check symbols in the corresponding rows of $U$. Write the $w_i$ in the remaining rows of $U$. We use $m = 3$ as an example for the rest of the development of the code. The parity-check bits are written in rows 1, 2, and 4 of $U$ because these columns of $H$ each have a single 1. The message bits go in the other rows of $U$.

$$U = \begin{bmatrix} p_1 \\ p_2 \\ w_1 \\ p_3 \\ w_2 \\ w_3 \\ w_4 \end{bmatrix}$$

(c) If the message $p_1 p_2 w_1 p_3 w_2 w_3 w_4$ is received correctly, the product $HU$ will be equal to the null matrix because we are working with even parity. The equation $HU = 0$ gives the parity-check equations.

$$H_3 U = \begin{bmatrix} 0 & 0 & 0 & 1 & 1 & 1 & 1 \\ 0 & 1 & 1 & 0 & 0 & 1 & 1 \\ 1 & 0 & 1 & 0 & 1 & 0 & 1 \end{bmatrix} \begin{bmatrix} p_1 \\ p_2 \\ w_1 \\ p_3 \\ w_2 \\ w_3 \\ w_4 \end{bmatrix} = \begin{bmatrix} 0 \\ 0 \\ 0 \end{bmatrix}$$

$$\begin{aligned} p_3 + w_2 + w_3 + w_4 &= 0 & & & p_3 &= w_2 + w_3 + w_4 \\ p_2 + w_1 + w_3 + w_4 &= 0 & \text{or} & & p_2 &= w_1 + w_3 + w_4 \\ p_1 + w_1 + w_2 + w_4 &= 0 & & & p_1 &= w_1 + w_2 + w_4 \end{aligned}$$

These equations can be used to encode the message. As an example, let us encode 1011.

$$w_1 = 1 \qquad w_2 = 0 \qquad w_3 = 1 \qquad w_4 = 1$$

$$\begin{aligned} w_1 + w_2 + w_4 &= 1 + 0 + 1 = 0 \longrightarrow p_1 = 0 \\ w_1 + w_3 + w_4 &= 1 + 1 + 1 = 1 \longrightarrow p_2 = 1 \\ w_2 + w_3 + w_4 &= 0 + 1 + 1 = 0 \longrightarrow p_3 = 0 \end{aligned}$$

The message is 1011 $\longrightarrow$ 011001, and the encoding is completed.

*Check Your Understanding*

5. Use the parity-check equations to complete the following encoding table for the sixteen possible four-bit messages.

| Message | Code Word | Message | Code Word |
|---------|-----------|---------|-----------|
| 0000 | | 1000 | |
| 0001 | | 1001 | |
| 0010 | | 1010 | |
| 0011 | | 1011 | 0110011 |
| 0100 | | 1100 | |
| 0101 | | 1101 | |
| 0110 | | 1110 | |
| 0111 | | 1111 | |

The format of the code word that is used here is different from the other codes we have developed using parity-check equations. The other codes had the message bits at the beginning of the code word and the parity bits appended to the message. Here, the parity-check bits are intermingled with the message bits, making the code somewhat more difficult to read—for a human but not for a computer. The reason for writing the code word this way is to make decoding much more convenient. The codes generated here can be shown to be equivalent to the codes in which the message bits were listed first.

## Decoding with the Hamming Matrix

The parity-check matrix, *H,* is useful in decoding a received message. Let *r* be a received message written in matrix form. For example, suppose that the received message is **0110111**. Then *r* is the following matrix:

$$r = \begin{bmatrix} 0 \\ 1 \\ 1 \\ 0 \\ 1 \\ 1 \\ 1 \end{bmatrix}$$

The matrix product $H \cdot r$ is called the *syndrome* for the message. If $H \cdot r = 0$, the message is correct; if $H \cdot r \neq 0$, an error has occurred and the syndrome indicates which bit is in error. In the case of the received message **0110111**,

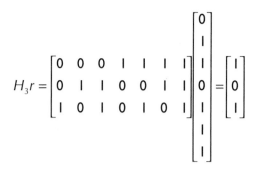

Note that the syndrome corresponds to the fifth column of $H_3$. When a single error has been made, the syndrome will always point to a column of $H$, which is the position in which the error has been made. Recall, however, that we designated the fifth column of $H$ as the integer 5 in binary notation; thus, comparing the syndrome with the columns of $H$ to find where the error occurred is unnecessary. The only remaining step is to convert the syndrome to its base-ten form:

$$101 = 1(4) + 0(2) + 1(1) = 5$$

To correct the message, we go to the fifth position and change the 1 to a 0; the result is **0110011**.

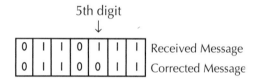

*Check Your Understanding*

Use the matrix

$$H_3 = \begin{bmatrix} 0 & 0 & 0 & 1 & 1 & 1 & 1 \\ 0 & 1 & 1 & 0 & 0 & 1 & 1 \\ 1 & 0 & 1 & 0 & 1 & 0 & 1 \end{bmatrix}$$

to decode the following messages:

6. **1101011**

7. **0011001**

8. **0100110**

9. **1111110**

10. *Challenge:* Develop the parity-check matrices for a Hamming code with eleven message bits and four parity-check bits. (Do not attempt to encode all the messages.) How many possible messages exist with eleven message bits?

## Using Hamming Codes to Derive Other Codes

The Hamming code we just created is called a *perfect code* because it has the property that every possible received message is a distance of 1 from one and only one code word. These perfect Hamming codes exist only when the number of parity-check bits is $m$ and the number of message bits is $n = 2^m - 1 - m$. However, the possibility exists to obtain good, although not perfect, single-error–correcting codes for any value of $n$ by deleting certain columns of the matrix $H$.

Suppose that we want a single-bit error-correcting code for $n = 2$ message digits. We saw previously that two parity-check bits are needed to correct one-digit messages, whereas three parity-check bits give single-bit error correction for four message digits. Because $1 \leq 2 \leq 4$, we need the Hamming code matrix for $m = 3$. But because our message contains only two message digits, we need to transmit $m + n = 3 + 2 = 5$ bits: three parity-check digits and two message digits. To accomplish this task, we use the matrix $H_3$ and delete the last two columns so that the new matrix $H$ has three rows and five columns. Form $HU$ as before, and find the parity-check equations.

$$HU = \begin{bmatrix} 0 & 0 & 0 & 1 & 1 \\ 0 & 1 & 1 & 0 & 0 \\ 1 & 0 & 1 & 0 & 1 \end{bmatrix} \begin{bmatrix} p_1 \\ p_2 \\ w_1 \\ p_3 \\ w_2 \end{bmatrix} = \begin{bmatrix} 0 \\ 0 \\ 0 \end{bmatrix} \qquad \begin{aligned} p_3 + w_2 &= 0 \\ p_2 + w_1 &= 0 \\ p_1 + w_1 + w_2 &= 0 \end{aligned}$$

The encoding table for this code is shown below.

| Message | Code Word |
|---------|-----------|
| 00 | 00000 |
| 01 | 10011 |
| 10 | 11100 |
| 11 | 01111 |

$Hr = 0 \rightarrow$ Message is correct.  $\qquad Hr \neq 0 \rightarrow$ An error has occurred.

Compare this code with the five-bit code that was generated previously using the code word $m_1 m_2 p_1 p_2 p_3$. Are the parity-check equations the same?

To decode a received message, we proceed as we did before by forming the matrix $r$, where $r$ is the received message written in matrix form. We then check the syndrome, $Hr$. If the syndrome corresponds to a column of $H$, the bit that is in error can be corrected. If the syndrome does not correspond to a column of $H$, an uncorrectable error has occurred.

Even though this code is not a perfect code, it has been shown to be the best single-error-correcting code we can derive for two message bits and three parity-check bits. To see why a perfect code cannot be obtained for two message bits, consider that we need four code words and that for each code word are five possible messages that are at a distance of 1 from that code word. For example, the messages 10000,

01000, 00100, 00010, and 00001 are distance 1 from 00000. The twenty messages that are at distance 1 from a code word, together with the four code words, account for only twenty-four of the thirty-two possible five-digit messages. Thus, eight of the possible thirty-two messages are at a distance greater than 1 from any code word. When one of those eight messages is received, decoding it is not possible. Codes for other values of $n$ message digits can be similarly generated by omitting appropriate columns from the Hamming code matrix.

*Check Your Understanding*

11. Use the foregoing technique to generate a single-error–correcting code for three message bits.

12. Use the foregoing technique to generate a single-error–correcting code for five message bits.

# Extension 3—Codes in Use

Codes are used to protect data, to compress data, and more traditionally, to hide data. The science of *cryptography,* the study of secret codes, goes back to ancient times and has been of great interest to both individuals and governments. One of the earliest and easiest methods of coding messages is the *substitution cipher,* in which each letter in the alphabet is substituted for another letter. This method is used in the cryptoquotes found in daily newspapers. The substitution cipher is fairly easy to decode using letter-frequency tables and knowledge of word formation in the English language. This activity outlines a method using matrices that makes a more secure secret code.

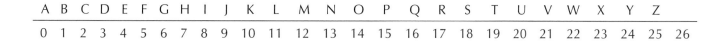

| A | B | C | D | E | F | G | H | I | J | K | L | M | N | O | P | Q | R | S | T | U | V | W | X | Y | Z |
|---|---|---|---|---|---|---|---|---|---|---|---|---|---|---|---|---|---|---|---|---|---|---|---|---|---|
| 0 | 1 | 2 | 3 | 4 | 5 | 6 | 7 | 8 | 9 | 10 | 11 | 12 | 13 | 14 | 15 | 16 | 17 | 18 | 19 | 20 | 21 | 22 | 23 | 24 | 25 | 26 |

Task: Encode the message "ONE SMALL STEP FOR MAN."

Procedure: For convenience, use a calculator that does matrix operations; if this technology is not available, the task can be done by hand without much difficulty.

1. Write the message down the columns of a matrix or matrices with three rows; the number of columns in the matrix is not relevant. Using more than one matrix may be convenient. In this example, we use two 3-by-4 matrices. Empty elements in the matrix at the end of the message can be filled in with spaces.

$$\begin{bmatrix} O & & A & \\ N & S & L & S \\ E & M & L & T \end{bmatrix} \begin{bmatrix} E & F & & N \\ P & O & M & \\ & R & A & \end{bmatrix}$$

2. Using the encoding chart above, translate the matrix letters into their numerical equivalents.

$$\begin{bmatrix} 14 & 26 & 0 & 26 \\ 13 & 18 & 11 & 18 \\ 4 & 12 & 11 & 19 \end{bmatrix} \begin{bmatrix} 4 & 5 & 26 & 13 \\ 15 & 14 & 12 & 26 \\ 26 & 17 & 0 & 26 \end{bmatrix}$$

3. For each of these matrices, multiply on the left by the matrix

$$C = \begin{bmatrix} 1 & 2 & 0 \\ 0 & 1 & 3 \\ -1 & -2 & 1 \end{bmatrix}$$

to get

$$\begin{bmatrix} 40 & 62 & 22 & 62 \\ 25 & 54 & 44 & 75 \\ -36 & -50 & -11 & -43 \end{bmatrix}\begin{bmatrix} 34 & 33 & 50 & 65 \\ 93 & 65 & 12 & 104 \\ -8 & -16 & -50 & -39 \end{bmatrix}.$$

4. To get numbers in the code range (0–26), reduce the numbers in the above matrices to their equivalents mod 27. This calculation yields the matrices below.

$$\begin{bmatrix} 13 & 8 & 22 & 8 \\ 25 & 0 & 17 & 21 \\ 18 & 4 & 16 & 11 \end{bmatrix}\begin{bmatrix} 7 & 6 & 23 & 11 \\ 12 & 11 & 12 & 23 \\ 19 & 11 & 4 & 15 \end{bmatrix}$$

5. Use the coding chart and the matrices to write the coded message NZSIAEWRQIVLHMTGLLXMELXP. Note that spaces between words are not the same as in the original message; this message will definitely be harder to decipher than a simple substitution cipher.

To decode a message using matrices, follow the steps in the encoding procedure except that in step 3, multiply on the left by the inverse of matrix $C$. Try this procedure with the encoded message from task 5, and verify that the original message is obtained.

*Working with Secret Codes*

1. Make up a message and encode it. Give the message and the matrix $C^{-1}$ to a friend to decode.

2. What is the determinant of matrix $C$? What is the determinant of $C^{-1}$?

3. Can you find other matrices that will work in the same way as matrix $C$?

4. Can you determine the conditions that are necessary for matrix $C$ to be an encoding message?

5. If the code has more than twenty-seven characters, what must change in the procedure above?

6. Can you use matrices with more than three rows?

7. Will this procedure work if the message is written across the rows of the matrix instead of down the columns?

8. Decode the message HJOCODTKHHSIJVRDXAHE.

## The ISBN Code

*ISBN* stands for International Standard Book Number, which is a code used internationally for recording information about books. For example, the ISBN for the book *Fractals for the Classroom: Strategic Activities, Volume Two* is 0-387-97554-3 (Peitgen, Heinz-Otto, and Dietmar Saupe [New York: Springer-Verlag, 1991]).

The ISBN always consists of ten digits. The first digit is used to code the language of the publisher's readership. In our example, the first 0 indicates that the book is designed for English-speaking readers. This particular book actually has two ISBNs because it is also published in German. The ISBN for the German version is 3-387-97554-3.

The second block of three digits identifies the publisher, and the third block gives the publisher's item number for the book. The last number is a check digit. The check digit scheme is as follows: Let $d_1$, $d_2$, $d_3$, ... , $d_9$ represent the first nine digits of the ISBN. The tenth digit, $d_{10}$, is chosen so that the linear combination of digits

$$10d_1 + 9d_2 + 8d_3 + 7d_4 + 6d_5 + 5d_6 + 4d_7 + 3d_8 + 2d_9 + d_{10}$$

is a multiple of 11.

For our number, $10(0) + 9(3) + 8(8) + 7(7) + 6(9) + 5(7) + 4(5) + 3(5) + 2(4) + 3 = 275 = 25(11)$. Note that this system can produce a check digit of 10; in this instance the letter X is used instead to ensure that the number still has only ten digits. This code is designed to detect errors in which two digits are interchanged or a single digit is read incorrectly.

*Working with ISBNs*

9. Find the ISBN for your mathematics textbook. Verify that the check digit is correct.

10. Suppose the example ISBN code has been incorrectly read as 0-387-79554-3. Compute the linear combination sum. Is the result a multiple of 11?

11. Suppose the sample ISBN has been incorrectly read as 0-381-97554-3. Compute the linear combination sum. Is the result a multiple of 11?

12. The first nine digits of the ISBNs for several books are given below. Compute the check digit in each ISBN.

| | |
|---|---|
| —*The Mathematical Circus* | 0-394-50207 |
| —*Number Treasury* | 0-86651-078 |
| —*Creative Puzzles of the World* | 0-8109-0765 |
| —*Apollo 13* | 0-671-53464 |
| —*Genius* | 0-679-40836 |

# Selected Solutions and Teacher Commentary

## Investigation 4—Does a New Code Do the Trick?

1. This code solves the ambiguity problem.

2. { 0, 10, 11} has the prefix property.

   { 0, 100, 101, 11, 1011} does not have the prefix property, because 101 is a prefix of 1011.

   { 000, 001, 10, 111, 1101} has the prefix property.

   { 00, 11, 010, 100, 011} has the prefix property.

   { 00, 10, 11, 1101, 0011} does not have the prefix property, because 00 is a prefix of 0011 and 11 is a prefix of 1101.

3. Various answers are possible. One possibility is

   $$+ = 00 \quad - = 010 \quad \times = 011 \quad \div = 10 \quad \pi = 110 \quad \infty = 111$$

## Investigation 5—Data Transmission in the News: *Galileo*

1. 134,000 bits per second

2. 16 bits per second

3. 160 bits per second

4. About 0.0012, or 0.12 percent

5. 5,120,000 bits

6. About 38.2 seconds

7. 1,919,448 seconds, or about 531 hours, or about 22 days

8. 320,000 seconds, or about 89 hours, or about 3.7 days

9. $1.6 \times 10^{10}$ seconds = ~4,450,000 hours = ~185,000 days = ~507 years

10. ~8.9 hours

11. 35,555 hours = ~4 years

## Investigation 6: Letters! We Get Lots and Lots of Letters!

See the letter-frequency chart on page 165.

## Investigation 7—Show Your Encoding Expertise

1. At the right is the Huffman tree for the letters on page 164. The Huffman code is as follows:

A = 00
E = 10
L = 1101
N = 111
P = 1100
T = 01

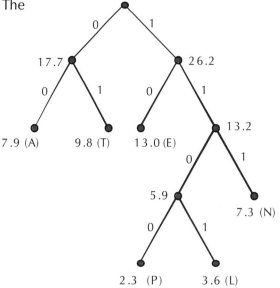

2. PLANET = 1100110100111001

   PATENT = 1100000110111101

   0100110110111101 = TALENT

   1100110100000110 = PLATE

3. Various answers are possible. Example: JOHNSTONE = 010011101011100110011111010. (See figure below.)

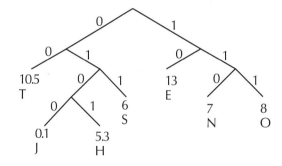

Words:  NOTE = 1101110010

TON = 00111110          HOST = 010111101100

SON = 011111110          NOSE = 1101110110

## Investigation 9—Wheel of Fortune

1. A cat has nine lives.
2. A bird in the hand is worth two in the bush.
3. It's raining cats and dogs!
4. You can't divide by zero.
5. A miss is as good as a mile.
6. Been there! Done that!
7. Mathematics is not a spectator sport.
8. Space exploration opens new horizons.

## Investigation 10—Speeding the Mail with ZIP + 4

1.  e 90210     g 39048
    i 53981     c 29857
    h 69794     f 45046
    a 12882     d 03823
    b 78964

2.

| Decimal Digit | Bar Code | Binary Code |
|---|---|---|
| 1 | ııı‖ | 00011 |
| 2 | ıı‖ı | 00101 |
| 3 | ıı‖ı | 00110 |
| 4 | ı‖ıı | 01001 |
| 5 | ı‖ı‖ | 01010 |
| 6 | ı‖‖ı | 01100 |
| 7 | ‖ıı‖ | 10001 |
| 8 | ‖ı‖ı | 10010 |
| 9 | ‖ı‖ı | 10100 |
| 0 | ‖‖ıı | 11000 |

3.  (a) 74006–8956         (b) 49855–5394
    (c) 55437–1916         (d) 68137–0662
    (e) 53228–1044         (f) 94035–1000
    (g) 32816–1250         (h) 22091–1593
    (i) 61790–4520

4.  35812-0001     ‖ıı‖ıı‖ı‖ı‖ıı‖ıııı‖ıı‖ı‖‖‖ııı‖ıı‖ı‖ııııı‖‖‖ıı‖

5.  (a) Correctable error: 20191–1593

    (b) Correctable error: 06813–9763

    (c) Detectable errors in second and fourth digits; not correctable

    (d) Correctable error: 49008–9947

    (e) No detectable error. (Actually, two digits were transposed.)

    (f) An error exists somewhere because the ten digits sum to 42; which digit is in error is impossible to determine.

## Extension 1—Binary Trees

1.  Degrees of $A = 3$, $B = 3$, $C = 3$, $D = 3$, $E = 4$

2.  Various answers are possible. An example is shown.

3. Examples: *ABEDCA, ABDECA, ABDCEA*

4. Various answers are possible. An example is shown.

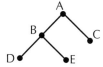

5. *C, D, E, F, G, H*

6. *E, F*

7 A, C, E, G, H

8. Various answers are possible. A sample answer is shown.

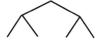

1. For the range 1–1000, the maximum number of guesses is ten.

3. The maximum number of guesses is sixteen for 60,000 words and seventeen for 100,000 words.

4. Answers will vary. The tree below is one example.

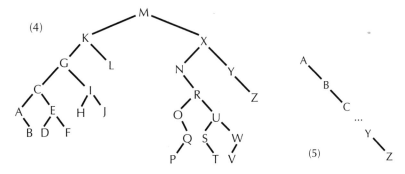

5. The binary tree above is equivalent to a sequential list. Before using a binary tree, you must have knowledge of the structure of the list. Computer science techniques can be used to help balance a tree.

6. (6a)

ONE
FOR
SMALL
FOR
MAN
STEP
GIANT
ONE
GIANT
MANKIND
LEAP

(6b)

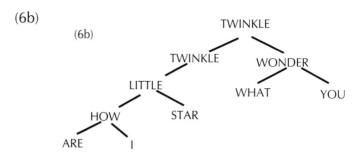

(6b)

7. (a) FOR, FOR, GIANT, LEAP, MAN, MANKIND, ONE, ONE, SMALL, STEP. (b) ARE, HOW, I, LITTLE, STAR, TWINKLE, TWINKLE, WHAT, WONDER, YOU. The words are in alphabetical order. The traversal given by the recursive commands "Go left, visit the node, go right" is called an in-order traversal.

## Extension 2—Other Coding Schemes

*Hamming Distance from Code Words*

### Summary of Hamming Distance from Code Words

| Number of messages at distance … | … from code word **000000** | … from code word **010101** | … from code word **101010** | … from code word **111111** |
|---|---|---|---|---|
| 1 | 6 | 6 | 6 | 6 |
| 2 | 15 | 15 | 15 | 15 |
| 3 | 18 | 18 | 18 | 18 |
| 4 | 15 | 15 | 15 | 15 |
| 5 | 6 | 6 | 6 | 6 |

*Check Your Understanding*

1. The binary linear codes satisfy all the properties under the operation of addition. The identity is **000000**, and each code word is its own inverse. A binary linear code forms a group under addition.

2.

| + | 00001 | 01010 | 10100 | 11111 |
|---|---|---|---|---|
| 00001 | 00000 | 01011 | 10101 | 11110 |
| 01010 | 01011 | 00000 | 11110 | 10101 |
| 10100 | 10101 | 11110 | 00000 | 01011 |
| 11111 | 11110 | 10101 | 01011 | 00000 |

This code is not a binary linear code; it is not closed.

| + | 0000 | 0110 | 1011 | 1101 |
|---|---|---|---|---|
| 0000 | 0000 | 0110 | 1011 | 1101 |
| 0110 | 0110 | 0000 | 1101 | 1011 |
| 1011 | 1011 | 1101 | 0000 | 0110 |
| 1101 | 1101 | 1011 | 0110 | 0000 |

This code is a binary linear code.

| +    | 0000 | 0010 | 0111 | 0001 | 1000 | 1010 | 1101 | 1111 |
|------|------|------|------|------|------|------|------|------|
| 0000 | 0000 | 0010 | 0111 | 0001 | 1000 | 1010 | 1101 | 1111 |
| 0010 | 0010 | 0000 | 0101 | 0011 | 1010 | 1000 | 1111 | 1101 |
| 0111 | 0111 | 0101 | 0000 | 0110 | 1111 | 1101 | 1010 | 1000 |
| 0001 | 0001 | 0011 | 0110 | 0000 | 1001 | 1011 | 1100 | 1110 |
| 1000 | 1000 | 1010 | 1111 | 1001 | 0000 | 0010 | 0101 | 0111 |
| 1010 | 1010 | 1000 | 1101 | 1011 | 0010 | 0000 | 0111 | 0101 |
| 1101 | 1101 | 1111 | 1010 | 1100 | 0101 | 0111 | 0000 | 0010 |
| 1111 | 1111 | 1101 | 1000 | 1110 | 0111 | 0101 | 0010 | 0000 |

This code is not a binary linear code.

3. The other possible messages are shown in the left column of the table below, together with their distances from each of the code words.

| Message Received | Distance from 00000 | Distance from 01011 | Distance from 10101 | Distance from 11110 |
|------------------|---------------------|---------------------|---------------------|---------------------|
| 00110 | 2 | 3 | 3 | 2 |
| 00111 | 3 | 2 | 2 | 3 |
| 01100 | 2 | 3 | 3 | 2 |
| 01101 | 3 | 2 | 2 | 3 |
| 10010 | 2 | 3 | 3 | 2 |
| 10011 | 3 | 2 | 2 | 3 |
| 11000 | 2 | 3 | 3 | 2 |
| 11001 | 3 | 2 | 2 | 3 |

4. Various solutions are possible. Two are given below. For the first code, let $p_1 = m_1 + m_2$, $p_2 = m_1 + m_3$, and $p_3 = m_2 + m_3$. For the second code, let $p_1 = m_1 + m_2$, $p_2 = m_2 + m_3$, and $p_3 = m_1 + m_2 + m_3$. The resulting codes are as follows:

| Message | Code Word | Weight | Message | Code Word | Weight |
|---------|-----------|--------|---------|-----------|--------|
| 000 | 000000 | 0 | 000 | 000000 | 0 |
| 001 | 001011 | 3 | 001 | 001011 | 3 |
| 010 | 010101 | 3 | 010 | 010111 | 4 |
| 011 | 011110 | 4 | 011 | 011100 | 3 |
| 100 | 100110 | 3 | 100 | 100101 | 3 |
| 101 | 101101 | 3 | 101 | 101110 | 4 |
| 110 | 110011 | 4 | 110 | 110010 | 3 |
| 111 | 111000 | 3 | 111 | 111001 | 4 |

5.

| Message | Code Word | | Message | Code Word |
|---------|-----------|---|---------|-----------|
| 0000 | 0000000 | | 1000 | 1110000 |
| 0001 | 1101001 | | 1001 | 0011001 |
| 0010 | 0101010 | | 1010 | 1011010 |
| 0011 | 1000011 | | 1011 | 0110011 |
| 0100 | 1001100 | | 1100 | 0111100 |
| 0101 | 0100101 | | 1101 | 1010101 |
| 0110 | 1100110 | | 1110 | 0010110 |
| 0111 | 0001111 | | 1111 | 1111111 |

$$\begin{bmatrix} 0 & 0 & 0 & 1 & 1 & 1 & 1 \\ 0 & 1 & 1 & 0 & 0 & 1 & 1 \\ 1 & 0 & 1 & 0 & 1 & 0 & 1 \end{bmatrix} \begin{bmatrix} 1 \\ 1 \\ 0 \\ 1 \\ 0 \\ 1 \\ 1 \end{bmatrix} = \begin{bmatrix} 1 \\ 1 \\ 0 \end{bmatrix}$$

6. We know that this message contains an error because the syndrome is not equal to 0 (see matrix at the left). Further, we know that the error is in the sixth bit because the syndrome is equal to 6. That bit is changed, and the correct message is 1101001.

7. $Hr = \begin{bmatrix} 0 \\ 0 \\ 0 \end{bmatrix}$ The original message is correct.

8. $Hr = \begin{bmatrix} 0 \\ 0 \\ 1 \end{bmatrix}$ The first bit is incorrect. The corrected message is 1100110.

9. $Hr = \begin{bmatrix} 1 \\ 1 \\ 1 \end{bmatrix}$ The seventh bit is incorrect. The corrected message is 1111111.

10.

$$HU = \begin{bmatrix} 0 & 0 & 0 & 0 & 0 & 0 & 0 & 1 & 1 & 1 & 1 & 1 & 1 & 1 & 1 \\ 0 & 0 & 0 & 1 & 1 & 1 & 1 & 0 & 0 & 0 & 0 & 1 & 1 & 1 & 1 \\ 0 & 1 & 1 & 0 & 0 & 1 & 1 & 0 & 0 & 1 & 1 & 0 & 0 & 1 & 1 \\ 1 & 0 & 1 & 0 & 1 & 0 & 1 & 0 & 1 & 0 & 1 & 0 & 1 & 0 & 1 \end{bmatrix} \begin{bmatrix} p_1 \\ p_2 \\ w_1 \\ p_3 \\ w_2 \\ w_3 \\ w_4 \\ p_4 \\ w_5 \\ w_6 \\ w_7 \\ w_8 \\ w_9 \\ w_{10} \\ w_{11} \end{bmatrix}$$

With eleven message bits, the number of messages will be $2^{11}$. The parity-check equations are as follows:

$$p_1 = w_1 + w_2 + w_4 + w_5 + w_7 + w_9 + w_{11}$$
$$p_2 = w_1 + w_3 + w_4 + w_6 + w_7 + w_{10} + w_{11}$$
$$p_3 = w_2 + w_3 + w_4 + w_8 + w_9 + w_{10} + w_{11}$$
$$p_4 = w_5 + w_6 + w_7 + w_8 + w_9 + w_{10} + w_{11} \, .$$

11. For three message bits, three parity-check bits are needed, and the first six columns of $H_3$ will be used.

| Message | Code Word |
|---------|-----------|
| 000 | 000000 |
| 001 | 010101 |
| 010 | 100110 |
| 011 | 110011 |
| 100 | 111000 |
| 101 | 101101 |
| 110 | 011110 |
| 111 | 001011 |

12.

| Message | Code Word | Message | Code Word | Message | Code Word |
|---------|-----------|---------|-----------|---------|-----------|
| 00000 | 000000000 | 01011 | 110010111 | 10110 | 011001100 |
| 00001 | 100000011 | 01100 | 110011000 | 10111 | 111001111 |
| 00010 | 110100100 | 01101 | 010011011 | 11000 | 011110000 |
| 00011 | 010100111 | 01110 | 000111100 | 11001 | 111110011 |
| 00100 | 010101000 | 01111 | 100111111 | 11010 | 101010100 |
| 00101 | 110101011 | 10000 | 111000000 | 11011 | 001010111 |
| 00110 | 100001100 | 10001 | 011000011 | 11100 | 001011000 |
| 00111 | 000001111 | 10010 | 001100100 | 11101 | 101011011 |
| 01000 | 100110000 | 10011 | 101100111 | 11110 | 111111100 |
| 01001 | 000110011 | 10100 | 101101000 | 11111 | 011111111 |
| 01010 | 010010100 | 10101 | 001101011 | | |

$$HU = \begin{bmatrix} 0 & 0 & 0 & 0 & 0 & 0 & 0 & 1 & 1 \\ 0 & 0 & 0 & 1 & 1 & 1 & 1 & 0 & 0 \\ 0 & 1 & 1 & 0 & 0 & 1 & 1 & 0 & 0 \\ 1 & 0 & 1 & 0 & 1 & 0 & 1 & 0 & 1 \end{bmatrix} \begin{bmatrix} p_1 \\ p_2 \\ w_1 \\ p_3 \\ w_2 \\ w_3 \\ w_4 \\ p_4 \\ w_5 \end{bmatrix}$$

$$p_1 = w_1 + w_2 + w_4 + w_5$$
$$p_2 = w_1 + w_3 + w_4$$
$$p_3 = w_2 + w_3 + w_4$$
$$p_4 = w_5$$

## Extension 3—Codes in Use

*Working with Secret Codes*

1. Answers will vary. The matrix $C^{-1}$ is shown. $\begin{bmatrix} 7 & -2 & 6 \\ -3 & 1 & -3 \\ 1 & 0 & 1 \end{bmatrix}$

2. $C$ and $C^{-1}$ both have determinants equal to 1.

3–4. Many other matrices will work. The determinant of $C$ must have an inverse mod 27 ($1 \times 1 = 1$ mod 27). To find other matrices with determinant 1, use row and column operations on the identity matrix.

5. The determinant of $C$ must have an inverse mod $n$ where $n$ is the number of characters in the code.

6. Yes

7. Yes

8. Have Fun! Happy Coding!

*Working with ISBNs*

10. 273; No

11. 231; No

12. 8, 8, 8, 5, 3

# Bibliography

"Astronauts Dodge Space Junk for Third Spacewalk." *CNN Interactive.* February 1997. www.cnn.com/TECH/9702/16/hubble/index.html.

Canadian Space Resource Centre. "The International Space Station (ISS) in Orbit." *Spacenet.* www.spacenet.on.ca/curriculum/iss2a/ observing_tea.htm.

Ferguson, Michael, Randy Kalisek, and Leah Tuck. *GPS Land Navigation: A Complete Guidebook for Backcountry Users of the NAVSTAR Satellite System.* Boise, Idaho: Glassford Publishing, 1997.

Graham, John F. "Navigation Satellites." *Space Exploration: From Talisman of the Past to Gateway for the Future.* www.space.edu/ projects/book/Chapter26.html. 1995.

Herring, Thomas A. "The Global Positioning System." *Scientific American* (February 1996): 44–50.

Hotchkiss, Noel J. *A Comprehensive Guide to Land Navigation with GPS.* 3rd ed. Leesburg, Va.: Alexis Publishing, 1999.

Huang, Jerry. *All about GPS: Sherlock Holmes' Guide to the Global Positioning System.* Taipei, Taiwan: Acme Services, 1999.

Larijani, L. Casey. *GPS for Everyone: How the Global Positioning System Can Work for You.* New York: American Interface Corp, Publishing Division, 1998.

Letham, Lawrence. *GPS Made Easy: Using Global Positioning Systems in the Outdoors.* 3rd ed. Seattle, Wash.: Mountaineers Books, 2001.

Liou, Jer-Chyi. Personal communication, June 20, 2002.

National Council of Teachers of Mathematics (NCTM). "Codes and Counting." *NCTM Student Math Notes* (January 1983).

National Space Development Agency of Japan (NASDA). "Follow-up Report on NASDA's Two Satellites, COMETS and ETS-VII." NASDA. www.nasda.go.jp/lib/nasda-news/1998/06/follow_e.html.

"Space Debris Creates Streaks across Sky." *USA Today,* December 2, 2001. www.usatoday.com/news/nation/2001/12/02/debris.htm.

"Space Station Dodges Floating Debris." *BBC News,* March 15, 2001. news.bbc.co.uk/hi/english/sci/tech/newsid_1221000/1221955.stm.

"The Spacecraft That Could." *Newsweek,* December 18, 1985.

Vest, Floyd, William Diedrich, and Kenneth Vos. "Mathematics and the Global Positioning System." *Consortium* (spring 1994).

Weinstock, Maia. "Orbiting Junk Continues to Threaten International Space Station." *SPACE.com,* September 5, 2000. www.space.com/ scienceastronomy/planetearth/space_junk_000901.html.

THREE ADDITIONAL TITLES APPEAR IN THE

# Mission Mathematics II

### Series
*(Michael C. Hynes, Project Director)*

### Mission Mathematics II: Prekindergarten–Grade 2
*Edited by Mary Ellen Hynes and Catherine Blair*

### Mission Mathematics II: Grades 3–5
*Edited by Mary Ellen Hynes and Donn Hicks*

### Mission Mathematics II: Grades 6–8
*Edited by Michael C. Hynes and Juli K. Dixon*

Please consult
www.nctm.org/catalog
·for the availability of these titles,
as well as for a plethora of
resources for teachers of mathematics
at all grade levels.

For the most up-to-date listing of NCTM resources on topics of interest
to mathematics educators, as well as information on membership
benefits, conferences, and workshops, visit the NCTM Web site at
www.nctm.org.